PÂTE DE VERRE

AND

KILN CASTING

OF

GLASS

By Jim Kervin and Dan Fenton

Fung's

Pâte de Verre and Kiln Casting of Glass

by James Kervin
and
Dan Fenton

Published by:

GlassWear Studios
1197 Sherry Way
Livermore, CA 94550
(510)443 9139

Copyright © 1997
First Printing 1997

Cataloging Data
Kervin, James E., 1950-
Fenton, Daniel M., 1950-
    Pâte de Verre and Kiln Casting of Glass
       by James E. Kervin and Daniel Fenton   214p
    Includes bibliographical references
    ISBN 0-9651458-1-6
    1. Glass blowing and working. 1. Title
TP859.K   1997

Library of Congress Catalog Card Number   97-093102

Front cover: "Maestro en Rouge" by Seth Randal
                 Pâte de cristal, 1991
                 10" high by 23" in diameter
                 Photographed by Roger Schreiber
                 Collection of Ginny Ruffner

Preface

This cooperative effort was established to develop a text on the complex glassworking technique of pâte de verre or kiln casting of glass. The process allows a small glass studio artist who possesses a kiln to push their artistic envelope into the fascinating world of three dimensional sculptural glass. This book, as would be expected of any book by Dan or Jim, is a very comprehensive presentation of the subject ranging from initial development of the model to final cleaning of the glass casting. It is loaded with detailed tips on the process as well as information pertinent to kilnworking of glass in general.

Dan Fenton is an internationally known glass artist who has been working in the field of glass since the sixties and with kiln techniques since the late seventies. He has long been known as a walking storehouse of detailed technical information on many small studio glassworking techniques and travels the country teaching pâte de verre as well as teaching it at his studio in Oakland, CA. Many other glass art subjects are also taught there. They include: stained glass, sandblasting, fusing, glass painting, dale de verre, neon, enamel work, beadmaking, etc. Dan is well known in the glass field for his many articles, willingness to share his vast knowledge and his own unique sense of humor. In fact, this work builds heavily on a series of articles he wrote on the subject of pâte de verre and kiln casting of glass for Glass Art Magazine.

Jim Kervin is a relative newcomer to glass, having only twelve years of experience in stained glass and eight in kilnworking. His strength is that with a Ph.D. in engineering, he tends to approach a subject from an orderly and scientific view point. He wants to know how and understand why things work the way they do. Some of you may already know him from his book on glass beadmaking entitled *More Than You Ever Wanted To Know About Glass Beadmaking*. He was interested in developing this book to make information on kiln casting of glass more available to the average glass artist. He had previously found himself frustrated when searching for information on this subject and wanted to make sure that the information was easily available to any budding artist seeking it.

Together, we have worked to compile all the information on the subject of pâte de verre and kiln casting of glass that we think the average glass artist could ever want. We hope that this book fulfills your needs for information on the subject and facilitates you in delving deeper into the possibilities available using this fascinating technique.

We wish to thank the many artists who have been so sharing in information on the techniques that they use in making pâte de verre and kiln cast glass. In particular we would like to thank Mark Abildgaard, Anna Boothe, Linda Ethier, Newy Fagan, Larry Fielder, Mary Fox, P. J. Friend, Robin Grebe, Lucartha Kohler, Boyce Lundstrom, Donna Milliron, Charles Miner, Seth Randal, Alice Rogan-Nelson, David Ruth, Kathleen Stevens, Janusz Walentynowicz and Mary Francis Wawrytko.

It should be mentioned that any discussion of particular equipment or supplies in this book does not constitute a recommendation. They are just some of those that we use in our work or know about from others. Results achievable with them may vary from individual to individual depending upon their skill level and the application technique; so no warranty is implied for these products. Instead we supply this information so that you, as an educated consumer, can make your own choices. Because of the nature of this art form, injuries can occur and you, the user of these products, have the sole responsibility for your safety as well as for other individuals that could be hurt by your actions. Neither we nor the equipment manufacturers are responsible for any injury resulting from equipment misuse. You need to learn as much about how your equipment operates as possible, read and follow all manufacturer recommendations, and take classes from qualified instructors. With this type of background, you will be able to safely enjoy pâte de verre and kiln casting of glass.

This book was designed to provide as complete an information source as possible regarding the subject of kiln casting of glass. Although this topic is presented in great depth, it is impossible to cover everything. You are urged to read all available material on the subject. Check out the many references listed herein to supplement this text. Be aware that, even though we have tried to provide as complete and accurate a source book as possible, **there may be some mistakes** present both typographical and in content. Therefore, use it as a guide and if something seems wrong, realize that it might just be so. This manual was written both to educate and to entertain the reader. The authors shall have neither liability nor responsibility to any person or entity with respect to any loss or damage caused, or alleged to be caused, directly or indirectly by the information contained in this book. **If you do not wish to be bound by these restrictions, you may return this book with a copy of your receipt to the publisher for a full refund.**

Jim Kervin and Dan Fenton

Table of Contents

Table of Figures

Table of Tables

12

Photography Credits

Introduction

Pâte de Verre is an ancient glassworking technique that was rediscovered in the art nouveau period of the late 1800's by Henry Isadore Cesar Cros. The term translates literally from French as "paste of glass." The technique produces solid glass objects with a rich translucent quality and was utilized by the ancient Egyptians to make glass amulets, scarabs and gems. Pâte de Verre techniques can be used to produce a wide range of objects from solid cast sculptures to hollow vessels. The technique can be used to produce glass objects with great surface detail and variation in coloration. The resulting glass surface is most often matte, but may also have a wet rough texture. Above all, it results in a work that begs to be held and examined.

The entire pâte de verre process is quite involved. It starts with the making of an original model of some material. Depending on the complexity of the model and your desire for multiples of it, you might next make a master mold of the model. With a master mold, you can cast as many wax replicas of the model as you desire. The replica, or original model, is then used to cast a refractory mold. After melting or steaming out any wax, following traditional lost wax techniques developed for foundry work, you air dry the mold and then fire it in your kiln to burn out any residual organic materials. Next a fine glass paste is packed or painted into the mold in a subtle blending of thin multi-colored layers. Of course you will have to make the paste yourself from colored glass or clear glass that you color and then frit (make into glass granules). After drying, the thin layers of glass paste are fired in a kiln until fused. Successive layers can be added and fused until the piece is complete. Once annealed, the mold is broken away to reveal the completed object of art. Lastly you clean the casting and sit back for a well deserved rest. Some artists though, may continue on and reinvest a casting as part of a larger work.

Although the whole process may sound complicated beyond your wildest expectations, don't let it scare you. If we can do it, so can you. Just read this procedure twice before bedtime and we will test you on it in the morning. Actually, you have nothing to fear, because the Art Police are on a fishing expedition to the South Pacific and will be gone for a long time. This should give you plenty of time to practice these procedures and to be honest you will probably need it. We suggest that you start off small before you proceed on to larger masterpieces. This will conserve on materials, help keep the initial messes down and prevent the vise grips of major failure from clamping down on your mental health.

The term, pâte de verre, is loosely used by many glass artists today, perhaps because of the romantic sound of the French term. They apply it to any artwork created by kiln casting glass frit in a refractory mold regardless of the size of the frit. Such "chunk de verre" is not really representative of what the old masters produced. It resembles something more like objects made from marble. It lacks the fine detail and the crystalline quality of the original work but does produce art objects with their own beauty. Such work should probably, as has been suggested by Boyce Lundstrom, be differentiated from the traditional pâte de verre work by use of a different term such as frit or kiln casting to avoid confusion. We try to make that distinction in this book.

You will find that most of the tools and materials that you will be using in pâte de verre are not available at your local stained glass retail store. Part of the adventure with starting out in this new process will be in seeking out sources for these new tools and supplies. You will also find yourself acquiring tools, supplies and skills that were developed by other artisans; such as: jewelers, sculptors, potters and glassblowers. As a result of this, you will probably make more than one visit to any of a number of new locations seeking out these materials. They may include: hardware stores, jewelers' supply stores, ceramic supply stores, flea markets, art supply stores and even your local supermarket.

The secret to producing highly detailed pâte de verre work in the average glass studio is the use of low temperature glasses that can be colored using common equipment and a mold material that remains stable in size during the process. This is because most of the investment mixtures (materials used to cast refractory glass casting molds) that will be described in this book are plaster-based and lose a great portion of their strength in the range of 1350 to 1400°F. But since these low temperature glasses tend to have a high lead content and are generally only available as clear frit, some artists have chosen to settle for slightly lesser detail in exchange for greater safety and a readily available color palette of higher firing-temperature glass to use in their work. It is these types of topics and more that we will discuss in this book.

Basic Kiln Casting Process

We were originally a little undecided on how to organize this book. Should we start right in with a step by step description of the pâte de verre process, presenting all the details along the way or give you an overview of the process and then go into more detail on the some topics. Sometimes we have found that even we are not interested in the details of a new technique until we have first developed an understanding of the basic process. So after much philosophical discussion, we decided that it was better to present you with the basics of the process itself here and then in later chapters to go back and wade our way through all those esoteric details. At that point you will better understand why they are important and they may make more sense. So let's get down to basics.

Glass types

Choosing the type of glass to use in your work is one of the most important decisions that you will have to make. The choice of glass dictates the processing temperatures, which in turn has a profound effect on the results that you will be able to achieve in a casting. The higher the fusing temperature of the glass, the more refractory the investment mixture has to be and the more likely it is to develop cracks. As will be discussed later, higher temperature refractory investment materials tend to retain less detail or can be so strong as to endanger the piece when demolding. These factors have to be weighed against other factors like cost, availability, and compatibility of the materials that you use. For now let's just assume that you are making a casting from a single piece of scrap soda-lime glass left over from your stained glass career which you are now going to break into pieces.

Frit preparation

The opacity in pâte de verre work is a result of fine air bubbles trapped between individual grains of the glass frit. In the kiln casting process, you do not usually get the glass hot enough for bubbles to rise to the surface of the glass. This result is contrasted to a typical casting process where the glass has been fined (debubbled) prior to pouring it into the mold. The number and size of the air bubbles trapped in the finished piece is dictated by the particle size of the glass frit used in its manufacture. Pieces made with particles the size of flour will end up looking more like alabaster than glass. Use of larger particles, the size of sugar, will result in a piece with more translucence but still with a definite opacity. Larger particles yet will continue to increase the translucence of the piece until in the ultimate limit of using sheets of glass. Here the final result looks essentially the same as the initial glass except for a few bubbles which get trapped at the interfaces of the sheets. For this first kiln casting project, we would suggest that you crush up part of that single sheet of glass by wrapping it up in a piece of newspaper, laying it on your garage floor and working out your frustrations on it with a hammer. This is an especially fitting end for one of those pieces of stained glass that just never cut like it should.

After crushing the glass, you will want to wash your frit to remove any dirt and organic material. This will also get rid of a lot of the really fine glass dust that some artists don't like and that is an inhalation hazard. Next spread the frit out to dry on some clean newspaper. You will want to run a magnet over it after it is dry to pull out any iron filings from the hammer. (This is normally done on any frit produced by mechanical methods.) Lastly you may want to divide the frit into different size grades to get different resulting opacities. This can be done by running your frit through various sized wire meshes or screens which can be purchased from a ceramic supply store.

Model making

The first basic step in the kiln casting process is to develop a model of the work you want to cast in glass. This is where we let the artist, or little kid, in us out of his or her cage to develop the theme for your work. The model, that he or she develops, is the original object that we will transform through the kiln casting process into glass. You can develop this model by working with any of a number of materials, the choice of which depends on whether you want to go directly into casting your refractory mold from your model or you want to add an intermediate step of making a wax reproduction. For now we will deal with the former and save the latter for the chapter on more advanced model making techniques. A good pallet choice on which to work your model is ¼ inch plate glass because it is easy to clean afterward with a solvent like alcohol. Dan prefers to use cardboard for reasons that will be explained later. A good pallet facilitates ease of casting your mold about the original model.

One of the things that you have to consider when making the original model is that the glass shrinks in volume by approximately 30% in going from the frit to the bulk fused piece. Therefore you have to plan for how you are going to add the extra glass needed to compensate for that shrinkage. If your piece is to have a large flat back like a bowl or medallion, you could just pile a lot of frit in that opening. Then later, after soaking at fusing temperature, you could peek into the kiln to see if you need to add more glass. If so, you turn off your kiln; don your protective clothing, gloves and glasses; and scoop some extra frit onto the pile. If you do not especially like to singe your eye lashes digging around in a hot kiln, you may want to plan on incorporating a reservoir into your mold to hold the extra frit that will be needed to fill the void volume inherent in the frit as it fuses. This reservoir can be incorporated in the form of a base that you retain as a part of the finished piece or as a temporary funnel that you grind off as desired later. This base or funnel is attached directly to your plate glass pallet during modeling.

There are many materials from which an original model can be developed. The traditional technique is to use wax like jewelers do for lost wax casting of metals. The beauty of this material is that the model is easily removed after casting the mold by melting out the wax. Alternatively the model could be made from any object that is combustible. In this case, the object can be removed from the mold by burning it out when you cure the mold. This can be a smelly and smoky process so be sure that your kiln is well vented. The model can also be constructed from clay. This is an excellent choice if you are making a large flat object like a medallion with a minimum of under cuts. After investing the mold around the clay, the clay can just be pulled out and the mold cleaned with water to remove any clay residue.

Mold construction

Upon completion of your original model, it is time to construct a plaster-based mold around it. In this section we discuss the basics of the mold making process that we present here. Later on, in the chapter on investments and in the one on advanced mold construction, we will delve deeper into the materials that go into an investment mix (which are usually plaster based), give some sample formulations and discuss more advanced mold construction techniques. In the basic process, the first step is to completely clean the plate glass pallet on which the original was made. This is done in order to be able to anchor down a mold frame to the glass pallet so that it will not leak. In this frame we will then cast the refractory investment mold around the original.

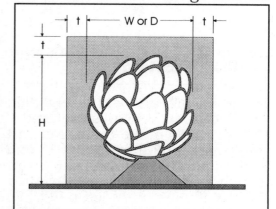

Figure 1. Sizing your mold.

So plan out the size of the investment mold to make around the original model. The mold, as illustrated in Figure 1 for an artichoke casting with an incorporated reservoir base, should typically be at least ½ inch thick (t) and at most about two inches thick. How thick you make your mold depends a lot on the exact process you will be using. If you are using traditional pâte de verre techniques as practiced by the old French masters where you will be firing the mold multiple times as you build up the thickness of the piece, you may want the mold to be on the thicker end of that range. If instead you are doing a one step casting of an object with a low firing-temperature glass, you can get away with making your mold on the lower end of the thickness range. Also as your model gets larger, your mold will need to be thicker and reinforced to resist the outward push of the molten glass.

Making a mold frame

To cast your mold, you need to first construct a mold frame or box around your model in which to cast it. Jewelers usually use a cylindrical metal frame referred to as a flask for this. Here we present a simple cardboard mold frame construction technique. Frames from cardboard and hot glue are good for small projects using up to about 5 to 20 lb. of investment material. Cardboard is

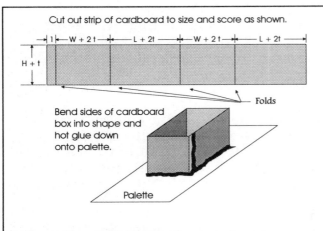

Figure 2. Constructing a simple cardboard mold frame.

easy to come by, but avoid any of the waxed cardboard like on fruit boxes because the hot glue will not stick to it. Cardboard is also easily cut with a standard utility knife. Dan's favorite is a Spyderco single serrated edge knife, but don't go running out to buy one because they are fairly expensive. The bottom of the box will be the plate glass or cardboard pallet on which your model is mounted. For the dimensions of your frame, length and width, envision the mold on the pallet of the decided upon thickness around the model as was illustrated in Figure 1. To make the frame, cut a strip of cardboard as is illustrated in Figure 2 that ½ to 2 inches wider than your model is high (again based upon the desired mold thickness, t) and at least 1 inch longer than twice the sum of the length (L+2t) and width (W+2t) of your intended mold. Fold the cardboard where each of the corners will be. This can be made easier by scoring fold lines on the back side of the cardboard prior to folding.

Figure 3. Placing the mold frame around the model.

Use a hot glue gun to attach the cardboard mold frame down to the pallet. Glue guns are easy to use. Choose the trigger type of glue gun available from any hardware store because it makes feeding of the glue sticks easier. The guns are an item that can be commonly found at the flea market for less than $3 and almost always work.

Glue sticks are a consumable item that you will find yourself going through like crazy. Each mold frame may require up to a half dozen of them. Some major hardware stores sell them in bulk and, if you can find them, buy the long sticks so that you don't have to reload the gun as often. The clear stick glue is stronger but the white "caulk" sticks set up faster. Be prepared to get an occasional "ouchie" and to exercise your vocabulary because in the frenzy of creativity, some of the hot glue invariably will get on your hands. It is never fatal and only rarely does it result in burns. It only hurts while you laugh or for a couple of minutes if you fail to have a sense of humor in this situation. If you are really sensitive about your lily-soft paws, you might want to wear dishwashing gloves while gluing.

Getting a good glue joint between the pallet and the mold frame is where it is critical that you did a good job cleaning your glass pallet before attaching the cardboard sides. Nothing is less amusing than having investment leak out under a side of your mold frame because of a poor pallet cleaning job. This is why Dan prefers using cardboard for a pallet—it bonds better. Jim prefers glass because it is stronger and allows picking the filled mold frame up for transport. To attach the final side of the frame to the first side use that extra one inch of length that we mentioned previously and which is shown on the left side of the illustration in Figure 2. Bend the frame into shape and glue it down to the pallet as shown in Figure 3 and Figure 4 respectively. If the mold will use more than about 5 lb. of investment, you may need to provide external reinforcement to

Figure 4. Gluing the mold frame to the pallet.

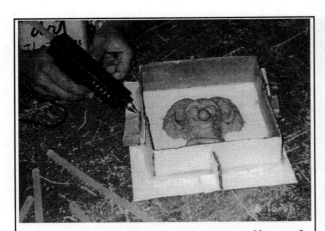

Figure 5. Reinforcing a cardboard mold frame.

the cardboard to help prevent it from bulging out and tearing away from the hot glue. Reinforcement can be in the form of cardboard buttresses or just piling bricks around the sides of the mold frame. (In case you are wondering, buttressing was an architectural technique used in building Medieval cathedrals and here refers to adding triangular pieces of cardboard attached perpendicular to a mold frame wall and attached with hot glue both to the wall and the pallet as shown in Figure 5.)

Once your mold frame is fully constructed around the model, lightly coat the pallet and the inside of the mold frame with a separator compound. This should be some hydrocarbon liquid of your choice. It is easiest if this coating can be applied as a spray. Products such as liquid dishwashing detergents, cooking pan coatings (Pam) or light machine oil sprays (WD-40) are suggested. Depending on what you used for your original model and how you plan to remove it from the mold, you may want to coat it also. For materials that you are going to burn or melt out this is not necessary. If you choose to use the separator on the original model, be aware that some surface detail will be lost. So paint it on thin and get rid of any bubbles. The separator compound will also assist in reducing bubble formation in the investment on the model surface by reducing the investment's surface tension.

Mixing the investment

Now it is time to mix up a batch of investment. Most investment recipes are plaster based and mixing them can take some practice. For this exercise, we suggest that you use what will be called investment mix # 1. It consists of a fifty-fifty mix by weight of Hydrocal plaster and 200 mesh silica flour. (Wear a respirator because the silica flour dust is hazardous.) Mixing plaster-based investment like this is often assumed to be elementary but there are really many different aspects that need to be addressed to do it right. Don't expect to necessarily get it right the first time. With a little practice though, you will soon become a professional. Try to mix enough to completely fill your mold in one pour as this will make the strongest possible mold. If this is not possible, allow the previous batch of investment to set up before adding the next batch. In mixing any plaster-based material by feel, as we describe here, there are a number of suggested rules that should be followed to achieve optimum results.

Always use cool, about 70°F, clean water to make up your mix. (Maximum plaster solubility occurs between 70° and 100°F.) Likewise try to keep your mixing bucket and tools clean. The presence of any old hardened investment will cause the new investment to set up faster, in as much as one half the expected setup time. In dirty water, new investment will also coat the old investment to form clumps. Water that is too hot will also cause investment to set faster. For those real control freaks out there, you can purchase an attachment for your sink from a darkroom equipment supplier to measure faucet

Figure 6. Sifting the investment into the mixing bowl.

temperature. Some people also swear that letting your water sit in a bucket for a few hours before use to be beneficial to final investment consistency. This allows a lot of the junk and gas that the city puts into your water to come out. (They also say that this also makes their water taste better.) If you want to go to real extremes you could use distilled water.

Add the plaster-based investment mixture to the water, not the water to the investment. Don't just dump it all in at once. Instead slowly sift the dry ingredients out onto the surface of the water as illustrated in Figure 6. An old flour sifter works well for this purpose. Slow sifting of the investment onto the water avoids

Figure 7. Investment peaking on the surface in the mixing bowl.

excessive air entrapment by the large surface area of the plaster particles. As the mixture settles onto the water, it will absorb enough water to displace the trapped surface air and sink. Some mix formulations give a suggested water to mix ratio. If so, add the dry mix until you reach that optimum ratio. (You will need to preweigh your dry and wet components ahead of time to get this right.) If mixing by feel, keep sifting investment mix onto the water until it "peaks" as shown in Figure 7. This is where it no longer sinks and the surface develops slightly dry islands or peaks as illustrated. This indicates a good dry ingredient to water ratio. Stop adding plaster-based investment mix at this point. Using this technique, your final wet mix will have approximately twice the volume of water with which you started.

Figure 8. Hand stirring the investment.

Next, allow the mixture to sit undisturbed and rest for about three minutes. This time can be varied from as short as one minute to as long as five minutes. This time period is called "slaking" and is necessary for the investment to set properly. During this time, the plaster in the investment is starting to chemically adsorb the water and becoming uniformly wetted. You may want to tap the edge of the container during this time to try to get the air bubbles out.

Now you hand stir the investment mixture being careful to avoid whipping any air into it. If you encounter lumps as you mix the investment, this may indicate that you added the plaster to the water too quickly or that not enough time was allowed for slaking. Of course, there is also the possibility that your investment was lumpy to begin with. Check it out. If there are lumps in your dry mix, you can screen them out next time. In such a case, you should also consider just getting a whole new batch of investment.

Slowly stir the investment mix from the bottom to the top allowing any trapped air to rise to the surface. The mold mixture should appear to be creamy at this point, not thin and watery but slightly opaque on the stirrer. Do not overstir. First, because all the time that you are stirring, the mixture is starting to set up and second, because the more that you stir, the faster it seems to set up. In fact you may want to undermix the batch to allow longer setting times.

Pouring the investment

After mixing, apply the investment mix to the model by slowly pouring it into the mold frame. Try not to trap bubbles. It works best if you pour the investment into an empty corner of the mold frame and allow it to flow around your model until you fill the mold frame to the rim. Afterward vibrate the mold gently by tapping on the edge of the pallet or shaking the work table to free any trapped air and allow it to rise to the surface. This is where Jim sometimes has trouble with the mold frame breaking free from his glass pallet and allowing investment to flow out from underneath. He then finds himself holding down the corners of the frame for the next half hour. So try to make sure something interesting is on the television or the radio, just in case. Bubbles can also be broken free from the model by careful stirring of the poured material, assuming that you can do so without touching the model. It is best to mix slightly more investment than you may think is necessary for the job rather than not enough. Otherwise if you have to mix more, the original batch will already be setting up just as the second batch is finished mixing and ready to pour. This will prevent the two layers from intermingling and they will then usually separate later. It is a good idea to have some small molds ready to pour just in case you mix way too much. Try to have your pour completed within about 10 minutes of initial mixing for best results.

If you have a lot of detail that you are trying to capture from your model, you may want to try and paint a thin initial layer of investment onto it with a small soft brush prior to pouring the bulk of the investment. Make sure that you fill any indentations that may trap air as you pour your investment. If you are fast enough, you may even be able to brush on your first layer on the model and then fill the rest of the mold frame all with the same batch of investment. If not, just take your time and let the painted layer set up before pouring the bulk of the mold.

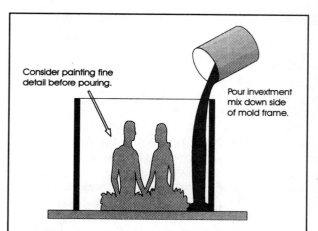

Consider painting fine detail before pouring.

Pour invextment mix down side of mold frame.

Figure 9. Pouring investment into corner of the mold frame.

If you end up needing to add a second pour of investment material, let the first pour set completely first. Then lightly scratch the top of the first pour to increase its surface area. This gives the next batch of investment material something to grab on to. Also saturate the material from the first pour with water or it will steal water out of the new batch, preventing it from setting properly.

Now that you are done with your pour, don't forget to clean your investment coated tools and bucket with water right away. Start by pouring off extra investment into some disposable trash container such as a plastic bag in a cardboard box as shown in Figure 10. Do not clean your equipment in your sink or other unmentionable plumbing fixtures. Never dump plaster or investment down a drain, unless you don't like your landlord and you are moving real soon. The investment particles are fairly heavy and will settle out in your pipes. There the plaster-based investment will set up even underwater and harden. This practice could eventually lead to complete blockage of your drain pipes creating problems for everyone but your plumber, who probably could use the work. Instead, always have another large plastic container, like a dishwashing pan, of water available in which to rinse everything off. Let the heavier plaster particles sink to the bottom of the plastic container. Then dispose of the water at top in some appropriate manner, like giving a tree a drink. Discard the plaster sludge at the bottom into your plastic bag for disposal. If any investment dries in the plastic container before you can clean it out, don't worry it won't stick to the plastic. Just kick the side of the plastic container and the plaster will come loose.

When first poured, the investment will look shiny and have a slight water film. Then as you watch, the shiny appearance will go away as

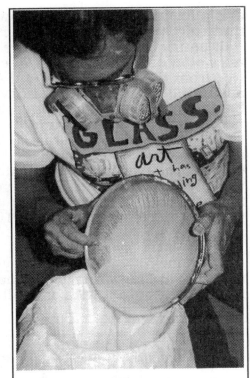

Figure 10. Disposing of excess investment.

the water is bound up by the investment. This phenomena is known as glossing off and should occur within about 12 minutes after mixing plaster-based investment. As the shine goes away and the investment starts to get mushy, you will want to screed what will later be the bottom of your mold, but is now the exposed top of your pour. Screeding consists of lightly drawing a flat instrument like a metal ruler across the top of your pour as shown in Figure 11 to form a nice flat bottom for your mold to sit on the kiln shelf. This is done by making a number of light passes to avoid ripping up the smooth investment surface and is complete when the investment is flush with the top of the mold frame. Clean the investment off your screeding instrument after each pass to avoid tearing of the investment surface. The results of investment mixes may vary, but most should start to harden up in about 20 to 30 minutes. If not, you may have gotten a bad batch of material or have somehow done something drastically wrong.

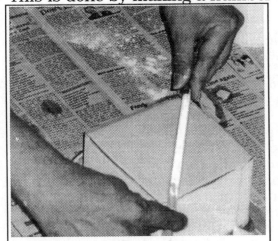

Figure 11. Screeding the investment pour.

Once the investment in the mold has initially set up, remove the mold frame from around mold and any hot glue stuck to the pallet. (Setup for plaster-based molds generally takes about two hours to develop the proper interconnective chemical bonding.) Then slide the mold off of the pallet. Next you should scrape all the edges of the mold and any visible joint locations of the mold frame with a sharp knife as illustrated in Figure 12. You are trying to remove any sharp edges or divots from the surface of the mold.

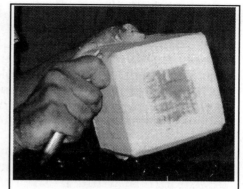

Figure 12. Scraping mold edges reduces cracking.

These may serve as a points for initiation of cracks during drying or curing and their removal generally results in reduced cracking of the mold.

Curing the mold

The investment casting around the model is what eventually goes into the kiln. So it will have to be carefully cured. After it has completely set up, it is time to remove your original. Since most plaster-based investment mixes expand slightly during curing, a solid model if properly designed should be easy to remove. (Assuming that you having plenty of draft and don't have undercuts as is shown in Figure 13.) You may be able pry the model out with a sharp tool around the edge of the model. Injecting compressed air under your model is also helpful in breaking the suction between it and the mold caused by the separator compound. A quick pull or jet of air may not always be sufficient to break this vacuum but a slow steady pull might. An easy way to apply a slow steady pull is to hang the whole thing by the model a small distance off the table and let gravity do the work for you. If your model is made of something like clay, you can carve out the bulk of it from the mold and wash out any residual with warm water. Here undercuts and draft are not of concern. All the clay must be removed or it will contaminate your final work.

If you used some form of wax to make your model, you can melt or steam it out after your mold has set. To do this, support your mold on a screen or rack over a pan of water in your kiln or on a hot plate. The pan should be big enough to catch all your wax. An aluminum pie pan works well for this. Fill the pan with water and slowly bring the kiln up to about 225°F. As the mold gets warm, most of the wax will melt and drip out into the water. If you are really frugal, this wax can be reused later but we do not necessarily advise it since the wax can pick up pieces of investment and get gritty. Don't let all the water evaporate, otherwise the wax will start to vaporize and create an explosive hazard. If you need to add more water, turn off your kiln and pour some into the pan. After you have melted out all the wax you think possible, you may have to burn out the rest. This wax residue is typically burned out to avoid staining your piece with carbon or having a reducing atmosphere in the kiln while casting your piece. (A reducing atmosphere can cause other problems, such as making lead precipitate out of lead-based glasses.) Once all the wax is burned out of the mold turn off the kiln and allow it to cool before removing the mold and the pan of water.

For best results the mold should be thoroughly air dried before putting it in the kiln for burnout and curing. Air drying reduces the amount of water in the mold so that it does not turn into steam when later heated in the kiln. Expanding steam stresses the investment matrix of the mold, thus weakening it. Air drying can be done in a number of ways. The easiest way is just to set it aside for about a week and let it air dry naturally. But if you are not the patient type, you can build a drying box as will be explained later to accelerate drying. This can reduce drying time down to a day or less depending on the size and the porosity of the mold. If this is still not fast enough, then throw the mold into the kiln on low and cross your fingers.

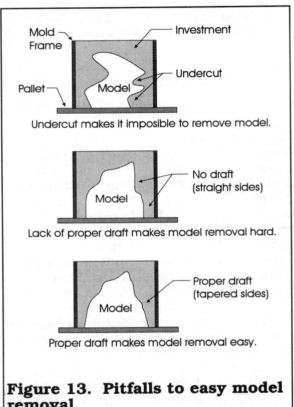

Figure 13. Pitfalls to easy model removal.

(within the figure:)
Mold Frame — Investment
Pallet — Model — Undercut
Undercut makes it imposible to remove model.

Model — No draft (straight sides)
Lack of proper draft makes model removal hard.

Model — Proper draft (tapered sides)
Proper draft makes model removal easy.

After air drying your mold, you may need to heat-cure it and burn out any organic remains of your original model such as wax. To do this place it in your kiln with model opening up as shown in Figure 14. Slowly heat the mold to drive out any remaining water, not too fast or steam could be produced. Of course slowly is a relative term. It is relative to how much time you have already put into this mold and how willing you are to take chances. You thermal soak the mold in the kiln first at 225°F to remove physically adsorbed water and then at 350°F to remove chemically bound water. After this you continue to slowly heat the mold up to about 1200°F to burn out any residual organic materials. This cure may take anywhere from hours to days depending on the size of your mold; hours for molds on the order a few inches, days for ones on the order of feet. You will develop a feel for what's needed with experience. The slower you go, the stronger the mold will remain. This is also a good time to go out to lunch or dinner because final model burnout can produce a lot of noxious fumes. Even well vented kilns and studios may become stinky for a while. These fumes will especially drive off your apprentices so don't count on getting a lot of work done during burnout.

After the mold is burned out, slowly cool it back down to room temperature. If you are able to remove all the modeling material from the mold without having to go into a burn out phase, then you have the option of curing your mold and firing your casting in the same firing cycle. At least air dry it though.

Firing casting

The bottom of your mold should be flat from the screeding that you did earlier. If it is not flat, the combined weight of the glass and the

Figure 14. Setting molds up in the kiln for heat cure.

mold may cause bending and can stress the investment material to failure, i.e. crack it. At this point you can still file or sand the mold bottom flat. This problem can also be alleviated by supporting the mold on the kiln self with a bed of sand. Be sure to use enough sand and to work the mold down into the sand to uniformly support it. If your mold is very large, it should also have internal support. Check to see that the top of your mold is level as you set it up in the kiln. Otherwise whatever you are making will vary in final thickness. This may not be apparent on small pieces but it certainly will be on larger bas relief ones.

You are now ready to fill your mold with glass frit. If the mold is in the kiln and hot, then this is done as shown in Figure 15. If not you have the luxury to set it up on your work table and take the time fill it by hand in a detailed manner. This process can be as easy as pouring in a single color and size of frit to as complex as using multiple colors and sizes of frit to achieve a variety of effects. For this demonstration piece, we recommend just using the homogeneous frit that you produced earlier when you crushed up that unruly piece of stained glass. If you graded the frit, you may want to place the finer grade first in any accent features.

Once your mold is filled with glass frit as desired and is in the kiln, it is time to cook. A basic firing schedule is sketched out in Figure 16. Slowly bring the mold up to the consolidation temperature for your glass. Ramp rates are controlled in order to prevent thermal shocking your mold. If you have not prefired your mold ahead of time, you will have to go slower and dwell at both 225 and 350°F to remove water bound in the plaster matrix as was described earlier. It is during the rise to process temperature that your mold is most likely to crack, because your glass is still fairly rigid and your mold is shrinking some as it reaches the neighborhood of 1200°F.

After reaching the consolidation temperature for your glass, you need to hold the kiln temperature constant until you are sure that your glass has equilibrated and consolidated inside the mold. The mold insulates the glass, causing its temperature to lag behind that of the kiln. You will have to hold the

Figure 15. Filling hot mold with single color frit.

temperature at the control point for about 1 to 2 hours per inch of mold thickness depending on how fast you heated up the mold. On the final firing of a piece, assuming that you are doing multiple firings for addition of detailed coloration, you will want to continue up in temperature to the full fuse point and hold for another hour per inch of mold thickness to get a full density piece. If you are only doing one firing, you would proceed directly up to the fusing point.

When you have finished your hold at process temperature, vent your kiln to rapidly crash its temperature down to near the annealing point. Then close your kiln. You will have to hold at this temperature to allow the glass to equilibrate, again for the same 1 to 2 hours per inch of mold thickness. We crash the kiln temperature down at this point to reduce the time spent in the 1000° to 1400°F range. This is where the glass can devitrify or crystallize on cooling. You now want to slowly lower the kiln temperature from the annealing point to the strain point for your glass. You will want to do this over a time period of 2 to 12 hours per inch thickness of casting. There you will need to hold the temperature constant for a while to again let the glass to equilibrate with the kiln, but this time the hold needs to be only about half as long as before because you have been lowering temperature slowly which already helps make the casting

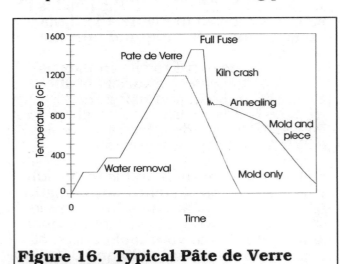

Figure 16. Typical Pâte de Verre firing schedule.

become more uniform in temperature.

Lastly you cool your casting back to room temperature. This can be done much faster than during the high temperature cooling because all the glass is now "hardened" and will no longer build up permanent stress. Just be careful that you do not proceed so fast that you thermal shock it. We will talk more of all this later. Allow the mold to remain undisturbed at room temperature for a couple of hours before you even think of demolding.

It is very important to precisely control kiln temperatures during the firing process. Temperature differences as small as 25 degrees can result in significant differences in the final product. Too high a process temperature allows the surface tension of the glass to reduce to the point were it starts to stick to the mold. This can be diagnosed by examining the edges of the final meniscus of the glass in the sprue. If slightly rounded, the temperature was okay; if sharp, the temperature was probably too high.

Demolding and cleaning your casting

To demold your glass casting, slowly break the mold away from the glass as shown in Figure 17. This can sometimes require great patience since you are understandably anxious to see your final product. A light touch is an asset at this point because it is here when breakage is likely to occur if you are heavy handed. Use a small hammer and chisel, if necessary, to slowly break the mold apart. Proceed gently since it is sometimes difficult to know exactly where the mold ends and the glass casting begins. If it starts to feel hot, stop and let it cool some more. Once the major mass of the investment is broken away, you can pick away at the rest using dental tools. The first sight of the glass will reveal the shape, but be prepared for the surface to look ugly. That's because there is still lots of mold material sticking to the surface. This is especially common with the soft low melting-point glasses or if you cook it at too high a temperature. After you have the casting free from the mold, don't stick it in water right away to wash off the remaining mold material. Let it sit for a couple more hours before you clean it. The key to the whole cleaning process is patience.

Figure 17. Carefully breaking the casting from the mold.

Once cool, wash the casting in water with a stiff vegetable brush. If you can not get all the mold residue off with a vegetable brush try a small stainless steel bristled brush. Do not use a brass bristled brush on a casting as the brass will rub off and will discolor your piece making it look like a brass sculpture. We have found that glasses with a high lead content seem to be more difficult to scrub clean because the glass is soft and you never seem to get a shiny surface without a lot of elbow grease. If you want a shiny surface, you may have better luck with a soda-lime glass like Bullseye. No we don't own stock in the company (and probably could not afford it), but Bullseye gives a surprisingly shiny surface relatively easily.

Once the casting is completely clean, look it over. Small imperfections can be removed by simply grinding them away or by sanding with 400 grit wet/dry sandpaper to mimic the natural matte surface texture of the casting. Dremel hand grinders or flex shaft tools with small diamond bits will help greatly with this task. Remember to keep things wet and to wear a respirator with a mist cartridge.

Figure 18. Grinding on a casting with Dremel tools.

Now that wasn't too bad was it. Did you get bogged down on some of those details. There sure are a lot of them. Don't worry we won't test you, the materials will do that. We will also try to keep the Art police at bay long enough for us to now go back over parts of the process and explain the fundamental details behind the them, so that you will be able to get through it better on your own later.

Glass

Almost any glass can be used for kiln casting regardless of particle size. It can be powdered, fritted (granularized), chunked or even slabbed. You can grind it yourself or buy it prefritted. Figure 19 shows three of the grades of Bullseye frit commercially available. As in our example of last chapter, glass used for kiln casting can be broken up soda-lime sheet glass or it can be specially purchased lead crystal cullet. The type of glass that you choose for your work dictates a number of factors, such as process temperatures, which in turn dictates the investment formulation. If you want color, you can use glass that is precolored or you will have to add color to a clear base glass of your choosing. If the

Figure 19. Some of the frit sizes commercially available from Bullseye.

prospect of mixing colors sounds daunting, then we know which direction you will choose to go. In that case, you will want to search out a line of glass to work with that has as many colors available as possible. As you start mixing different colored glasses, you will also have to be concerned with other factors such as their compatibility. We will discuss many of these decisions and factors in great detail in this chapter. There is a lot to learn about glass in order to work with it knowledgeably in kiln casting.

To begin our discussions on glass, let's review what this material that we have all grown to love really is and which two basic types are most appropriate for kiln casting. As part of this discussion, we will examine how a glass's chemical makeup affects the properties of interest to our work and what kinds are commercially available.

Chemistry

Glass is a material made up of a mixture of oxides. The main oxide used in most of the glasses of interest is silica or silicon dioxide (SiO_2). If it is the only oxide present, then the glass is known as fused silica or quartz. Glasses, rather than being composed of distinct molecules or atoms arranged into an orderly crystalline matrix, consist of atoms arranged in an interconnected, random three dimensional matrix. Figure 20 illustrates the difference in appearance between these two structures for a two-dimensional matrix of a boron-based glass where each boron atom (black dot) is bonded to three oxygen atoms and each oxygen atom (clear dot) is bonded to two boron atoms. You can see how the crystalline solid looks more rigid. This structure is also more stable and harder to break up once formed.

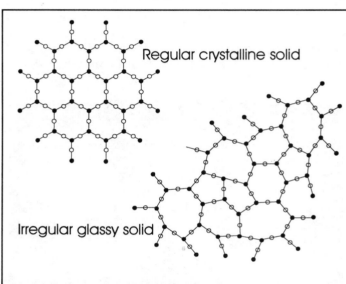

Figure 20. Disorderly structure of glass.

You can see from the figure that the structural component for these boron glasses is a flat platelet. The basic structural component for a silica based glass on the other hand is the silica tetrahedron. This is a four sided pyramid as illustrated in Figure 21 which has four oxygen atoms bonded to each silicon atom, one at each corner of the pyramid. Together the oxygen atoms shield the silicon atom at the center of the tetrahedron from the surrounding environment. Each oxygen atom is part of two tetrahedrons that are randomly orientated with respect to each other. For this reason, the oxygen atoms are commonly referred to as bridging oxygen atoms.

The bonds that hold the atoms together in a fused silica glass are a uniform network of strong covalent bonds (electron sharing between atoms) with a lot of crosslinking between chains. This results in a very sharply defined, high melting point (3115°F). This is a much higher temperature than anything you are used to working with in kilnworking. In

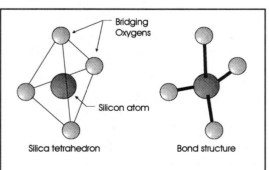

Figure 21. Silica tetrahedron.

fact most of the refractory materials used to line a typical electric kilns will not stand up to repeated exposures to such high temperatures and would self-destruct.

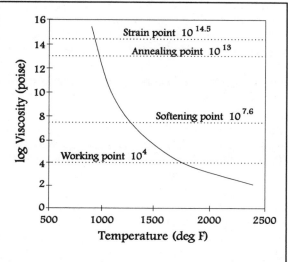

Figure 22. Typical temperature-viscosity relationship.

The uniform strong bond structure of fused silica causes it to expand and contract under the influence of temperature much less than most other glasses. The measure of this property is commonly known in engineering as the coefficient of thermal expansion (CTE) and is an important property to our work. You may be more familiar with one of the terms more commonly used in the glass media — the coefficient of expansion, COE, or the linear expansion coefficient, LEC. We have chosen to use the term, COE, because it is probably the term with which you are most familiar.

To lower the melting temperature of fused silica glass, other oxides are added to break up some of the bridging oxygen bonds by attaching them to a metal atom instead. This terminates one section of the tetrahedron chain making the matrix both less rigid and less viscous. Some of the oxide additives are more electro-positive than silicon which allows them to pull electrons away from the oxygen atoms. This results in forming weaker ionic bonds that lack the directionality associated with the stronger covalent bonds. The metal oxides can also strain the glass matrix if the size of the metal atom is large or small compared to a silicon atom. When heating up such a modified glass, the weaker ionic bonds and the less-rigid, strained structure allow the glass to become mobile or "melt" at much lower temperatures (about 1800°F). In addition, the variations in chain length of the glass matrix results in different portions of the interwoven chains becoming mobile at different temperatures.

On the macroscopic scale, the effect of this microstructure is manifested in glass by its getting soft gradually over a wide temperature range that spreads with increasing amounts of modifiers. Different types of modifiers, as you might guess, will effect this differently. The weaker the modified internal bonds, the lower the softening temperature. Additionally the more modifying oxides that are added to a glass, the shorter the resulting silica chains and the more fluid the molten glass. We refer to glasses that soften at lower temperatures as being "softer" than those "harder" glasses that soften at higher temperatures.

You have probably heard or read glass artists referring to glasses as frozen liquids. What does this mean? Ice is a frozen liquid but it has an orderly crystalline structure and is definitely not a glass. What is meant by this is that glass has a "frozen" random structure similar to that seen in the lower half of Figure 20. This kind of structure is typically associated with liquids, while solids usually have an orderly crystalline structure. The covalent bonds and long cross-linked chain structure of glasses are what causes them to remain disorderly. This structure causes glasses to gradually get more and more viscous (thick and gooey) as you cool them making it hard for them to form the lower-energy crystalline structure. (Crystalline structures can form easier at the surface of the glass because the chains are less restrained there. That is why you generally see crystallinity or devitrification as a surface layer on the glass which can be sandblasted off.) Unlike crystalline materials such as water, there is no single temperature at which glass makes essentially a step change in viscosity as it goes from a solid phase with a very high viscosity to a liquid phase with a very low viscosity. An example of this gradual transition in viscosity with temperature is graphed in Figure 22 for a typical soda-lime glass.

The gradual change in viscosity with temperature that you see in the figure is what gives glass the properties that allow us to work it like we do. If it was like water, instead of slumping, it would puddle. We would not be able to stretch and shape it if it did not soften gradually. Examine the graph of the temperature dependence of viscosity carefully to see the location of the different temperature reference points because we will be referring to them when we discuss high temperature properties of glasses.

Types of Glass

Let's compare the basic glass types that we are most likely to use in our work to fused silica glass and discuss how their composition affects some relevant kiln casting properties. The range of properties for each of the glasses is summarized in Table 1. Let's start by looking again at quartz glass.

Table 1. Range of properties of some basic glass types.

Property	Quartz glass	Soda-lime glass	Lead glass
Softening point (°F)	2876	1280-1350	820-1240
Annealing point (°F)	1983	960-1020	690-980
Strain point (°F)	1753	880-920	650-840
Coefficient of expansion (10^{-7} in/in/°F)	3.1	56-100	47-55
Density (lb/ft^3)	137	153-158	174-338
Refractive index	1.459	1.51-1.52	1.54-1.75

Quartz

Quartz, or fused silica as we have referred to it, is made by heating pure silicon dioxide to about 3137°F. The resulting liquid is so viscous that any gas bubbles trapped between the grains of sand as it melts, come out very slowly if at all. This high viscosity is a result of the rigid three-dimensional nature of the glass matrix. When cooled, the rigid three dimensional matrix of this material does not allow it to move around much to seek a minimum volume configuration. This explains its very low coefficient of expansion (COE). The rigid structure also accounts for quartz's relatively high softening, annealing and strain points listed in the table.

Soda-lime glass

The viscosity of molten fused silica glass can, as was discussed earlier, be decreased by adding fluxes or network modifiers in the form of metal oxides. The metal oxides that are added to make soda-lime glasses are sodium oxide (Na_2O) in the form of soda ash (Na_2CO_3) and calcium oxide (CaO) in the form of lime carbonates ($CaCO_3$). Both of these materials decompose to the oxide by releasing carbon dioxide (CO_2) gas as they react with the molten silica. Typical batch compositions for soda-lime glasses are in the range of 70 to 80 weight % silica, 12 to 17 weight % soda and 8 to 12 weight % lime. These materials modify the silica network to shorten and weaken it as seen in Figure 23. Varying these ratios will cause variation in properties; as an example, too much lime makes the glass susceptible to devitrification, too little results in a glass that is susceptible to chemical attack. In addition to the soda and lime, other additives are added in small amounts to make the mixture more workable. As an example of this, alumina or aluminum oxide is added to improve the chemical durability. The larger metal atoms of the modifying oxides help to lower viscosity making the glass flow into the molds easier. On the down side, they also result in a higher COE due to asymmetric vibrations of the molecules. This requires more careful thermal processing of the finished casting to minimize trapped stress.

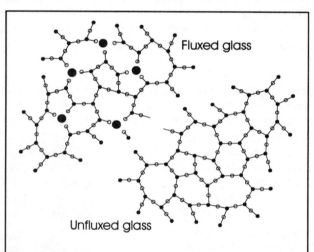

Figure 23. The effect of modifiers on glass structure.

The average warm-glass studio artist is probably very familiar with soda-lime glass from fusing. The brands of glass in common use require processing temperatures in the range of 1575°F to fully fuse. This is on the higher end of the working temperature range of investment materials for studio casting. Thus work done with this glass may not have the fine detail desired by some and will commonly have flashing lines caused by mold cracking. But on the up side there are many varieties of self-compatible soda-lime glasses (Bullseye, Wasser, GNA, Spectrum, etc.) available with an existing wide palette of colors. Compatible glasses are those with the same coefficient of expansion. Some of these glasses are also compatible between manufacturers, such as Bullseye, Wasser, and Uroboros. Look for the tested compatible label with Bullseye and Uroboros. Never assume that the glass will fit just by manufacturer alone. All GNA glass has to be tested; likewise with Spectrum. Besides color selection, there are other reasons that may cause you to want to mix glasses from the different manufacturers — changing the overall viscosity of the glass mixture is one. Adding softer Wasser frit to Bullseye frit results in a "softer" frit mixture that flows at a lower temperature. (Wasser flows at a temperature about 100°F lower than Bullseye.) These differences can be important when you are trying to kiln cast without too much flow that might ruin any design you are trying to introduce.

Some glass artists prefer using these common soda-lime glasses since they are trying to produce pâte de verre or frit cast objects that they can fuse together into larger pieces, although this could also be accomplished through the use of glass adhesives without having to worry about compatibility. This technique also allows joining together glass components made from other glassworking techniques such as the piece by Lucartha Kohler seen in Figure 24. This piece entitled "the Myth Maker" incorporates kiln cast, flame worked and sandblasted components. Soda-lime glasses should also be used for projects that might later be used as food bearing vessels where a lead glass may have toxic effects.

Figure 24. An example of a work bonded with adhesive.

Plate glass is one type of soda-lime glass that does not work too well in the kiln casting process because of its tendency to devitrify during the firing process and subsequent refusal to flow or fuse together. Attempts to try and alleviate this problem by fluxing the glass results in its sticking to the mold. Some glass artists on the other hand, like to use plate glass because of these properties. They like the porous look that they get in pieces made with fine plate glass frit. Another disadvantage of plate glass is that pieces made from it will have a definite green color from the iron impurities present in it.

Lead Glass

Lead glasses are formed by adding lead oxide (PbO) to silica. It is usually used as a network modifier of the silica matrix, but when added in high enough concentration, it can replace silica as the network former. Because of the large size of the lead atom, lead oxide is a good flux that bestows the glass mixture with a large working range over which the glass changes very little in viscosity. As seen back in Table 1, lead glasses tend to have a much lower softening point than either quartz or soda-lime glass.

One lead glass that may still be available from your local ceramic supplier is Pb 83 lead-based glaze frit from Pemco. Others with essentially the same characteristics are O'Hommel 33 and Ferro 3419-2. They are "colorless" base glasses which are used as ceramic glazes and contain about 60% lead oxide by weigh and can even set off the metal detectors at the airport. This has resulted in more than one embarrassing incident for Dan. Pb 83 is available as a fine-ground frit for about $2 a pound and fuses into an opaque alabaster-like piece. (It has a slight dirty yellow tint to it that is ignored in its intended function.) That's assuming you can find a ceramic supply company that will sell it to you with the current phobia of using lead. Most potters are now using lead-free glazes and ceramic suppliers are reluctant to sell lead-based ones to you because they are afraid of its misuse. If you explain what you are doing with it, you may have better luck. The frit is also available in a number of colors, not all of which may be compatible because they were formulated as glazes to be used in thin layers. It is suggested that, like for any fusing project, you check material compatibility out ahead of time before starting any masterpieces. An alternate option is to prepare your own colors by melting the frit and metal oxide colorants together followed by refritting. This process usually ensures the compatibility of your lead glass frit palette.

Lead glass's main appeal in pâte de verre work lies in its low fusing-temperature, 1040°F for Pb 83. This allows use of fine-grained, low-strength investment materials for development of crisp surface details. Plaster-based investments retain much of their strength at this temperature and therefore are much less susceptible to cracking. The low viscosity of high lead glasses once they are melted requires precise control of your firing schedule since variations as little as 15 to 25°F can result in rapid movement of the glass and loss of your image. Finished pieces made from lead glasses tend to have a matte surface to them possibly from mold interactions or ease of overheating.

Another medium low fusing-temperature (1425°F) alternative is a 24% lead crystal available from Ullmann glass of Germany. This is a true crystal glass without any tint of color. Finished pieces from it tend to have the typical semi-shiny surface of a lead crystal glass.

Some of the common colored glass (Kugler or Zimmerman) used for coloring glass in glassblowing can also be fritted and used for pâte de verre. Since this glass is formulated primarily for glassblowers, most of the colors should be compatible. But again you should probably check compatibility yourself to be sure.

Whenever firing a lead-based glass, you should ensure that you have a oxidative atmosphere (well ventilated kiln) or the lead will precipitate out of the glass and appear as dirty black specks in your finished piece. Your studio should also be well ventilated to get rid of any lead fumes which may be released from precipitates and are hazardous to your health. Ventilation should be done near the floor in addition to higher up since lead fumes are so much heavier than air.

Also lead glasses and fluxes, as was mentioned earlier, should not be used in any work that might be used as a food bearing surface. This is to avoid any chances of lead poisoning. Even though the lead is vitrified and is in a silicate rather than an oxide form, does not mean that the lead can not be leached out into foods. Foods that contain acids like acetic acid (vinegar) and citric acid (fruits and juices) can leach out lead. There are also other examples such as coffee, etc.

You may not be aware of it but even some Bullseye glass has a significant enough amount of lead in it that can be leached out. They report that both pink opal (#0301) and salmon pink opal (#0305) leach out lead to levels of 11µg/ml which is well above the 3µg/ml FDA compliance guidelines for flatware or the more restrictive 0.5µg/ml limit for cups, mugs and pitchers.

Frit

Besides what kind of glass you want to work with, you also have to chose what size frit you want to use based on the desired opacity for your work. You can chose to work with particles as fine as powders to large chunks. For traditional pâte de verre work, the glass should be finely ground and should contain granules of more than one mesh size to minimize shrinkage during firing. If you were packing perfect spherical particles, ideal packing would be achieved with what metallurgists call a body centered cubic cell structure. The spherical particles will be of two sizes that have a diameter ratio of 1.4 to 1. This combination, as seen in Figure 25, packs much denser than a single sized frit. If they are of the same glass, then you would use 1.87 times as much of the larger particles by weight as the smaller to get maximum packing.

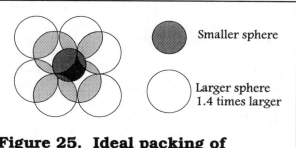

Smaller sphere

Larger sphere
1.4 times larger

Figure 25. Ideal packing of spherical particles.

Frit size is usually measured (or sized) by passing the frit through different sized metal meshes, or screens. These screens are characterized by the size of their openings. The openings are measured in the number of openings or strands of mesh wire per linear inch. From this you can not know exactly how big a particle can go through a given size mesh. If the wire was of zero thickness, then the particle size passed by a mesh would be the reciprocal of the mesh size. Thus a number 20 mesh would pass particles $1/20^{th}$ of an inch in diameter and smaller. But since the wire does have some thickness to it, a #20 mesh will only pass particles up to about $1/30^{th}$ of an inch in diameter. Table 2 lists example mesh data received from one mesh manufacturer.

Table 2. Mesh sizes from a typical manufacturer.

Mesh size	Wire diameter (in)	% open area	Mesh opening (in)
12	.023	51.8	.0600
14	.020	51.0	.0510
20	.016	46.2	.0340
30	.012	37.1	.0203
40	.010	36.0	.0150
50	.009	30.3	.0110
60	.0075	30.5	.0092
80	.0055	31.4	.0070
100	.0045	30.3	.0055
120	.0037	30.7	.0046
200	.0021	33.6	.0029
325	.0014	30.0	.0017

The mesh sieves can be purchased at your local ceramic supply store but are not cheap. A complete set is typically composed of the following meshes: 4, 6, 8, 12, 16, 20, 30, 40, 50, 70, 100, 140, 200, and 270. Because of their expense as well as the wear and tear that these screens can see from pushing glass frit through them, you may want to consider "calibrating" some common cheap and expendable alternatives. As an example, a spaghetti strainer is about a #10 mesh. You can also use hardware and window screens from your local hardware store. Be creative and save money.

Some glass artists, when using a fine mesh frit (80-100 mesh) will wash the frit in water to get rid of the extremely fine dust sized particles. They then drain the washed frit on a screen that is a grade finer than the last screen used (such as a 120-mesh one in this example). Alternatively you could just screen out the finer particles on a finer mesh and use what remains behind. Those extremely fine particles trap extremely small air bubbles. These small bubbles don't have enough buoyancy to rise out of the melt on their own during the casting process and thus increase the opalescence of the final work.

If you decide to make your own frit, you should be aware that whatever manufacturing technique that you choose to use will produce frit with a predictable size distribution. Although the distribution produced by each technique may vary from glass to glass depending on the variations in their physical properties. To get near ideal size packing ratios may require using more than one technique and some extra work sizing your frit. But if you are not trying to achieve fine color detail or are not concerned about movement of glass and the resultant blurring of color during firing, then you do not have to be concerned with trying to get dense packing.

To test for how well any mix of frit you make packs prior to filling a mold, you can measure what is called its tap density. This is done by putting the mix into a jar or glass. (Scientists generally use what is called a graduated cylinder—a test tube like container with volume markings on the outside.) Then you gently tap the container on the table to get the frit to settle. The tap density is then calculated by dividing the weight of the frit mix by the volume of the container it occupies after tapping. (The same ratio before tapping is called the free flowing density.) The higher the tap density the better the packing.

Temperature regimes of glass

To successfully kiln cast glass, you need to understand how its physical properties vary with temperature. This will help you to comprehend why it behaves the way it does and when you have to treat it with kid's gloves or when you can really push it around. An effective way to think of glass is as a material whose properties vary in different temperature regimes, the ranges of which vary for each type of glass.

The brittle solid temperature regime

You are probably most used to working with glass around room temperature where it is in this temperature regime. Here we see glass as a solid material that breaks in a brittle manner when stressed. Small scratches or cracks propagate through the material with ease.

Glass in this temperature regime expands and contracts in a predictable manner with changes in temperature. The amount of expansion is, as was explained earlier, quantified by the glass's coefficient of expansion (COE). This number which is expressed in units of 10^{-7} inches per inch per degree centigrade, is the average expansion of the glass over a given temperature range. This value is usually determined in the laboratory over the range of 0 to 300° C (32-600°F). The upper end of the brittle solid temperature regime is somewhat higher than this. For soda-lime glasses, it is on the order of 700°F while for lead glasses it is on the order of 600 °F.

As the temperature of a piece of glass is changed, the edges of the piece get warmer faster and will try to grow in size relative the cooler glass around it. This causes the silica tetrahedron chains to try to slip and stretch past each other. These slippage's build up, straining the natural order of the atoms in the glass and resulting in thermally induced stress. In the brittle solid temperature regime, the only way that stress in the glass can be relieved is by fracture.

The non-brittle solid temperature regime

As the temperature of the glass is increased, the tetrahedral chains become more mobile from increased molecular thermal vibrations and rotations. They start to be able to twist around any obstructions that may have pinned them previously in the brittle solid regime. This does not happen all at once but gradually as vibrations of the glass atoms increase with increasing temperature. A measure of this change is the decrease in the glass's viscosity with increasing temperature as seen back in Figure 22. This increased mobility allows any stress that may have built up in the glass to relieve itself. The temperature at which the stresses start to flow in a reasonable amount of time for a given glass is commonly referred to as its strain point. Technically this corresponds to the temperature at which a glass thread has a viscosity of 4×10^{15} poises when measured while cooling at a rate of 4±1°C/min. At this viscosity, the stress in a piece of glass takes on the order of hours to relieve itself.

The non-brittle solid temperature regime for soda-lime glasses ranges roughly from about 700 to 1000°F. In this temperature regime, the glass still expands and contracts with temperature change but the COE is different than it was in the brittle solid regime. In fact, a glass's COE is never constant and varies continually throughout all temperature regimes as is illustrated for a typical soda-lime glass in Figure 26. What you know as the COE is, as we said before, the average value of the COE measured over the shaded region of 0 to 300°C. This value is illustrated as a tiny dot on the curve. As you can also see in the figure, COE increases

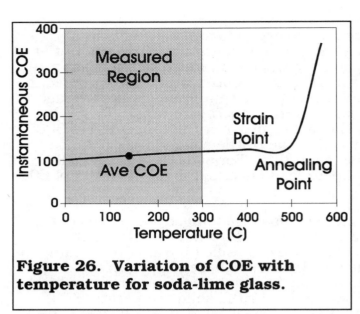

Figure 26. Variation of COE with temperature for soda-lime glass.

rapidly at higher temperatures where viscosity is also changing rapidly.

Although the higher mobility of the tetrahedron chains in this temperature regime allows any build up of stress to relieve itself over time, it is still possible to change the temperature of the glass faster than the stress can be reduced (in other words you can still thermal shock glass in this temperature regime). This is also the temperature regime in which glass is annealed. Many artists have been taught to think that annealing (stress relief) takes place at a particular temperature called the annealing point, but that is not quite correct. What that temperature actually represents is a compromise. The compromise is that it is a temperature at which the tetrahedron chains are mobile enough to allow relief of stress in a more reasonable time, minutes, without being so high that the bulk glass itself starts to flow in the same time scale. The annealing point technically refers to a temperature at which the viscosity of the glass is 2.5 x 10^{13} poises measured while cooling at 4±1°C/min. At this viscosity, the stresses in your work will be relieved in about 15 minutes. We will discuss annealing in greater detail in a little bit.

The flexible solid temperature regime

As you continue to raise the temperature of a piece of soda-lime glass above 1000°F, it starts to become more and more pliable. If left at this temperature, the glass will start to droop under the influence of gravity or muscle power. The transition point between this temperature regime and the previous one is commonly referred to as the softening point. It varies from glass to glass and refers to the temperature at which a viscosity of 9.6 x 10^7 poises is reached during the usual prescribed cooling. The chains of silica tetrahedrons are now so mobile that it is no longer possible to thermal shock the glass. Its properties start to resemble something more like taffy and its surface also starts to get sticky. It will stick to another piece of glass or to other materials such as separator coatings or kiln wash. These attributes become more pronounced with increasing temperature until about 1400°F and higher when the glass starts to enter the last temperature regime.

The fluid temperature regime

In this temperature regime, hand manipulation of the glass becomes possible. The glass exhibits fluid-like properties and will puddle out if left unconfined. This is the regime in which glassblowers are working when they blow glass and form it into complex shapes. This is also the temperature regime where full and flat fusing takes place in a kiln. The lower end of the regime is bounded by what is commonly referred to as the working point. It varies from glass to glass and refers to the temperature at which the glass has a viscosity of 9.6×10^4 poises.

Glass compatibility

A glass property near and dear to every hot glass artist's heart is compatibility. Glass compatibility means that glasses like to work with each other. If you put them together in a piece they won't fight each other and break everything up as you cool them down. This is the kind of glass that we like to work with because if its happy, we're happy. If you intend to mix colors and different types of glass, you will have to be concerned with compatibility because two or more incompatible glasses cast into the same mold is an invitation to disaster. They may be agreeable with each other at high temperatures but will quarrel violently at terrestrial ones where they are not likely to stay together long and their divorce will not be amicable. In order to better understand this disagreement, let's look at the whys and wherefores of glass compatibility.

Coefficient of expansion (COE)

As mentioned earlier, the kinds and amounts of oxide modifiers used in making a particular glass, break up and strain the silica matrix differently. These changes in turn affect the rate at which the glass shrinks when cooled. This rate, as discussed earlier, is commonly known as the coefficient of expansion (COE) and is usually expressed in the fusing community as a whole number coefficient between 0 and about 120; zero representing the ideal of no expansion and 120 being about the largest value seen. As an example, the Bullseye compatible glasses all have a COE of about 90. What this means is that in the solid regime, a 1 inch long piece of one of these glasses will shrink on the average 0.0000090 inches (90×10^{-7}) for each 1°C reduction in temperature. This is good information to know in case you are ever trying to impress someone at a cocktail party.

Thus a 10 inch piece of this glass will shrink about 0.046 inches in cooling from its annealing temperature (about 950°F) to room temperature. Similarly a 10 inch piece of Moretti glass with a COE of 104 would shrink 0.051 inches. Therefore, if you were trying to fuse together 10 inch strips of these two types of glass, the difference between the shrinkage of one strip and the other is

0.008 inches. This is about the thickness of 5 sheets of paper. That may not seen like much on our ordinary macroscopic level, but when you compare it to the size scale of reference, atoms, it is enormous. As a result, the piece would literally pull itself apart trying to separate the two types of glass.

Table 3. Coefficient of expansion (COE) of some common art glasses.

Manufacturer	COE (10^7 in/in/°C)
Fused silica (quartz glass)	3
Pyrex, Northstar	32-33
Float glass	81
GNA (Antec 76)	86-88
Kugler, Zimmerman (lead based)	87
Bullseye, Wasser, Uroburos	90
Lenox crystal	94
Spectrum	96
Moretti	104
Pemco Pb83	108
Satake	120

Thus as anyone who has done hot glasswork before knows, you have to make sure that whatever glasses you use in your work expand and contract at nearly the same rate to be compatible. This will avoid breakage upon cooling or sometime later. Some manufacturers cater to hot/warm glass artists and have initiated good quality control measures to ensure a consistent self-compatible glass line. For small work, small variations (1-3 points) in COE will probable not cause any major problems, but as most good fusing manuals will recommend, you should probably check the compatibility of your glass yourself for large work especially in the light of the fact that COEs at high temperatures may differ. Remember the COE of a glass is not really a constant (although nearly so at low temperatures) but instead is an average over the temperature range of 0 to 300°C. Outside this region, the COE starts to increase rapidly with increasing temperature such that in the annealing temperature range the COE may be as much as 3 times the reported value. If the COEs of the two glass are not matched in this region, this may also cause incompatibility. Luckily if they are of similar composition (i.e. both soda-lime glasses or both lead glasses), they will probably match in that region also. Table 3 lists reported COEs for a number of common art glasses.

Determining glass compatibility

The easiest way to be sure that your glass is compatible is to buy glass whose compatibility has been verified by the manufacturer. Many of the expansion 90 glasses are tested by the factory. Look for the tested compatible label. If you are using frit, they can be a point or two off without encountering any real problems in reasonably sized work. But what should you do if you want to be sure of a glass's compatibility?

The most accurate way of ensuring that two glasses are compatible is to fuse up a test strip. To run a test strip requires a clear compatible base glass against which to test. What you are really doing is testing the compatibility of each of the other glasses to this base glass. Then by using the Transitive Property of Glass Fusing (i.e. if A is compatible to B and C is compatible to B then A must be compatible to C) we can presume their compatibility.

To run a test strip on sheet glasses, you start by cutting a strip of the clear base glass about 1½ inches wide and about 1½ inches long for each specimen that you are going to test. Thus if you are going to test 6 specimens, the strip should be at least 9 inches long and 1½ inches wide. Next cut ½ by ½ inch square specimens of each of the glasses you want to test for compatibility. (Although Dan swears that triangular specimens work better to show up incompatibility stress because of their sharper corners.) Wash, clean and dry the glass carefully to prevent any contamination from biasing your results. Space the specimens out on the strip of clear base ½ inch from the edges and 1 inch from each other. Keep track of which glass is which since sometimes they change color during firing. It helps to mark both the glass sheet and the test strip by the specimen to ensure no mix-ups. Some marking pens are available (Steel Paint marking pens made by the Alton Company are one version) that have a metallic based ink that will not burn off the glass during the firing and will work well for this process. It can be easily removed after the test if desired. Now fire the test strip to a flat fuse. This will require a processing temperature somewhere in the range of 1450 to 1650°F for most soda-lime glasses depending on their hardness. After this firing, the thickness of the strip should be almost constant all the way down the strip.

Now examine the test strip for signs of incompatibility by looking for residual stresses in it. To do this we use polarizing filters like those on expensive sunglasses. You will need two of these filters to conduct the test. These filters have fine parallel crystal assemblages in them that only let light through that is vibrating in one direction, say left-to-right. If you rotate these filters relative to each other over a light table, you will see that they will get dark and light periodically. They are dark when the filter on the bottom only lets light vibrating left-to-right through and the second filter only lets light vibrating top-to-bottom through. As you rotate the top filter 90° relative to the bottom filter, the crystal assemblages on both are now aligned such that both filters now allow only light that is vibrating left-to-right through. This configuration allows the maximum amount of light through. As you turn the top filter further, they will again get darker until at another 90° the light is again at a minimum.

You are probably wondering how these filters are going to be used to measure residual stress in the glass. To understand how this works, you have to know that light which is passed through glass that is stressed is twisted so that the direction of its vibration changes. Light that passes through unstressed glass is not twisted. With this in mind, put one filter below the test strip on the light table (or over a light bulb) and the other filter on the top of the glass. Rotate the top filter to the position that lets through the minimum amount of light. Any signs of incompatibility that exist in the test strip will be visible as a halo of light around the test specimens where the light has been twisted by stress in the base glass. Figure 27 illustrates what this will look like for varying amounts of stress in the glass. The bigger the halo, the greater the amount of stress. The only exception to this rule is for strips that have cracked. In this case stress will be relieved in the vicinity of a crack. Of course the development of cracks should also give you a clue that something is wrong. Specimens that show only slight stress or less are considered to be compatible with each other.

When doing this test, it is much easier to work with large polarizing filters on a light table rather than those smaller ones on the commercially available "Stressometer." Large filters are available from Edmund Scientific Company and you don't need a letter from the governor to buy them.

A similar test that works well when testing frits or solid sheet glass against a clear control base was suggested by Gil Reynolds and seems to make a lot of sense. It gives a larger interface over which the strain can develop, thus making detection of incompatibility more likely. Assuming that glasses are 1/8-inch thick, cut two 1 by ½-inch rectangles of each kind of glass to be tested. Place piles of the pieces doubled on a kiln shelf with doubled clear rectangles of your reference glass between each doubled test piece and at the ends of the strip. If the glass that you want to test is frit, pile it between piles of the clear reference glass. The mass of the piles should be sufficient to allow them to spread out and edge fuse to the adjacent clear stack. The frit pile has to be about 1½ times as high as the base glass pile to accommodate for shrinkage as it consolidates. The interfaces between the clear base and the test glass are then examined for residual stress using polarizing filters as before.

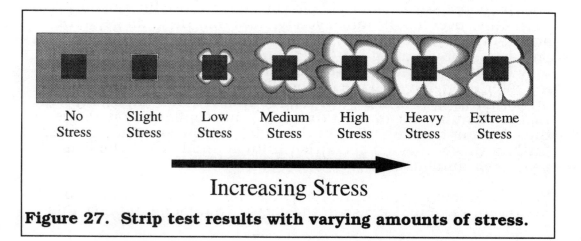

| No Stress | Slight Stress | Low Stress | Medium Stress | High Stress | Heavy Stress | Extreme Stress |

Increasing Stress

Figure 27. Strip test results with varying amounts of stress.

Getting around incompatibility

Sometimes artistically you really want to use two glasses that you know are slightly incompatible together in a piece. Is there anything that you can do to get this to work or are you just courting disaster? Well there are somethings that you can do to minimize the effect of this decision. The first is to always try to minimize the use of the incompatible glass. Second, if fusing to full density, you can completely encase the incompatible glass with a fairly thick layer of the compatible glass that makes up the bulk of the casting. This works best if the incompatible glass that you are encasing is of a lower COE so that the interface between the two glasses is under compression after cooling to room temperature. The third thing that you can try to do is to cast at a lower temperature. Here you will get a sugary like casting where the fused portions of the individual grains are fairly small resulting in lower stress between them because the small area of contact. The last thing that you can do to minimize the stress present in the piece is by annealing it very well as we discuss next.

Annealing glass

Annealing is the process of taking a material to a high enough temperature where its molecules are sufficiently mobile to relieve internal residual stress and then slowly cooling the material in a way to minimize build up of any new stress. In pâte de verre or kiln casting work, we are not usually removing stress from a piece. Instead what we are trying to do is minimize the amount of stress that gets locked into a piece during the cooling process. To learn how to accomplish this, you have to understand how stress gets locked into a piece.

Theory of annealing or stress minimization

As you remember, glass expands when heated and contracts when cooled, so any temperature gradients in the glass result in differences in length of adjacent portions of the glass. These difference in lengths of nearby sections are commonly referred to as strain. They can, in the limit, be thought of as differences in distances between adjacent glass atoms. Atoms in any material stay together because they are attracted to each other and these attractive forces can be thought of as rubber bands. So as you stretch (strain) the rubber bands, they build up forces (stress) in them that want to push or pull the atoms back to their optimal position. For rubber bands, if you hold them stretched for long periods of time, they start to grow in length and loose much of the force on them. For glass, this happens at higher temperatures where the attractive forces become weaker.

In cooling the glass back down from the process temperature to room temperature, the glass cools from one or two outside surfaces as pictured in Figure 28. This process sets up temperature gradients in the glass such that the outside is cooler than the inside. The optimum distance between glass atoms increases with temperature as seen by the fact that glass has a positive COE. So the temperature gradient sets up a density gradient which causes the adjacent atoms to yank and pull on each other. At high temperature where the atoms are still relatively mobile, they will flow around to relieve this stress just as the rubber band stretches with time. Thus they will move into an area where the rubber bands, or forces, between the atoms are stretched or are in tension. Likewise they will flow out of an area where they have been squeezed together, commonly known as compression. So at high temperature of the fluid and flexible regimes, you don't have problems with stress. The glass just flows to relieve it.

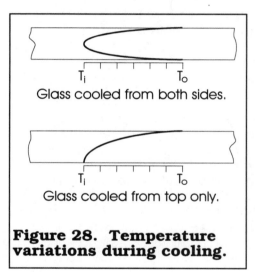

T_i T_o

Glass cooled from both sides.

T_i T_o

Glass cooled from top only.

Figure 28. Temperature variations during cooling.

At temperatures in the brittle solid regime, which are low relative to the melting point of glass, bonds between the atoms can no longer stretch relative to each other. So when temperature gradients cause stress in this temperature regime by differential heating or cooling, they are stuck with it. But this stress state is temporary and goes away as soon as the temperature gradients go away and all the rubber bands become the same length again. Of course you have to make sure that the stress in the rubber bands never gets so great that they break or in this case causes the glass to crack.

The situation where you run into trouble in cooling your glass is when the outside is cool enough that the atoms can not move much but the inside is still hot enough that the atoms are free to move. So when the outside squeezes on the inside, the atoms on the inside will move around to push back evenly on the outside like air pushes on the sides of a balloon. Then as the inside cools a little more, these atoms get locked into position based upon the existing temperature gradient. As the temperature gradient gets reduced during cooling, the atoms in the center of the glass find themselves farther apart than the desire spacing on which the atoms on the outside of the glass are located. Thus they will be in tension, pulling against the surrounding glass with a residual stress, while the outside will be in compression, trying push back against the inside. If the glass on the outside or the inside is not strong enough, the glass cracks apart. This may happen immediately upon returning to room temperature or, if just barely strong enough, it can occur at a later time when subjected to a stressful environment. This can be in the form of a thermal variation or an insignificant physical impact.

Before you can start annealing, you have to know the annealing temperature range for your glass. As we have discussed, there are three commonly defined points that are important in defining the annealing range — the softening point, the annealing point and the strain point. The softening point marks the transition between the flexible solid temperature regime and the non-brittle solid temperature regime for a given glass. It is the lowest temperature at which a rod or strip of glass will slump over an extended heat soak of a reasonable length of time (an hour.) The annealing point is that temperature at which the atoms are mobile enough to allow all stress to quickly flow out of the glass but not so mobile that the bulk glass will flow. Lastly there is the strain point, this marks the temperature at which the atoms are no longer mobile enough to allow the stress to flow out of a piece in a reasonable length of time. This, as mentioned earlier, serves as the boundary between the brittle solid and the non-brittle solid temperature regimes. The region in which you have to be careful during cooling is from the annealing point down to the strain point. The softening point is important because it is an easily measurable temperature that can, as we shall see, serve as a good sign post for the location of the other two points.

Allowable high temperature cooling rates (that between the annealing point and the strain point) are dictated by the chemical composition of the glass, the mass and thickness of the glass, and the mass and type of investment material surrounding the glass. Of these it is the composition of the glass that determines boundaries of the temperature regimes for the glass (annealing and strain point) and the ultimate tensile limit that the glass can accommodate. The mass (thickness) and type of investment material used for a casting affects the rate at which heat can be transferred into and out of the glass. They help define how large of temperature gradients and thus strain will be set up in the glass.

The classical analysis of residual stress and strain resulting from cooling at a given rate through the annealing range was developed for plate glass cooled from both sides by Lillie in 1950. (If you want the gory details of this analysis look at his paper listed in the reference section or one of the other technical references such as "Glass Practice" or the "Glass Engineering Handbook." If you want details on the modern theory of annealing, get a lot of No Doze and check out Narayanaswamy's paper.) Although not quite correct because it does not take phase changes of the glass into account, Lillie's equations can be used to estimate the residual stress and strain that will result from cooling a glass of a given thickness and properties down through the annealing range at a chosen cooling rate. This rate dictates the thermal distribution during cooling and thus the resultant stress. The formula for stress in layman's terms can be approximated as:

$$\text{Stress} = 0.926 \, (\text{COE}) \, (\text{thickness}^2) \, (\text{Cooling Rate})$$

where stress is in pounds per square Inch (psi), thickness is in inches and cooling rate is in degrees Fahrenheit per minute. We are not going to try and explain where this equation came from to you with any rigorous mathematics (at least as long as you don't encourage Jim). It is based on assumptions of the shape of the temperature distribution in the glass, the heat transfer rates and the relationship between the high temperature COE and the low temperature COE as well as approximations of the stress/strain relationship. Solving for cooling rate we get the relationship that:

$$\text{Cooling Rate} = 1.08 \, (\text{Allowable Stress}) \, / \, (\text{COE} * \text{thickness}^2)$$

In the case where you are dealing with something like a bas relief casting, you are really only <u>cooling from one side</u> and should treat the glass as if it were a sheet of glass of twice the thickness (T=2t). This is the typical case in fusing or in bas relief castings where you are only cooling through the top surface of the glass. Making this substitution into the cooling rate equation results in the following relationship which is applicable to our single sided work:

$$\text{Cooling Rate} = 0.27 \, (\text{Allowable Stress}) \, / \, [\text{COE}* \text{thickness}^2]$$

We apologize to many of you who may have just had this fly over your head, but Jim is an engineer after all and these are the basic equations that you can use to calculate your own high temperature cooling rate tables. So all you have to do to apply them is decide what level of residual stresses or strains you are comfortable with and plug in that value along with your glass properties. From this you can develop cooling rate tables for your work. Plate glass companies usually hold the residual strain left in their glass to below 10 µ strain (0.00001 inches/inch) to ensure good cutability of their glass. This corresponds to a stress of about 100 lb/in^2 (psi). If we impose similar requirements on strain and use the COE of Bullseye glass, the following table of appropriate cooling rates can be generated.

If you want less residual stress or strain by a given factor, cool through the annealing zone by a directly proportional slower rate. Thus in optical glass manufacture, where they want strains on the order of a twentieth of the above 10 µ strain to avoid optical distortions, you would have to cool twenty times slower. (You can probably get away with a little more strain than 10 µ strain, so if you are in a hurry you might be able to double these given rates without disastrous results.) If you want to develop a table for a different type of glass for which you only know the COE, divide the values in the rate column by the ratio of the new glass's COE to that of Bullseye. Thus for float glass, you would divide each rate by 81/90 or 0.9. (This is the same as multiplying by 1.1.) So the lower the coefficient of thermal expansion, the faster the allowable high temperature cooling rate.

Table 4. High temperature cooling rates for Bullseye glass.

Glass Thickness (inches)	Two Sided Cooling		Single Sided Cooling	
	(°F/Min)	(°F/Hr)	(°F/Min)	(°F/Hr)
1/8	76.5	4608	19.2	1152
1/4	19.2	1152	4.8	288
3/8	8.5	512	2.1	128
1/2	4.8	288	1.2	72
5/8	3.1	184	0.88	46
3/4	2.1	128	0.53	32
7/8	1.6	94	0.39	24
1	1.2	72	0.30	18
2	0.3	18	0.08	4.5
3	0.13	8	0.03	2.0
4	0.08	4.5	0.02	1.1
5	0.05	2.9	0.012	0.72
6	0.03	2.0	0.008	0.50
8	0.02	1.13	0.005	0.28

As we have discussed, this situation is for the general case where we are considering cooling semi-flat pieces from one side. Sometimes we have shapes that are considerably different from this. Are any modifications needed for these cases? Engineers, like Jim, can calculate the temperature gradients and resulting stress gradients that are generated in cooling a mold full of glass. All they need is a complete definition of the glass and investment properties, and a large enough computer. (They sure enjoy their computers.) Jim ran a series of calculations to examine the effect of different cooling rates on molds and castings of different shapes and sizes. What he was trying to do was demonstrate how the temperature distributions vary as these conditions change. In the first portion of this study, he looked at how temperature variations develop in three basic glass configurations: large flat sheets, long cylinders and spheres. For this study, he looked at how the different shapes affect how fast the center of the glass cools down during an instantaneous crash cooling of a kiln from 1400°F to 1000°F. This means that the outside surface of the piece is instantaneously reduced.

As you might expect, each of these shapes cools somewhat differently because their surface to volume ratio increases as you go from a large sheet to a long cylinder and then on to a sphere. Since cooling occurs from the surface, the higher this ratio; the faster the object cools. Figure 29 illustrates the difference that shape plays on cooling of the center for these three different shapes: a 6" thick sheet (cooled from both sides), a 6" diameter cylinder and a 6" diameter sphere. From this graph, we see that the temperature variations in large sheets are more than about twice those in spheres and one and a half those in long cylinders. Thus you should be able to cool spheres twice as fast or cylinders one and a half times as fast as sheets to get the same temperature gradient. Since residual stress is a direct result of the temperature gradient in the glass as it cools through the annealing zone, this

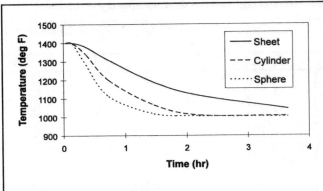

Figure 29. Change of temperature at center with time for different shapes.

means that you will then get the same residual stress in each of these cases too.

The next question to ask is what affect does the addition of a mold and its thickness have on cooling of a piece. For this portion of his study, Jim took the simplest possible configuration, that of a spherical glass casting in a spherical mold. To further simplify the problem, he assumed that the mold wall was continuous all around without any reservoir or gating. He then ran calculations on how the temperature variations in the casting developed as it was again instantaneously crash cooled from 1500°F to 1000°F. Here it is the outside of the mold that is instantaneously changed. You can see the results of these calculations again for a six inch diameter glass sphere inside spherical plaster molds of various thickness. Let's look at how fast the center of the glass's temperature drops to 1100°F for the different mold thickness. Look at the lowest curve in Figure 30, which is the curve describing the temperature drop for the normal ½ inch thick mold. The curve shows that it will take the six inch diameter casting 2 hours to drop to 1100°F. If the mold thickness is increased to 1 inch, the required time increases to 2 2/3 hours. Increasing the thickness to 1½ inches increases the required time to 3 1/3 hours. Lastly if you used a 2 inch thick mold, you would be required to hold for 4 1/8 hours to allow the temperature to drop to 1100°F. If for some reason you were to decide to use a 4 inch thick mold, the center of the casting would still be at 1265°F after a 5 hour hold.

The purpose of this example is to illustrate to you the importance of keeping your molds thick enough to have enough strength to contain the glass but not to go overboard. Try to stick near the recommended thickness of ½ inch as much as possible. If you need more strength, reinforce your molds as described in the section on mold reinforcement in the chapter on advanced mold

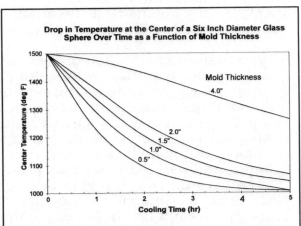

Figure 30. Mold thickness' effect on cooling.

construction techniques. Otherwise you will find that you have to go to extremely long firing cycles.

Determining annealing properties

There are several different ways to determine the annealing point of a glass. The easiest way is to just ask the manufacturer. They usually know their glass better than anyone else since they make the darn stuff. But keep in mind that their interest in annealing is making a product, whether it is blown vessels or sheet glass. What we are doing in kiln casting typically involves greater localized mass and more thickness variations of glass. This situation requires greater control of the high temperature cooling or annealing cycle than a constant thickness regular shape object does. For this reason their annealing requirements are usually less stringent than ours and they can get away with ramping down through the annealing range faster without having to establish an exact annealing point. We will also want a nice soak before proceeding into our annealing cycle to reduce thermal gradients as much as possible.

As we stated earlier, the annealing and strain points of a soda-lime glass can be approximated from the softening point. So if we can determine it, we can estimate the annealing point and the strain point. There is a test that you can run in your own studio kiln to determine the softening point. It can take some time to get accurate results though, sometimes as much a full day with an additional day to test the test. This test is called a slump test. You start by cutting several strips of the test glass ¼" wide and at least 12" long. Place one strip in the kiln with one end sandwiched between two pieces of soft fire brick, so that most of the strip hangs out horizontally over the shelf. Now heat the kiln to about 100°F below the suspected softening temperature and hold it for about an hour to stabilize the temperature distribution in the kiln. Then slowly raise the temperature at a rate of about 50°F/hr. Occasionally observe the strip through the peek hole to see what is happening. (This will disturb the temperature distribution in the kiln much less than lifting the lid.) When the test strip appears to show signs of movement, hold the temperature steady to see if it really is slumping. If so, this will be close to the softening point.

To zoom in on the softening point a little more accurately, insert another strip into the kiln and preheat as before. Then slowly heat the kiln to bring the temperature up to 25°F below the previously determined slumping temperature and hold for three hours. If there are any indications of slumping, repeat the test again another 25°F lower. If the test strip doesn't slump, then you know that the softening temperature is somewhere in the middle of the two previous tests. You can make a more accurate measurement if you want by running more tests but that is usually not justified. The test is easy to run when your starting material is sheet glass but frit requires an extra firing. The frit must first be fused into a sheet that can be cut up into strips.

The annealing point for soda-lime glasses can for all practical purposes be defined to lie about 50°F below the softening point and the strain point is commonly considered to lie 150°F below the annealing point.

The preceding overview is based on our extensive experience in fusing soda-lime glasses. If you venture into casting of lead glasses, you might find some interesting variations on this. For example, the lab report on Lenox heavy lead crystal indicates a 1161°F softening point, a 826°F annealing point and a 750°F strain point. That's a little bit different than what we just described but lead glasses have a larger working range. Besides what do those guys at the lab know anyway? There just a bunch of scientists and engineers like Jim. Dan's observations on GNA (and he uses a lot of it) are that it softens at 1010°F, has its annealing point at 960°F and its strain point at 800°F.

Colorants

If you choose to work with one of the high lead glasses, you may not have the advantage of a ready-made color palette. Instead you most likely will have to make your own colors from clear lead-based frit. Colors in glass are formed by three major processes: dissolved metallic oxides, colloidal suspensions of particles, and inclusion of crystalline materials.

Metallic oxides can be dissolved uniformly into molten glass just like sugar in water. They actually become part of the solution and will not settle out again. When the molten glass is cooled and allowed to solidify, the oxides remain dissolved in the solid glass phase. These metallic oxides absorb different wavelengths of light as it passes through the glass. Each metallic oxide absorbs certain characteristic wavelengths of light and pass the rest through.

A second way that glass is colored is to disperse tiny particles uniformly throughout the melt. Although this may seem the same as the previous method, it is not. This is more like the mix of fine silt in river water. Here the particles are suspended because of the motion of the water molecules, they never really become part of the solution. If you were to take that water and run it through a centrifuge, you would be able to separate them out. In this situation, the size of the suspended particles dictate the wavelengths of light that they can reflect. The remainder of the light is absorbed.

The third way that glass is colored is through addition of materials, that when the glass cools, form tiny crystalline inclusions in the glass. Because they have a different structure they will refract the light differently than the bulk of the glass. This leads to opal-like effects.

The method that we will discuss for coloring your glass is not exactly making it from batch as any self-respecting glassblower will be glad to tell you but is closer to batching from cullet. To color your base frit, first grind it to a fine powder, about 350 mesh, next mix it with a given amount of whatever material you are adding to color it, then pour the mixture into a crucible and remelt it. Once the melt is very fluid and most of the trapped bubbles have come out, pour it into a bucket of water to refrit it. It is now ready to use. There is a singular joy in realizing that you developed the color in the glass that you are using. We sometimes get off on simple things like that. Of course we've made some good colors and some so bad that we couldn't even blame the dog. The actual color that you end up with after adding a colorant to the glass may vary depending on a number of factors such as: the composition of the base glass, the concentration of the colorant, the temperature to which you took the melt, the atmosphere of your kiln (reducing or oxidative), and the time at temperature.

Since the main thing that you will be coloring is lead based glasses, let's review some safety procedures for their use. The lead oxide is a flux added, as you should remember, to make the glass melt at a lower temperature. Since it has been integrated into the silica matrix, it is now a lead silicate which is relatively inert compared to the original oxide. But we still advise caution in handling it, especially as a fine powder, because it can be easily inhaled or ingested and once into the body, lead may be leached out of the powder just as it can be by some foods. So wear a respirator whenever dealing with these fine powders, especially when pouring them into a hot crucible. Not only can some of the lead be released as fumes but also some of the coloring oxides that you will use. Many times these are more toxic than the lead. Vent your kiln and your studio, or at the very least use a fan and an open window. For the lead glaze bases that we have discussed — Pemco Pb 83, O'Hommel 33 and Ferro 3419-2 — you will only have to heat them to about 1600°F to get good dispersion of the colorants within the glass and at this temperature they can be poured like honey on a hot day.

Table 5 lists some color recipes that we have found work fairly well for us. The exact amount of colorant to add may take a little experimentation. You may be surprised how little is actually needed to color your glass. The amounts that we give are for coloring 2 cups of glaze base which will just about fill the average crucible to the top. The colorant amounts are given as ½ gram measures but are actually added as medium size palette knife measures. Hey what the heck, we are usually in a hurry and we cook the same way too. Besides a little uncertainty usually won't hurt. If you come up with a good recipe, you may want to dust off the old triple beam balance and make more accurate measurements later.

Table 5. Metal oxides commonly used as colorants .

Color	Shade	Colorant	Measures
white	opal	vanadium pentoxide	12-15
yellow	pale to mid	silver nitrate	1-3
	yellow-green	potassium dichromate	2-3
	champagne	cerium oxide titanium dioxide	60 20
purple	pale	manganese oxide or manganese carbonate	2-3
	grayed	manganese carbonate & copper carbonate	10-12 4-6
blue	light turquoise	copper carbonate	2-3
	med turquoise	copper carbonate	6-8
	deep turquoise	copper carbonate	10-12
	pale	cobalt oxide	¼
	medium	cobalt oxide	½
	deep navy	cobalt oxide	1-2
green	yellowish	iron chromate	5
	jade	vanadium pentoxide	6-8
	dark green	chrome oxide	2-3
	dark grass green	chrome oxide	6-8
	rich green	cerium oxide & vanadium	10-12 2-3
black	purple	manganese carbonate	12-16
amber	yellow	potassium dichromate	6
	medium	iron oxide red	6-10
brown	dark	red copper oxide & nickel carbonate	2-3 2-3
	dark amber brown	lithium carbonate & nickel carbonate	30-40 4-6
gray	pale	nickel carbonate	4-6
	medium	nickel carbonate & manganese carbonate	8-10 4-6
	gray-blue	potassium nitrate & cobalt carbonate	20-30 2-3

More on Modeling

The model is the original object whose shape you want to cast in glass and can be constructed from a number of different materials. Since many glass artists do not necessarily have an extensive background in common modeling materials, we decided to expand in further detail upon this subject in this chapter. The materials most commonly used for modeling in direct casting of single part expendable molds are wax, clay and organic materials such as small vegetables or for the more gruesome of you, small animals. All but clay can be burned directly out of the mold. If you make multi-part molds, then almost any object can be used to form an impression in a reusable mold as long as there are not undercuts that will trap the model in the mold. Let's now look at each of the main modeling materials and discuss how they are used.

Modeling With Wax

Wax has been used for modeling effigies for thousands of years. Wax models of religious figures have been found in tombs of ancient Egyptians. Wax has many properties that makes it the ideal material for modeling. It is durable, lightweight, clean working and does not shrink, crack or dry out. The media can be worked in a number of ways: sawing, carving, casting, handworking, etc. Wax has the advantage of allowing development of intricate details even down to fingerprints. (That's one way to prove you did the work.) The process of making an original out of wax, then melting the wax out of the mold is the basis of cire perdue or lost wax casting. The technique is used by craftsmen in a number of trades (bronze sculpture, jewelry, glass, etc.).

Direct working of wax can sometimes involve a considerable amount of time depending upon how detailed you care to get and quite a few tools depending upon how much of a tool collector you are. You don't have worry about undercuts or draft in wax work because you just melt the model out and can burn out any residue that might get trapped in the mold. You will want to learn a little about the chemistry of wax in order to understand which additives are added to the wax to soften it and make it more flexible. Additives are also added to change other properties such as melting temperature and plastic range. These additives include such things as animal fats, oils, tallows, gums, resins and fillers.

Types of waxes

The term wax is loosely applied to describe many different oily solids and there are many different kinds of waxes. They vary in a number of properties; the most important of which are slipperiness, plasticity, melting temperature and hardness. Waxes can also be classified according to how they have been prepared, as being either natural, modified or compounded. Natural waxes are those that can be directly found in nature from animal, vegetable or mineral sources. When such a natural wax is chemically or thermally altered in some way, it is said to be a modified wax. Then by mixing a number of different waxes together to get the properties that you want, you end up with a compounded wax.

The choice of which wax to use depends upon how you prefer to sculpt or the process that you are using. Most glass artists prefer working with microcrystalline wax, which is also used by most bronze sculptors, because it is cheap and easily available. For fine detail some of the harder jewelers' waxes, of which there are two major manufacturers — Kerr and Ferris, may work better. Even beeswax and paraffin can be used for modeling. It is all right to mix waxes, you will just get a new compounded wax formulation, with a new properties. Most have already been blended to give them specific properties such as toughness, flexibility, viscosity and melting point but slight changes should not hurt. Just take care that you keep them clean and try not to overheat them when blending. Besides being available in different formulations, waxes are also available in different shapes: sheets, blocks, rods, wires, bars, tubes, etc. Feel free to use whatever shape or formulation that works for you. The Art Police will not cite you if you decide to construct different portions of the model out of different types of waxes.

If you're thrifty like us, you can try to reuse as much of your wax as possible but you will invariably end up with small investment fragments in your wax that can make modeling more difficult over time. For this reason, many glass artists choose not to reuse any of their wax and advise others against doing so. After all, wax is probably one of the cheapest materials that we are dealing with in the whole kiln casting process so trying hard to save it may not make sense if it results in losing a piece of work.

Microcrystalline Wax

Microcrystalline wax is a relatively recent natural wax with properties similar to natural beeswax and was originally an unwanted petroleum by-product. In order to keep motor oils fluid at low temperatures, the relatively high molecular weight materials had to be removed. This resulted in a hard waxy material that at first no one knew what to do with. Now-a-days the production quantities of this unwanted material exceed that of any of the other natural waxes. It is the standby, as was previously mentioned for those craftsmen that do bronze casting in a real foundry situation, even if they only cast baby shoes. It has good strength, fairly high melting point and is relatively flexible. Three types of microcrystalline wax are available from our local arts supplier (Douglas and Sturgess) under the name of "victory wax." Heck if we know who won what, but it saves harvesting honey combs. The three types, white, yellow and brown, differ in hardness and melting temperature. White is the hardest of the three. Yellow is slightly softer and also works well as an easel wax for stained glass. (You do remember stained glass, don't you?) Dark brown, the softest of the three, is the one preferred by foundry personnel and sculptors. This is the reason that it is the type of microcrystalline wax that can usually be found in the larger art supply stores.

Microcrystalline wax is typically sold in 1 or 10 lb. blocks and is cheaper than the jewelers waxes that we will soon discuss because of the larger volume of wax produced helps bring down its price. You can also order wax directly from the petroleum manufacturers but you will have to be prepared to specify it by complex technical jargon that we do not intend on presenting here. Good sculptural microcrystalline wax will have a melting point in the 140° to 180°F range. In addition it will be fairly soft. Hardness of a wax is determined by measuring how many tenths of a millimeter a "standard" needle will penetrate into wax that has been warmed to a given test temperature (usually 77°F) — the higher the number, the softer the wax. For sculptural work, you want a wax with a needle penetration in the 20 to 40 tenths of a millimeter range

Red Wax

Another sculptural wax that is a little harder than microcrystalline wax is red wax. It is also sometimes referred to as "French" wax. We guess that this means it goes well with wine and can only be used a little at a time. It is commonly used in sculpture by building it up over a soft wire backbone and appears to be particularly suited for casting. Red wax is more expensive than microcrystalline wax and because of its hardness needs to be worked with sharp or worked heated tools. It is similar to the carving waxes which we discuss next.

Carving Waxes

Carving waxes are hard waxes, hard on the order of a hardwood, able to hold sharp details. Unlike a hardwood, they do not have any grain to them but can be worked with many of the same tools. They cut cleanly with a knife or a saw as well as file like a metal.

Their melting temperatures are so high that they can even be worked with powered hand tools. The harder they are though, the more brittle they are. You have to be careful not to inadvertently split them during carving. They are available in blocks, tubes, rods and sheets of various thicknesses. Ferris makes three different carving waxes for jewelry work that have been dyed different colors, green, purple and blue, each with slightly different properties. Green is the hardest, allowing the development of greatest detail, but is also the most brittle which usually limits its use to small objects. It melts at 220°F, and immediately becomes very fluid. Purple is more flexible and a little softer, making carving a little easier. It melts at 230°F and first becomes viscous before becoming fluid. Unlike green wax though, once melted, it becomes too soft to hold fine detail. Blue wax is the most flexible and carvable of the three. It melts at 230°F and remains very viscous. This allows control when adding wax to a modeling project as will be discussed later.

Mold-a-wax

Mold-a-wax is another wax type produced by Ferris. This wax is generally used by cutting it into thin sheets or slabs. These sheets are then softened in warm water and pressed into molds or shaped around objects. This allows construction of thin walled objects or vessels. The wax is made in two types. The first, black, is the harder and higher melting temperature of the two. The other, red, is very soft. The problem with using this wax is its softness. It can inadvertently become distorted as you as you remove it from whatever you formed it on. This problem can be minimized by prior application of a release agent on the object you are modeling but even with this precaution it can still be a problem. It is hard to put further detail in a model of this wax because it is so soft, and it is hard to add extra wax to a mold-a-wax model because it melts at so low a temperature.

Casting Wax

Casting or injection wax is a hard wax which melts at a relatively low temperature to form a low viscosity fluid and also sets up quickly to its original hardness. It is used primarily for casting duplicates from a master mold as will be discussed later and is often introduced into the mold by injection.

Set-up Wax

Set-up wax is primarily used for wax build-up. It is a low melting temperature wax that is used by melting and the dripping it onto your work. It is too soft for filing or carving and melts at too low a temperature to use motor tools on it. It is primarily worked with hot tools, although it can be carved with a sharp knife while still warm. Ferris makes two types of setup wax, blue and Perfect. Of the two, blue is the harder and most workable with carving tools which makes you wonder why they call the other Perfect. A hard yellow microcrystalline wax also works well for this purpose.

Sticky Wax

Sticky wax is a soft, gummy wax that melts at fairly low temperature. Its main purpose is to act like an adhesive in bonding pieces of wax together. You can use it to bond individually constructed components together into a single model. To use it, simply warm one of the objects that you want to bond in one hand and a little sticky wax on the end of a tool in the other. Spread the sticky wax onto the piece. Then rewarm the sticky wax region of this piece and the other piece that you want to bond to it. When ready, press the pieces together. This should hold them together well enough to cast a mold around it. Sticky wax is very similar to the wax that is used in stained glass work to hold pieces of glass to a glass easel or to a lamp mold.

Water Soluble Waxes

Water soluble waxes are used in situations where you may want to create an object with a hollow portion. It is brittle and cannot be carved or filed easily, but it can be built-up like a set-up wax. Other waxes can be added around it. When your object is finished, you just place the whole thing in warm water and the water soluble wax will dissolve away. This is especially useful in making things like beads where you want a hollow in the model to make it lighter. You will probably never use this wax though because even for beads it is easier and cheaper to insert a hole former of something like fiber paper into your finished mold.

Paraffin

Paraffin, another petroleum byproduct, is the hard white wax that is commonly found in your supermarket. Besides being used for sealing the tops of jelly jars (which in itself is a use that we highly approve, especially if we are on your mailing list), you will use this hard wax primarily as an additive in compounding other waxes to harden them or to lower their melting temperature. Paraffin is so hard because it has been highly refined to contain only the higher molecular weight material. If you want, you can try to model with it directly. Try working it as if it were a carving wax. Be warned that it tends to be even more brittle than most carving waxes, so work carefully. It can also be used as a cheap substitute for a casting wax because of its hardness and low melting temperature.

Beeswax

Lastly, if you want that back-to-nature feeling, you can work with the real thing, beeswax. It is a nice soft wax available in a number of different flavors if you so desire. (This can make melting it the first couple of times a fragrant proposition that everyone will enjoy.) You can get it from a number of sources but price may vary considerably. It was twice as expensive as microcrystalline wax at one art supply store visited during preparation of this work.

Plastecine

One wax-like material that is not compatible with wax is plastecine. This material is actually more like a clay. It should not be mixed or compounded with your other waxes if you plan on trying to recover and reuse them because it will not really mix with waxes. Instead of getting a smooth uniform mixture as you do when mixing other waxes, you will end up with a crumbly material sort of like pie dough that is completely unusable for anything and will have to be discarded. (Unfortunately our pie crusts are not usually much better.) If you do not reuse your wax, as is recommended, you are not bound by any such restrictions.

Modifying waxes

You may want to modify your wax to try to make it more suitable for whatever process with which you have chosen to work it. You can modify your waxes in a number of ways. To soften them, try adding squishy oily materials like petroleum jelly or cocoa butter. To harden them try adding harder waxes. To give them more body, try adding sawdust. (For purely sculptural wax, clay or whiting are traditionally added but these will not burn out. So we do not recommend their use.) To color them, try adding oil-soluble dyes like wood stains. To lower their melting point or viscosity, try adding a low melting temperature wax like paraffin.

Working with wax

Wax can be worked in a lot of different ways. We'll go over some of them but we guarantee that you will come up with other ways to abuse this material. Try to choose a technique that is appropriate for the wax that you choose to use. Wax is fun to work with and if nothing else you can always use it to make candles.

Melting Wax

Wax can be melted and cast into shapes to be used in modeling such as sheets, rods, blocks, bowls, etc. There are wax melting pots available from jewelers' supply houses but they tend to be rather expensive. An old pot on a hot plate will work in a pinch, but must be watched so as not to overheat the wax and possibly start a fire. This problem is further aggravated if you use a burner with an open flame like a gas stove or propane camping stove to heat the wax. It is hard to tell by eye what the temperature of the wax is because wax at 500°F looks exactly like just melted wax at 150°F. Forgetting the wax on the stove can be definitely bad for business, unless you have a very understanding insurance agent. If you melt wax directly on the burner, there is also the possibility of it reaching its flash point and exploding into flames. To avoid this use a double boiler arrangement when heating wax. This prevents overheating the wax to the point where it starts to vaporize and create an explosive hazard. Remember to add more water to the bottom boiler pan as it boils away otherwise you can really ruin that pot. (This is one of Jim's standard cooking tricks.) One economical way to safely melt wax is to use a cheap crock pot. It will take a while for the wax to melt, but you can depend on it not to boil the wax even if you leave it on all day. You can usually get a good used crock pot for about $5.

Never leave hot wax unattended especially if any small children have access to the studio. Even if not a fire hazard, it is still a dangerous burn hazard. When melting wax, make sure that it is dry prior to being added to the melting pot. Water is heavier than wax and will immediately sink to the bottom of the pot. There it will flash boil and splash hot wax all over the place. Unfortunately this is also probably the one time that the watched pot actually boils and you end up with a face full of 400°F wax. Even dry wax can be hazardous when reheated because it expands as it melts. On a burner, the bottom portion melts first and builds up pressure. Then when the top layer gets thin enough, hot wax may erupt through it. For both of these reasons, we suggest that it may be a good idea to keep a cover on your wax pot to prevent accidents. A clear lid is preferred so you won't always be taking it off to see what's happening. You might also want to consider wearing safety glasses. Hot wax will stick to your skin and continue to burn you until you can cool it off. So keep some cool water around to cool off any body parts that may get splashed with hot wax.

Also don't spill any hot wax on your carpet. Wax exploding in your face may be preferable to your spouse's or landlord's response to wax stains in the carpet. Residual coatings of wax can be removed from tools and pots with mineral spirits but it is hard to remove from carpet. The only way that we know to do that is to first dig the bulk of it out with a dull butter knife or popcycle stick. The rest can sometimes be wicked out by placing a plain paper bag over the spot and running a medium iron over the bag. Good luck if this happens to you But having a pot of hot wax around is so handy for many things that you may want to risk it.

Casting Wax Shapes

To cast wax into sheets, pour hot wax from your pot out onto a wet slab of plaster that has ridges around its edge to contain the wax or out onto waxed paper. Also if you melt wax out of a mold into a pan of water, it forms sheets of wax that could be reused. These sheets of wax can be warmed and shaped. They are especially useful in developing cloth-like textured objects. Rods of wax can be made by pouring wax into soda straws and cutting the straws away after the wax is cool.

All sorts of wires can be made from soft waxes using an extruder such as is used for cake decorating. As suggested by Tim McCright in his excellent book on casting metals and illustrated in Figure 31, this tool can be constructed by using a section of pipe about an inch in diameter and about a foot long to form the barrel of the extruder. The plunger is made from a tight fitting piece of doweling with a tighter fitting rubber washer screwed to its end to prevent wax from leaking out the back end as you depress the plunger. Brass dies of 18 gage or greater can be mounted on the end of the barrel using bolts which have had their heads cut off and have been soldered to the sides of the pipe with their ends extending past the end of the barrel. Then using heavy gloves and safety glasses, molten wax is poured into the barrel and forced out through the die with a slow uniform pressure into a dish of cool water. If the wax in

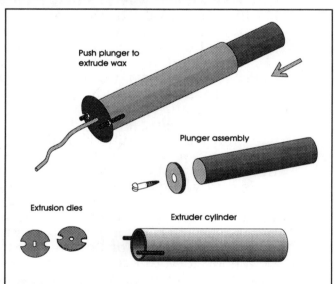

Push plunger to extrude wax

Plunger assembly

Extrusion dies

Extruder cylinder

Figure 31. Home made extruder for making wax wires.

the extruder hardens up on you, heat the whole extruder's worth back up in a pot of boiling water.

For casting more complex shapes, you can make quick molds out of clay. The rough clay shapes can be carved to include detail into your wax. To cast a wax in the mold, you pour in some molten wax from your double boiler and roll it around the surface until it completely covers the inside of the mold. The extra wax can be poured out and the remaining wax allowed to cool for a couple minutes. This process produces hollow castings as done with slip casting in ceramics. You continue to build up the thickness of your wax original by repeated applications until you get the desired thickness. You can use this same technique to cast wax into those pottery slip molds if they are well coated with a release agent prior to introducing the wax. Otherwise the wax will stick to the plaster mold.

For developing good control in casting wax, it helps to get a feeling for your wax's plastic range. This is the temperature range from the liquidus point at which the solid wax will melt down to the solidus point at which a molten pool of wax will start to skin over and harden. The larger this range the easier it will be to work with your wax. This range can be measured using a candy thermometer.

Carving Wax

Hard carving waxes are worked by various cutting techniques. They can be sawed roughly to shape using a coping saw frame. The friction from the saw blade sliding through the wax actually melts the wax as it cuts.

If an ordinary coping blade is allowed to stop for any length of time, the wax can harden and trap the blade. The most versatile saw blade for use in wax work is a spiral wax blade which has been manufactured such that all its teeth project outward from the blade in a spiral. It cuts a wide enough curf through the wax that it does not lock up in the wax. But unfortunately, it also wanders some as it cuts and therefore is only good

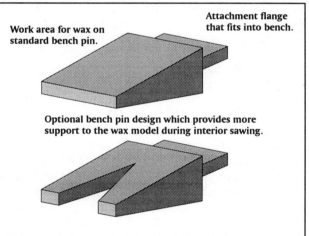

Work area for wax on standard bench pin.

Attachment flange that fits into bench.

Optional bench pin design which provides more support to the wax model during interior sawing.

Figure 32. Bench pin support system used by jewelers.

for roughing. For sharp corners, you might like to use a #4 piercing blade. They are used because coping saws and hacksaws can not get into tight corners. For removing interior areas, you can drill the wax to form a starting hole, thread the blade through the hole and connect it to your saw frame. Always try to support your work as much as possible when working on it to prevent cracking the wax. This can be accomplished by using a V shape bench pin support setup like jewelers do. Two versions of these bench pegs are illustrated in Figure 32. The peg in the back of the picture fits into a hole in your bench. This frees your hands and allows better access to all sides of the wax piece as you carve, saw or file it. Sharp details can be carved using an X-Acto knife. Be careful or you may fracture the wax. Take only small short cuts. By holding the sharp edge of the blade perpendicular to the wax and dragging the knife across the surface of the wax you can shave small amounts off the surface in the form of fine curls of wax. This leaves a nice smooth finish to the surface and allows a lot of control as you work. Unless of course you are the heavy-handed type like Jim and always nicking yourself in the morning when shaving.

When carving wax, try to keep the wax flexible or you may snap it. As you cut, make sure that your blade is sharp and new as they dull quickly, especially if you are using a plate glass pallet. When you make a cut be aware that many times you will leave a wax burr on the side of the cut. This can be removed by cutting parallel to the back

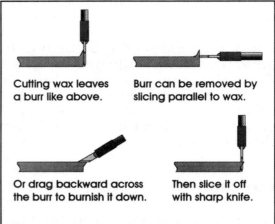

Cutting wax leaves a burr like above.

Burr can be removed by slicing parallel to wax.

Or drag backward across the burr to burnish it down.

Then slice it off with sharp knife.

Figure 33. Removing a burr from a wax model.

surface or by burnishing it to the side with a backward scrap of your blade before cutting the burr off the side as illustrated in Figure 33. Cut away from corners to avoid fractures. Do not try to cut all the way through in one pass. Instead, make a number of shallower cuts which end up being easier to control. Do not hurry too much or the blade may wander, but at the same time try to work quickly because too much handling at one time will result in leaving finger prints in the wax.

Even though you can cut almost any shape from a single block of wax, sometimes that is not the best use of your time, much less the expense of a large block of wax. Many times it makes more sense to cut a number of small blocks of wax and stick them together to rough out the shape of your piece. The techniques for joining wax together will be described shortly. Allow the wax to completely harden before you start carving it. This will be apparent from its returning to its original color and will take a couple of minutes.

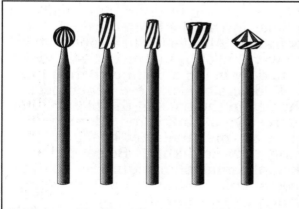

Figure 34. Power tool bits usable with wax.

Motor driven tools and burrs can be used on hard carving waxes. The burrs should be coarse-toothed such as those illustrated in Figure 34. Special three-bladed burrs shaped like small propellers have also been designed for use on wax and are available from your friendly neighborhood jewelry supplier. Even these burrs heat up quickly and can clog, but this can be avoided by working them in short strokes where you lift the burr off the work between strokes. You can also just repeatedly touch the same spot lightly allowing the burr and wax to cool between touches. If you can control the speed of the shaft, slow it down. If you need to hollow out areas, this can be done using miniature gouges like those used in woodcarving or turning.

Softer wax, like sheet wax, can be carved with a sharp X-Acto knife after it has been softened by dipping it in hot water.   Dental tools are also commonly used to shape wax and are handy for scraping, carving and scratching the wax just like they are used on teeth. You can even pretend to be a deranged dentist as you work. "Oh, you wanted that tooth! That's too bad!" Dental tools can also be used for melting detailed designs or applying wax. Never buy your dental tools new, they are too expensive. Instead ask your oral hygienist to save you old ones that are ready to be retired from regular service. They don't have to be sharp to work well on wax. Dental tools can also be found at flea markets but still tend to be overpriced. Wood carving or linoleum carving tools also work well on soft or hot wax. Don't heat them in a flame though if you are ever planning to use them again for their original purpose as this will cause them to lose their temper.

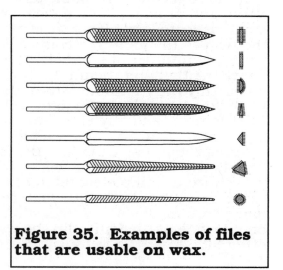

Figure 35. Examples of files that are usable on wax.

Once the carving wax model is cut roughly into shape, you can then use one of the many files available, some of which are illustrated in Figure 35, to remove saw marks and finish shaping it. Coarse-tooth files are best because they cut quickly and are resistant to clogging. For those hard to reach places, you can get a set of really small wax working files from a jewelry supply house. For final smoothing, switch back to a fine-tooth metalworking file. These will cut slower but will leave a smoother final surface. For smoothing fine details in your final polish, we suggest using a set of rifling files. Fine toothed files will have to be cleaned often using a file cleaner to prevent clogging. This is a flat wood brush with short metal bristles. Clogging of your files can be minimized by applying a light coating of a powder like talc, cornstarch or whiting to the file. A light spray of silicone lubricant or mold release also works well. Softer wax pieces can be made hard enough to file or carve by sticking them in the freezer for a while before you start working on them and recooling as necessary.

To get a final polished finish on the wax, you may want to touch it up with a little bit of fine sandpaper. Be careful though because it can leave grit in the wax. A final buff can also be done using a soft cloth or nylon stocking. The open mesh acts as the sanding instrument. Again you may have to cool that wax as was recommended for filing.

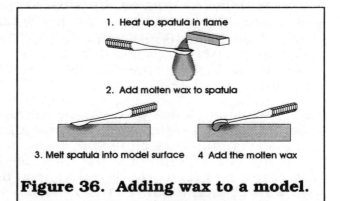

Figure 36. Adding wax to a model.

Adding Wax

If you need to bond or add wax to a model, this can be done with the judicious application of heat. To apply the heat, small spatulas heated in an open flame are usually used. The simplest flame source is one of those short stubby candles available from the supermarket. Most artists prefer to use an alcohol lamp like those available from jewelers' supply houses. They burn denatured alcohol, available as shellac thinner from the hardware store, and provide a much cleaner flame than candles. You bond small delicate wax pieces together using these spatulas to apply the heat to the joint in a controlled manner. You first tack the joint at a number of points by touching it with the hot spatula. To permanently bond them together, you take the hot spatula and repeatedly bury it about 2/3 of the way into the joint. Continue to work your way along the joint, reheating the spatula as necessary. After joining, add any extra wax needed to fill any depressions in the joint by heating some wax in the bowl of the spatula and again burying the full spatula into the crack. When you pull it out, it should leave most of the wax in the bowl behind. Use this procedure to completely fill in cracks or to build up areas with extra wax. This technique is necessary because just like flameworking glass, hot wax will not bond to cold wax. •When done on one side of the joint, flip the wax over and do the same to the other side.

Cheap soldering irons make good hot wax sculpting tools and can be temperature controlled by hooking them up to a plug with a dimmer switch. For attaching larger pieces of wax, try heating up the surfaces to be joined together in a flame and then pushing the two molten surfaces together. Touch up of the joint can then be done with a spatula as described above. Be careful with the molten wax though, because as we said before, it can stick to your skin and burn you.

Handworking Wax

Handworking of sculptural waxes, is done when they are warm and pliable. Start by getting a flat surface to cool the molten wax on like a marble or plaster slab. Apply oil to the slab to act as a release agent. Ladle out as much molten wax as you want to work with onto the slab. Allow it to cool slightly, but do not let it harden. Lift and flip the sheet on the slab trying not to crack it.

Cool the other side slightly. Now with oiled hands, knead the wax into a malleable ball and work it until it has the right texture, that of soft candy. Model the wax into your basic shape. Use your hands and tools to develop this shape. Add more soft wax as necessary using your fingers and pressure. More wax can be added with a hot spatula as described before in areas where pressure is not appropriate. Heated small loop-ended clay tools can be used to shape the wax by melting it and causing it to flow. They can also cut really soft wax just like clay.

An alternative method to warm wax for handworking is to stick it in an old coffee can and warm it with a reflector-type drop light, like used in photography. Use the drop light like a lid for the can with the bulb on the inside. The reflector should be slightly larger than the can so it will not fall in and if it has a spring clip on it that can serve as a good handle to lift the light. By a little trial and error, you may find that you will be able to control the softness of the wax by the wattage of the light bulb that you use and the length of time that you apply it. This will vary with the amount of wax you are heating and the desired working temperature. You can tell when microcrystalline wax has been warmed sufficiently because it will change from the dark chocolate color to a milk chocolate one.

There are a number of ways that sculpture wax can be worked. It can be rolled out between your hands like clay to form elongated shapes. It can be pinched between the fingers to form flat details. It can be twisted and stretched to elongate it. It can be worked with pointed objects like pencils. It can be smoothed with your fingers. It can be bend or folded. It can be sliced with knives, gouges or carving tools. (It might help to cool the wax before trying to carve it.) What you can do to it is only limited by your imagination.

Flame polishing

After you are done modeling, you may want to flame polish the surface of your wax piece by passing it over a flame. You can do this with an alcohol lamp. The cheap ones that look like Austrian crystal with multiple surfaces as shown in Figure 37 work well because you can tilt them and work on both sides of the flame. There are also alcohol lamps with little nozzles where you can blow through a hose to direct the flame. If you want to really get fancy and have about $50 burning a hole in your pocket, you can get an adjustable micro-torch called a Blazer Piezo from a jewelers' supply house. This torch has a fast and focused little flame, so go slow when fire polishing the wax or you

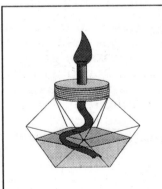

Figure 37. Alcohol lamp used to flame polish wax.

may have a professional overrun. It is fueled by the same butane cans used for filling cigarette lighters.

Texturing a wax surface

Instead of flame polishing the surface of your wax model you may want to texture it. This can be done by heating up the wax to about 300°F where it gets uniformly shiny and then pressing whatever has the texture or design that you are trying to imprint on the wax surface into the wax. You could use leather working dies to put in letters or decorations. You can also press found objects or rough textures from nature like rocks into it. Avoid any object with undercuts or you will find yourself breaking off wax as you remove the object. Also be careful not to burn yourself. We suggest that you wear some heavy gloves when trying this.

Modeling With Clay

Let's now look at our second modeling material — clay. Modeling with clay is less complicated than working with wax. There is no melt-down or burnout, no hot caldrons of volatile material and no fumes. Clay is cheap and can be recycled, as long as it is not allowed to dry and you keep mold chips out of it. There are many artists who prefer the feel of clay and find wax difficult to control. The disadvantage to clay is that there are limitations to the shape or detail that can be put into it and cast as part of a single part mold. Because it does not melt like wax, it has to be dug out of a mold. This is an important consideration and access must be provided to all clay. Jim has literally spent hours digging clay out of tight deep spots in learning this point. For this reason, we use clay mainly as a modeling material for open face castings.

What is clay

As James Mitchner would probably explain to us in excruciating detail, clay is a natural decomposition product formed by the weathering of granite and igneous rock. This decomposition is primarily brought about by the action of water over years and years. Water, as rain, abrades the rock just as sand does glass in sandblasting. In changing from water to ice during freezing, water that has seeped into cracks in rocks will expand and further crack the rock into smaller and smaller pieces. As ice or glaciers, water grinds the rocks upon each other to form fine gravel Plants also assist in this process by sending roots down into the cracks which expand as they grow to help break the rocks apart. Some minerals in the rock are soluble in water and once exposed end up being leached out by it, thus further weakening the rock matrix. Finally when the rocks become small enough they get ground further up by the tumbling action of streams and surf. During transportation by streams, the individual grains of rock are also sorted by size. As the water slows down, it drops bigger grains first while carrying the smaller grains further downstream.

Since the weathering process happens everywhere on earth, clay is quite common. Its composition is primarily determined by the original rock composition and this composition really does not vary much from place to place because the composition of the earth really does not vary all that much. It is about 58% silicon and 15% aluminum, in the form of silica (SiO_2) alumina (Al_2O_3), and is chemically combined with water in the ratio of 2:1:2. Note this chemically combined water is not the water which gives clay its plasticity. If you allowed the clay to get bone dry, the chemically combined water will still be present. Clay also contains oxides of other materials such as iron, magnesium, calcium, sodium etc. in smaller amounts. These other materials add to the color and physical properties of the clay.

The purity of a clay depends on whether it was formed in place or whether it was formed during transportation from one site to another. A clay that has been formed in place is called a primary or residual clay. The primary mechanism for this formation is through chemical action of water on the rock, most commonly on feldspar. Because primary clays have not received the added benefit of mechanical action and sorting that takes place during water transport, they are composed of a mixture of grain sizes both large and small. Also because they have not been mixed with other materials during transport, they tend to be whiter and purer than other clays. Both of these factors make them coarser in texture, more difficult to work and gives them higher refractivity. For this reason, as we will see in the next chapter, one common residual clay (Kaolin clay) is often added to investment mixes to make them more thermally resistant.

The other clays, those that have been formed and transported by the forces of nature, are referred to as secondary or sedimentary clays. They are more common than primary clays. But because they have been transported and mixed with materials from many locations, they have a more complex composition than a primary clay. This leads to inclusion of impurities like iron oxide which give many clays their reddish color. It also leads to inclusions of organic materials which increase their plasticity. As mentioned earlier, the transportation also results in segregation of the size of the grains of sedimentary clays making them finer and more pliable. All of these differences affect the properties of a clay.

Desirable clay properties

The primary property of interest for modeling is a clay's plasticity. This refers to the ease with which a clay can be shaped and how well it retains its shape. Plasticity is believed to be a function of the distribution of size and shape of the individual grains within a clay. The grains are thin plate-like structures surrounded by an even thinner layer of water. The layer of water is held in place by the attractive adhesive forces of the large surface area of the grains. Clays with a higher content of fine grains are more plastic because the grains slide over each other easier. A clay's organic content also adds to its plasticity by inclusion of many smaller softer particles made by bacterial action on the organic content that act as lubricants to the clay particles. The reddish brown clay that reminds Dan of dirty baby diapers is a good one for modeling.

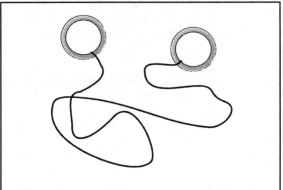

Figure 38. Wire tool used to cut slabs from block of clay.

Most of the clays that you will find are actually a mixture of a number of different types of clays and have been formulated to get the optimum properties for one of a number of ceramic process. Such mixtures of clays are referred to as clay bodies and are formulated to control factors such as color, plasticity, shrinkage, firing temperature and surface properties. The type you should ask for are throwing or modeling clays. These will have good plasticity and have been formulated to minimize the cracking that occurs during drying. Stay away from stoneware and porcelain clays because they are less plastic and more coarse. If you want to know more about clay see "Clay and Glazes for the Potter" by Daniel Rhodes.

We don't think we need to tell you where to buy your clay. We hope! While you are there you might want to buy some of those wire tools as seen in Figure 38 to cut slabs off a big block of clay. They are inexpensive and work great. And don't forget some of the loop tools that we will be taking about in the next section. You will need them for working those fine details that are too small for fingers.

Working With Clay

Working with clay is easy. It is no harder than making the mud pies that we probably all did as children. (Did yours taste as bad as ours?) Any clay can be used, but water-based products rather than the oil-based plasticine types are usually preferred. This is because the plasticine type are harder to clean out of the mold and any residue can cause carbonization on the surface of the glass.

In working with a water-based clay, you can make it softer and more plastic by adding additional water. When storing your clay, encase it in plastic bags or sealable boxes to prevent it from drying out. If it does dry out, it can usually be reconstituted by adding a little water and working the water in. As clay dries it also shrinks. This can cause cracking between sections of varying cross section or from shrinkage down upon some internal support. You can help keep your clay moist by wetting it with your fingers or by spraying a mist of water on it. An old perfume bottle, plant spray bottle or an air brush works well for this task. If you have to leave a clay model on which you are working out for a while, cover it with a plastic bag to help prevent it from drying out.

Clay can be worked in a number of ways, many of which we all learned as children. One of the easiest is with coils. Make coil from the clay by rolling it between your hands or on a flat surface. These serpentine coils can then be formed into other shapes like pots. In kindergarten you probably made such masterpieces by starting with a small circle and successfully building up layers of damp clay coils of larger diameter circles until you had a bowl. You may have even been one of those advanced students that then added coils of successively smaller diameters to form a pot. If you were even more advanced, you probably then smoothed out the coil texture to a nice smooth surface. But if you were like Jim, you probably had big gaps between your coils and they probably weren't circular either. So what, that's art too.

Another way to form clay into shape is to pinch or press it together with your fingers. As you squeeze the clay, the grains will flow and come into intimate contact with each other to form a uniform mass. This causes it to stick together. It can be further shaped by bending or folding. After you stop pushing, it retains its shape. To help prevent the clay from cracking as you pinch it thinner, it helps to keep your fingers damp.

When working to make flat clay shapes of multiple layers, the best technique is that of slabbing. Flat slabs of clay can be formed by flattening it out with a rolling pin. Uniform thickness can be achieved by using guides of constant thickness under both ends of the rolling pin as illustrated in Figure 39. To prevent the clay from sticking to the surface on which you are rolling it out, you can dust the surface ahead of time with something like finely-ground fired plaster or you can roll it out on plastic wrap which can be removed later. The slabs are cut into two dimensional shapes and overlaid upon one another to form three dimensional shapes. As you lay

one slab layer on the next, moisten the contact surfaces to allow them to stick better. If you are going to stand these shapes on edge, allow them to stiffen a little before cutting them out. To join slabs on end, roughen the surfaces that you are going to join and bond them with a layer of clay that has been

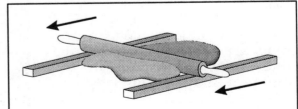

Figure 39. Rolling clay slabs out to uniform thickness.

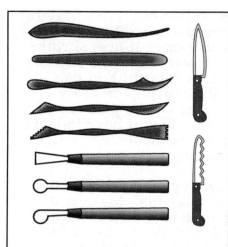

Figure 40. Various clay modeling tools.

mixed with so much water that the mixture is almost creamy. Smooth out any of the bonding cream that seeps out of the joint with your finger tips.

In making clay vessel models you may sometimes want to use a bowl for an aid which you cover with clay and shape as desired. When you do this there are two things that you need to do. The first is make sure that your mold will not trap the vessel because of a small opening. Second apply a coating of oil to the vessel so that it can be easily removed from the clay after casting of the mold. If you forget this the vessel or any other object can still be worked free from the mold by getting the clay very wet and gently rocking the object back and forth. You will have to continue adding water to the clay as it will seep away though the walls of the mold. This will leave some pretty mushy clay and hard to clean out of the mold though.

The most versatile tools of any clay modeler are his or her fingers. There are details though that are hard to put in with fingers. Those finer details can be carved into clay using knives and some of those inexpensive wooden modeling tools that are illustrated in Figure 40. You can also use common objects like popcycle sticks, pins and nails to carve details. To smooth out areas of a model use a flat spatulas or rounded spoon-like objects. Wire loop tools are good for carving out bits of clay. They come in different shapes and sizes.

Mark Abildgaard likes to make fairly large kiln cast sculptures such as the one he is standing

Figure 41. Large cast sculpture composed of bonded pieces.

next to in Figure 41 that he forms by bonding several components together using Hxtal epoxy. To ensure that the final cast pieces will fit well together, he works with a fine textured sculptural clay and lets the components dry to a leather hard state before casting the investment molds. This allows him to play with the fit and ensure that it is true.

After investment, any residual clay has to be cleaned out of the refractory mold or it can stain the final glass casting. This process is made easier if a little separator compound was added to the outside of the clay model. Remove it as soon as possible after the investment sets while it is still moist. You know when the investment is set because it is hard and no longer warm to the touch. If the clay is allowed to dry in the mold, you may never get it out. Remember clay can not be melted and burned out like wax. It has to be carved and washed out. Start removing it by using the loop tools to dig it out in chunks. Then wash out whatever residual clay remains on the plaster mold. This can be done using cool running water and a soft brush like a tooth or paint brush.

Models From The Real Thing - Organics

Don't worry. You don't have to go to the health food store for this option, although we all could probably benefit from frequent visits there. Organics in this context means anything that was once a living organism and can be burned out of a mold. This eliminates things like sea shells or coral which are primarily calcium deposits left behind by once living organisms. If you really want to

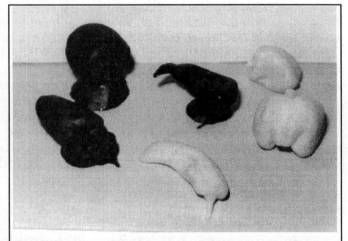

Figure 42. Collection of Pate de Verre peppers.

capture their shape, they can be used to construct master molds from which you can cast wax reproductions.

Of the organics that can be completely burned out, vegetable matter seems to be the most popular one used. (I guess because most of us don't like handling dead animals and insects.) Of these, the vegetation to which we relate best is food. In other words, this means vegetables or fruits. Many vegetables have very interesting shapes and textures. We are sure that you have noticed this during your many years of playing with your food and now pâte de verre gives you the perfect excuse to further partake in these mealtime games. Go to your supermarket and browse the fresh vegetable section with a new eye. Some vegetables, like brussel sprouts, have boring shapes and are better left for eating. (Dan says that he actually likes them.) Look carefully, pickling cucumbers have a nice texture that can prove interesting. Asparagus always works as does cauliflower. Watch out for things like broccoli or artichokes though because cleaning out the fine details in the investment mold after burnout is difficult. Figure 42 shows a collection of Pâte de Verre peppers that Jim put together.

Be wary of using woods or nuts. They can be used as models but they can smoke up your studio if you attempt to burn them out of a mold. Burn a walnut out in your studio and your neighbors will have the fire department down on your case in no time flat. If you must do so, be sure to vent your kiln area. Woods also swell when exposed to water and could thus crack your mold. This can be prevented by coating a wood model with a sealer such as a spray on lacquer. Two light coats will usually be sufficient. Keeping these comments in mind, carved woods can produce some interesting patterns. It is best to use the softer woods, like pine, balsa or cedar, because they burn out more easily. Fir has too much pitch and like oak is not all that easy to carve.

The other thing to be aware of with organic models is that during burnout some them can be quite fragrant. Most will just steam but there are a few, like garlic, that beside driving away the vampires will also drive everyone else out of the studio in a matter of minutes. Curiously enough some of the ones that you would think might be problematic, like hot peppers, have no impact at all. Anyway, it is always good practice to vent the kiln and the kiln area, even if you have to open all the windows and use fans. Otherwise apprentices and employees will consider switching to something like a career in advertising. The worst part about bad burnout fumes is that they always seems to happen right at lunch time, leaving your stomach a little unsettled.

You might want get out into your garden to search for inspirational specimens. Some suggestions might be an unopened rose or other flower buds. Look for that oddly shaped vegetable or fruit. A favorite is peppers that have grown with shapes like faces, complete with noses and mouths. Dress them up a little with some wax eyes and glasses and they make great novelty pieces. Also think about what might fit into local events. How about making small pumpkins with faces carved into them around Holloween or corn on the cob at Thanksgiving. Maybe you have some sort of local festival that will provide inspiration. In our area we have garlic, pumpkin, artichoke and asparagus festivals. We also have festivities like the erotic-exotic ball but those subjects may be better left unhandled.

On a walk in the woods, you can find an abundance of possible specimens. Young pines cones, small twigs or tree bark are just a few of the many candidates. Small animals like banana slugs, the unofficial California state mollusk, are also fair game. Tree leaves are usually too thin to work effectively, but they can be dipped in wax to give them more mass. Unfortunately this will result in loss of detail, so break out the wax carving tools to carve them back into the model.

A trip to the sea shore or lake may uncover other great finds like driftwood, fish, seaweed or shells. The great part about any natural thing is that the viewer can easily relate to it. For a really eye catching piece, you might try juxtipositioning natural objects. How about a fish swimming through pine cones or birds flying through coral and seaweed.

The advantage of replica casting is that you can be creative by selection. Just because you can not draw (stained glass) or carve (clay, wax or wood) doesn't mean that you're out of the ball game. Some of the finest photographs have been made by just looking at nature and trying to capture what already exists. Edward Weston (he was one of those great photographers) said, "Composition is only the strongest way of seeing." He never did fish — just nudes, bell peppers and portraits. But, these like fish and the rest of nature, are not copyrighted. Don't be afraid to reach out and explore what's around you.

Models from other materials

Other materials, like plastics and styrofoam, can also be used to form models which, like the natural organic materials, can be burned out afterwards. Plastic objects of all kinds can be used and these days there are a lot of interesting plastic shapes out there. How about a glass Barbie ® doll. (You should probably try to get permission from the manufacturer before you sell something like this but anything is fair game for personal consumption.) You can also use plastic models, like most of us put together as kids, as the basis for your design. Avoid ones with tiny details though, as these can be hard to reproduce in glass.

Be aware that some plastics may not burn out completely but will instead leave a gummy residue. So you may want to consider test burning a small piece of the object in your kiln ahead of time. To prevent messing up your kiln, put the plastic in a small tin can (not aluminum) and place the can on the center of your kiln shelf, well away from the elements. Cover the can with a small piece of non-aluminum scrap metal and heat it up to about 1200°F to see how cleanly it burns out. If it does, go with it. If not, try making a master mold of the object and casting the shape in wax as will be described later.

When burning out plastic from a mold, be sure to ventilate the kiln and the studio well. The fumes produced when burning many plastics are very toxic and can be a serious health risk.

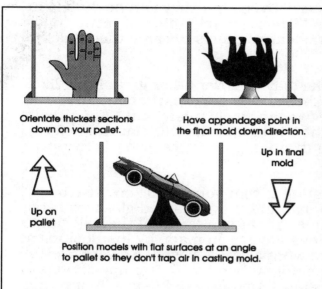

Orientate thickest sections down on your pallet.

Have appendages point in the final mold down direction.

Up in final mold

Up on pallet

Position models with flat surfaces at an angle to pallet so they don't trap air in casting mold.

Figure 43. How to orientate models for casting.

Preparing models for casting

The final steps in preparing your model for casting is to decide on an orientation for it in the mold and to develop the gating system for delivery of the glass into the mold as well as that to allow air to escape.

Model orientation

When placing the model in the mold, you would like all parts of the model as much as possible to point down into the final mold as illustrated in Figure 43. This allows gravity to assist in filling of the mold. Try to position flat surfaces of the model in an off-horizontal orientation so that they will be less likely to trap air. Also, try to orientate the thickest sections of your model up in the finished mold (or down on the pallet). This prevents having to feed the glass to the thicker casting sections through thinner sections where flow will be slower. Realize too that what is down when setting up your model on the pallet is actually up in your final mold.

Gating your model

Now that you know how to orientate the model, you have to work out a gating system to carry the glass from the sprue cup or reservoir, that funnel at the top of the finished mold, down into the model cavity and allow trapped air to escape. Since glass frit shrinks in volume during the casting process, you need to provide a fair sized reservoir to feed your mold. This reservoir should hold the extra frit needed to fill your mold as the bulk volume of the glass frit shrinks in the casting process. The top of your funnel should be sized to provide enough extra frit to allow for the approximately 30% reduction in bulk glass volume during the kiln casting process.

If the mold is an open bas relief, this is no problem. You just pour the glass frit into the open face of the mold and mound it up to allow for shrinkage. If this is not the case, you will need to include a reservoir and a gating system in your mold plan. This system can be as simple as a single sprue (channel through which the glass flows) from the reservoir to the model. Alternately you could have multiple sprues feeding different sections of the mold from a central runner and multiple riser vents to allow air escape as shown in Figure 44. As you design this system, there are a number of principles to keep in mind. First as just stated, the cup or reservoir should be one-quarter to one-third of the volume of the whole piece. Reservoirs of wax can be cast in small paper cups which if too big can easily be carved down. Often the reservoir will be incorporated into the design as a base for the piece as seen in Figure 45 that will only need smoothing after casting. Otherwise it will have to be cut off at the sprue and polished up. The cutting can be done with a diamond saw of which here are now many affordable types on the market such as table, band, ring and chop saws.

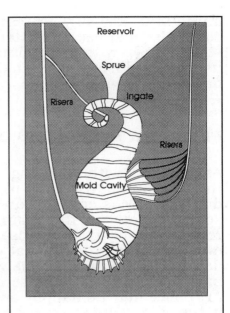

Figure 44. Components of a gating system.

Sprues should be made as smooth as possible to prevent glass from hanging up in them. For the same reason, make them as short and as large as possible. Have them be at least one quarter of an inch in diameter. If they are to be removed, try to place them in areas without too much detail that you will be able to clean up later by polishing. Attach the gating, which is usually made from wax wires and rods, securely to the model using hot wax that is dripped onto the connection and shaped with hot tools. Clay can also be used to make gating, but it is harder to clean out afterwards. If you do use clay, make sure that you clean it all out.

Smooth the ingates, those connections between the sprues and the model, and taper them slightly toward the model to allow easier removal later. Vents or risers should be attached to any features that are higher up in the model than the area that feeds it. This will allow the glass to push out the air in these areas as the model fills. They only need to be between 1/16 and 1/8" in diameter to do the trick.

Figure 45. Pepper mounted on clay reservoir base.

The next step in preparing a model for casting is to firmly attach your model down to the pallet to prevent it from floating up into the plaster. If the model is of wax, this can be accomplished in a number of ways. The first is to just go around the edge of your reservoirs with an old soldering iron. You could also just get the bottom hot and stick it down or you could stick it down with low melting temperature sticky wax. If you are using a cardboard pallet, like Dan prefers, you can attach the model down with hot glue.

Making wax replicas of models

As you work with modeling, you may develop an original model that you find particularly pleasing and which you would like to duplicate. Master molds are used for this purpose, they form a spatial negative of the original model in which multiple wax replicas are cast. Otherwise you can imagine toiling hours, days or even weeks to produce that perfect masterpiece only to see it melt down or go up in smoke as your investment mold cracks. A master mold gives you a second chance to get it right. While the Art police may be happily away on a fishing trip, that lawyer by the name of Murphy is always lurking in the shadows.

So all you need to do in order to cast wax replicas of a model is to make a master mold of the original. A master mold needs to allow easy removal of the original model and casting of new wax models. Before starting construction of a master mold, examine your model and think where you would put the parting plane. This plane will be where you will try to cut the master mold apart after you have cast it around your model. It should minimize undercuts and allow easy removal of the replica from the mold. Try to make sure that the parting line does not run through some point where you have a lot of detail because there will usually be a little flashing at the parting point that you will have to remove from the wax casting. The best places for parting of the mold are along edges or on broad smooth areas that can be smoothed afterwards. Some models because of their geometry have very easily defined parting planes, other do not.

The kinds of materials that work best for making master molds are flexible materials. The perfect materials that we suggest for doing this are clay, alginate, room temperature vulcanizing (RTV) rubber and latex. Why do we use these materials? They are simple to work with and all will reproduce detailed images, even those with mild undercuts. Once formed, they are easily flexed and distorted to remove the model, although some may be more durable than others. Lets look at each of these materials in turn.

Clay master molds

Perhaps the easiest way that a master mold can be constructed of some models, especially flat, hard medallion-like ones, is by making an impression of the model in clay. This can be done by either making a small clay pancake and pressing the model into it or by building up the clay around the model bit by bit. The model is then removed by flexing the clay as necessary and lifting it out. A little mold release or powder such as talc if applied ahead of time will assist in removal of the model. Master molds of clay are of rather limited use because the are easily damaged and stretched out of shape. The stretching could be used to good advantage if you want to distort the shape of your original model.

Alginate master molds

The use of alginate in making master molds is usually restricted to limited-use, short-term molds. Those of you who did not take very good care of your teeth in your youth may already have some familiarity with this material. It is the material that dentists use to make impressions of your mouth and teeth when they are making plates or dentures. It is a natural substance that is extracted from the gelatin-like algae or kelp that we find at the seashore. You can purchase the material from dental, jewelry or art supply stores.

As purchased, the material is a light tannish powder that, if purchased from a dental supply store, may even be flavored. (Anyone miss lunch?) The powder is mixed with water to make a mush with the consistency of creamy mashed potatoes. It must then be quickly applied to the model because it has a very short set time—on the order of two minutes. Apply it by scooping it out of the mixing container and either pouring it into a casting frame, or pressing it around the model. After application, allow 5 to 10 minutes for full curing of the mold.

Alginate can be used to make very exact and detailed molds of you original models but because of its relative fragility, it is not the best mold material of choice for convoluted models. A lot of flexing in trying to free the model or wax replica can result in ripping or tearing of the mold. For that reason, you may only get between one half to two dozen wax replicas (depending upon the complexity of the model) from such a mold before they start to break apart. Addition of a little bit of separating compound will help maximize the number of replicas achieved.

Another limitation with alginate master molds is that they rapidly dry out and shrink. This will usually happen over about a twelve hour time span during which they also get more rigid and brittle. Their useful life can be extended somewhat by trying to minimize water loss either by sealing the mold in a plastic bag or by storing it in water. Best results are achieved if the replicas are made within the first couple of hours after making an alginate mold.

RTV master molds

One room temperature vulcanizing (RTV) rubber that works well in making master molds is Poly 74-30 made by Polytek Development

Corporation. This material comes in a two part mix that when mixed together hardens to a make a lasting mold that is both strong and flexible. Unopened, the two parts are usable for at least a year from shipment. After opening, both components tend to absorb moisture from the air and should be used as soon as possible. The two parts are mixed by weight in inert containers. They are then poured into a mold frame constructed around your model. The model should also have a sprue for filling the master mold. The size of the sprue depends on whether it will also be used in the refractory mold filling with frit or is only to be used for filling the master mold with wax and is then to be removed or added to. Because of the expense of RTV, the reservoir is usually added later. Once a master mold is cast, it is usable within 48 hours but the material really takes 7 days to reach optimum cure. These molds should be cured in a warm location (60-140°F).

At this point you will need to make a couple of cuts into the master mold to get your original model out. The object is to cut into the master mold in such a way that the mold is never completely separated or that it is cut in such a way that it is easy to put back together. Keeping the mold in one piece allows you to cast your duplicate wax models easier. To cut the mold apart, hook the rubber down to your bench with something like a bent nail. Then with a sharp hobby knife start by cutting some male-female alignment features or natches into the corners of the mold. Then slowly cut the model out of the mold trying to use your memory of where the model is to guide you in your cutting as near to the previously considered parting plane as possible. As you start reaching the model, bend the mold open as much as possible to help guide you in your last few cuts. You may also find it helpful at this point to make some cuts into the inside surfaces of the flexible mold to help make it easier to open and remove the model. This is especially helpful around delicate areas of the mold. If you can free the model without completely cutting the mold apart so much the better. The difficulty of this process depends a lot on the form of the object. A simple object like a marble is easy to do. Something like a hollow vessel is much harder and of course there are also some things for which it just may not be possible to keep the mold in one piece.

If you have any chambers in the mold cavity above the entrance sprue, you may have to drill a small hole through the RTV to the top of the cavity to act as gating for venting during wax injection. You should then insert some small brass or copper tubing like that used for hinges in making stained glass boxes to ensure that the hole stays open. The RTV master mold is now ready for use.

Latex rubber master molds

Liquid latex rubber compounds are another master mold option. These solutions are available from a number of different manufacturers. We have found that you don't have to buy the most expensive kind, because the cheap kinds seem to work just fine. "Mold-It" from a hobby craft store has worked the best. Another good one is D & S 74 from Douglass and Sturgess in San Francisco. Like the RTV rubbers, latex's can reproduce great detail from a model. On the down side, they are a little less rugged than the RTVs but on the other hand they are much more flexible than RTVs. Latex master molds can even be turned inside out. They also are a little cheaper which always helps. One thing that they do not accommodate well is inside passages that go through the mold. Don't confuse latex mold material with latex paint. You won't find this at your hardware store. The latex for mold making, such as "Michael's", can be found at sculpture supply, plastic's supply and hobby craft stores.

Construction of a latex master mold is simple. Latex's are applied by painting them onto the original with a cheap disposable brush like the ones used for applying soldering flux. Its sometimes easier to throw the brushes away than to clean them up afterwards if you forget to pretreat them. If they are in short supply, they can be cleaned with mineral spirits. Latex is used as follows:

1. Place your original model on some base surface like glass or linoleum which will provide easy release afterward. Coat base and model with a light coating of some mold release compound. Murphy's oil soap or Pam spray both work well for this.
2. Ready a small soft bristled brush for application by precoating it with liquid soap. This helps prevent the latex from sticking to the brush.
3. Apply a light coat of latex to the base surface in an area at least 1" around the model to anchor the mold to the base.
4. Apply a light coat of latex to the entire model taking care to cover all detail. The detail that you will achieve in the master mold depends on the smoothness of this first coat. You may even want to thin out the latex a little for this first coat with distilled water. Also if you trap any air bubbles in the first coat blow on it to release them.
5. Drying of each coat is usually fairly rapid and can be accelerated by blowing on it with a fan or by heating with sunlight, a hairdryer, oven, kiln, or other heat source. Use a low heat setting. The popular question is how do you know when a coat is dry? Usually when it dries, it changes tone and becomes slightly less translucent. Of course this will vary depending on the exact product used.
6. After each coat, soak the brush in soapy water to keep it clean and precoat it again with detergent prior to adding each successive coat.
7. As soon as the first coat is completely dry, at least to tack free but never over 24 hours, add a second coat of full strength latex solution all over the model and some extra to the apron on the base extending the apron slightly on each coat. Brush out pools and drips of latex so that each coat will dry completely. Be sure to replace the lid on the latex container between applications. Prolonged air exposure can greatly alter the material's performance.

8. For a single use mold, you could probable stop after about four coats. For a semi-permanent mold to make many replicas, you want to apply up to 8 or 16 coats. After adding your last coat, allow the latex 24 to 48 hours to cure completely. If you want to really speed up the drying process you can always use a hair drier.

9. Strength can be added to a mold by embedding a cloth mesh backing into the mold after about 6 coats and continue on with about 8 to 10 more coats. For a mold that will see a lot of use or for larger molds, you may also want to cast a two part plaster mold around the latex mold to give it strength during filling.

Figure 46. First layer of latex painted on models.

After the final latex coat is completely dry, slowly and carefully remove the latex coating from the model as was explained for the RTV mold. If you find a snag, work it out carefully. Snags, areas sticking to the model, occur because of a gap in the mold release or from a thin spot in the latex coating. If you end up with a hole in the latex, it is usually possible to patch it by painting on some more latex. Snags may also be an indication that the shape that you are trying to duplicate is much too complex.

When trying to separate a latex master mold from an original wax model, it often helps to try and harden the wax by sticking it into the freezer for an hour or two. Then when ready to cut it free, briefly warm the latex with a hair drier, but not too much. You are just trying to take the brittleness out of the latex without softening the wax. Like with RTV molds, it may be necessary to add vents to your latex molds to ensure complete filling when injecting them with wax. Prior to injecting wax into a latex mold you may want to close cuts made in it by painting on a little latex along the cut like adding glue and letting it dry. This will make the latex master mold more stable during wax injection.

Using master molds

Now that you have your master mold, you can make as many wax replicas as you want. Generally speaking, the way that you do this is to inject molten wax into the master mold. Jewelers use hydraulically powered wax injectors for this operation. But a simple kitchen turkey baster is a good alternative, especially if your model is not very small. Special casting waxes have been developed for this process that melt and set quickly as well as being more fluid. These waxes when set are fairly hard and slightly brittle. You can use these waxes or some other hard one of your choice. Heat the wax to temperatures between 100 to 250°F before injecting it. Then let the hot wax to cool back down to the solidus point, the temperature where a skin just starts to form on it and inject it into the master mold. Otherwise, if too hot, the wax may dissolve some of the mold release and stick to the mold. This can ruin some master molds and will surely scar the wax casting. Another problem with injecting your wax too hot is that it will shrink more as the bulk cools down and this can cause cracking or other imperfections in the replicas. The way Dan can tell if the wax is cool enough to pour is when he sees a slight film starting to form on the wax. He next waits about 10 minutes and sticks his finger in it. If he ends up performing the "hot wax dance," he realizes that it was still too hot. We do not really recommend this practice unless you have chrome-molly finger tips. You may want to try a candy thermometer instead.

Once you have injected wax into your mold give it a little time to start to set but try to remove it from the mold while still flexible to make removal as easy as possible. Be very careful when injecting the wax that you do not spray it around and burn yourself. This can especially be a problem if you push the injector against the mold and back pressure builds up as the master mold fills up. Take it easy. Next let the wax set up some before disassembling but removal is easier if the wax is still warm and pliable. Some people find it easier to cool the wax until it is hard before removal. This can be hurried by putting the mold into the freezer for a half hour or so.

For alginate molds, the walls are usually thick enough to be self-supporting. If need be you can set them up in sand like the more flexible latex molds that will be described shortly. No release agent is required but it will prevent sticking and will allow casting more wax replicas from a mold. After the wax has hardened, flex the alginate mold as necessary to release the replica.

For a thick RTV box mold, clamp the mold together between two flat plates using spring or C clamps. No release agent is needed in the mold for casting your wax models but a little silicone spray or cornstarch would not hurt. Then inject the wax, allow it to cool and remove it by opening the mold.

Casting wax into a latex mold needs to be done a little more carefully but it is not too different. The latex is flexible and therefore needs to be supported by a cradle mold during injection. Otherwise it may slump and distort or worse yet, roll over and dump hot wax all over. A box of sand is usually just the ticket to serve as a cradle. Use 80 or 100 mesh silica sand. Avoid "sand-box" sand because it is too dusty and presents a silicosis danger. (Talk about dangers on the playground.) Press the latex mold into the sand and adjust to shape. This may be done easier if you slightly dampen the sand. It is possible to creatively alter the shape at this point but most artists choose to be true to the original model. When the latex is set up in the bed of sand, spray the inside of the mold with a little mold release and inject the wax. Once cool, roll the latex mold off the wax replica.

One thing that you may notice after removing the wax replica from the mold is that it will be slightly smaller than the original model. This is because the mold material shrank around the original model and the melted wax shrank while solidifying in the master mold. This will probably result in a copy that is about 5% smaller in volume than your original. This new wax model is now ready to invest for frit casting. Although you may find that you also have to clean up the casting in the parting region of the master mold where the pieces come together by scraping across it as discussed earlier by using a sharp X-Acto knife.

If your model is fairly large, you may not want to deal with all that wax. In this case you may want to make a hollow wax multiple with a method similar to slip ceramic casting. To do this, first paint on a layer of hot fluid wax into your rubber mold, paying special attention to any areas of great detail. Areas with sharp angles will need to be built up even thicker as the next step may erode some of this away. Now close up the master mold and fasten it shut using rope, tape, C-clamps, etc. Next pour some hot wax into the mold that has been cooled back down to just barely over the solidus temperature so that it will harden quickly. Roll the wax around in the mold for a few seconds if it is not enough to fill the cavity. Then pour out the excess wax. After the wax has completely hardened, you can pull back some of the master mold to determine if the wax is thick enough. You would like it to be about 1/4" thick to hold up under the weight of the mold material during investing. If not, repeat the process until you reach the desired thickness.

If you are using a number of copies of an original model in one work, one thing that you can do is to flex and shape each of them into a slightly different pose. They can then be grouped or cast singly.

Plaster master molds.

We have already talked about how we use plaster-based investment molds for casting glass in the kiln, but we can also use plaster to make master molds for casing wax models that we then invest in waste molds. The simplest of these plaster master molds is a single-piece, open-face one. To make such a mold, the original model must have a flat back, no undercuts and good draft. Draft as you remember means that the sides of the original have to be tapered to allow easy removal of the model once the plaster has been cast. Because plaster expands when it sets, the mold will compress down upon the model. You cast a single-piece master mold just like you cast a regular waste investment mold — by gluing the model down to a pallet, building up a mold frame, coating everything with mold release and then casting away. You do not need to add any refractory materials to the plaster or chamfer any of the edges after casting. You may still want to screed it so that the wax castings you make in it do not vary in thickness from the mold not being level.

Once finished with the master mold, coat it completely with a release agent, such as Pam, to allow easy removal of the wax multiple. If you don't, the wax may penetrate into the plaster attach itself firmly to the surface of the plaster and you may not be able to remove it from the mold. Some of us had to learn this lesson the hard way. (Right Jim.) Casting wax into plaster master molds is not as delicate a process as it was with latex master molds. It is still a good idea to let the wax cool to the solidus point before pouring, but that depends upon the shape. A more complex pattern with small passages might be more easily poured if the wax is a little warmer but you stand the danger of it not separating well. The plaster will absorb heat from the wax while the latex acted as more of an insulator. If you happen to forget the mold release, don't panic, just steam the wax back out and try again.

Mark Abildgaard

"Ancestor Boat" 1996
Bonded kiln cast glass
Size: 28" x 28" x 9"
Photo by: Mark Abildgaard

Anna Boothe

"Neo-Flower Bowl" 1996
Pâte de Verre
Size: 8" x 8¼" top x 3½" bottom
Photo by: Eric Mitchell

"NASA Notwithstanding" 1993
Lost wax kiln cast glass
        with copper and steel
Size: 36" x 8" x 4"
Photo by: Eric Mitchell

Linda Ethier

"Ancient Athletes" 1992
Kiln cast glass and neon
Size: 60" x 84" x 36"
Photo by: Michael Mathers

"In The House Of Voices" 1993
Kiln cast irridized glass
Size: 24" x 45" x 15"
Photo by: Roger Schreiber

Newy Fagan

"Cactus #1" 1992
Kiln cast glass
Size: 13" x 9½" x 1"
Photo by: Mike Barrett

"Horse Head #2" 1988
Kiln cast glass
Size : 8½" x 1½"
Photo by: Mike Barrett

Mary Fox

"The Determined Veteran" 1996
Lost wax kiln cast & blown glass
   with gold and copper
Size: 18¾" x 4" x 4"
Photo by: Bill Bachhuber

"The Breadwinner" 1996
Lost wax kiln cast & blown glass
   with silver, gold and copper
Size: 18¼" x 4" x 4"
Photo by: Bill Bachhuber

Robin Grebe

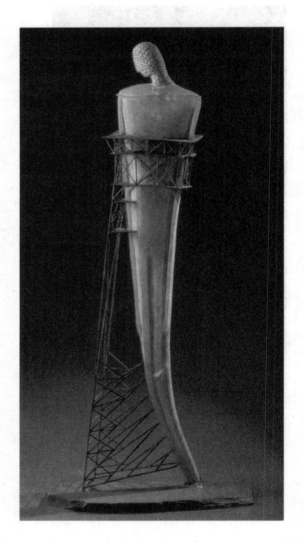

"Mind's Eye" 1994
Kiln cast glass and metal
Size: 32" x 15" x 10"
Photo by: Will Howcroft

"Building Tradition" 1994
Kiln cast glass, metal and slate
Size: 37" x 10" x 11"
Photo by: Will Howcroft

Rachel Josepher Gaspers

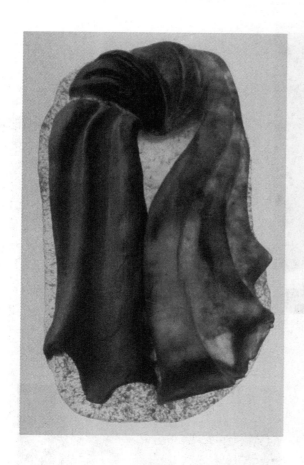

"Twist" Series #1
Pâte de Verre
Size: 12" x 6" x 2"
Photo by: the artist 1986

"Twist" Series #3
Pâte de Verre
Size: 10" x 7" x 2"
Photo by: the artist 1986

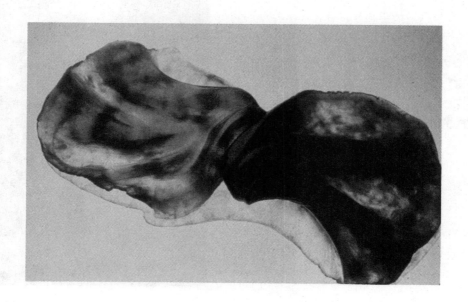

Lucartha Kohler

"The Language Of The Goddess"
Kiln cast glass with slumped &
    sand carved plate glass
Size: 17" x 12" x 20"
Photo by: the artist 1994

"Love Story III" 1994
Kiln cast glass with brass
Size: 20" x 12" x 12"
Photo by: the artist

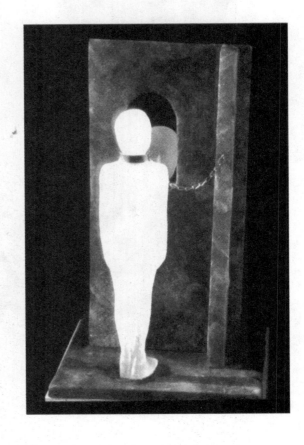

Donna Milliron

"Cityscape, Whisper and Dreamscape Beads" 1994
Pâte de Vere / Cire Perdue
Photo by: Christopher Marchetti

"Strong Women Series Necklace"
Pâte de Verre / Cire Perdue 1996
Photo by: the artist

Charles Miner

"The Ladies" 1996
Kiln cast glass
Size: 13" x 13" diameter
Photo by: Addison Doty

"Tarpon School" 1996
Kiln cast glass
Size: 13½" x 18½" diameter
Photo by: Carol Wright

Seth Randal

"Double Cage Cup" 1994
Pâte de Cristal
Size: 19" x 9" diameter
Photo by: Roger Schreiber
Collection of Antonio Amado

"Amphore Classique D' Albrâtre"
Pâte de Cristal 1993
Size: 23" x 10" diameter
Photo by: Roger Schreiber
Collection of Mr & Mrs Marvin Weis

Alice Rogan-Nelson

"Mythical Setting: 1995
Cire Perdue kiln cast crystal
    with copper and silver
Size: knife   3½" x 6½" x 2"
        goblet 5¼" x 4" x 4"
        plate   4" x 9½" x 6½"
Photo by: Richard Nelson

"Celestial Explorers" 1995
Pâte de Verre
Size: 9" x 18" x 4"
Photo by: Richard Nelson
Collection of Michael P. Curry

David Ruth

"Nebula" 1995
Kiln cast glass
Size: 49" x 40" x 11"
Photo by: the artist

"Baltra" 1996
Kiln cast glass
Size: 16½" x 10" x 9"
Photo by: the artist

Kathleen Stevens

"Tree Dancers" 1996
Lost wax kiln cast crystal
Size: 15½" x 8" x 8"
Photo by: Arthur Probst
Shown at: The Divine Gallery

"Promises" 1996
Lost wax kiln cast crystal
Size: 15½" x 10¾" x 10¾"
Photo by: Arthur Probst
Shown at: The Divine Gallery

Janusz Walentynowicz

"Seagull" 1992
Lost wax kiln cast glass
Size: 29" x 22" x 19"

"Carousal" 1993
Lost wax kiln cast glass
Size: 30" x 18" x 15"

Mary Frances Wawrytko

"Diva" 1994 (Edition of 8)
Cire Perdue kiln cast glass
Size: 7" x 9" x 4"
Photo by: the artist

"Edris" 1995 (Edition of 8)
Pâte de Verre
Size: 9" x 8"
Photo by: .the artist

Investment Materials and Formulations

Success in pâte de verre and kiln casting depends a lot on how strong your casting molds are which in turn depends upon what investment materials and formulation you use. The term investment is derived from a term once used to describe special apparel such as cloaks. Thus when a model was "cloaked" with a mold it was said to have been invested and the material came to be called investment.

Whether you should formulate your own investment or purchase a commercially prepared one becomes a matter of choice based upon convenience and availability. In most cases a commercially prepared investment will have more consistent results because the manufacturer has facilities to carefully control its manufacture. Also since they are a large company they can purchase the components in enough bulk that they may be able to sell it to you at a price below that with which you could formulate it yourself. On the other hand you may be located a great distance from a manufacturer or distributor of investment which would require considerable shipping cost to purchase it. In this case you may be forced to formulate and mix up your own investment. So let's learn more about the materials used in investment formulation.

Investment materials

There are a number of factors that have to be considered when choosing a investment formulation for use in your work. The first is based upon your glass choice — at what temperature will you be processing the glass? How fine of surface detail are you trying to capture in your work? Is your work so large that it requires very strong molds to hold it together, or so delicate that you cringe while breaking it out of the mold? Are you having problems with molds cracking during firings? Those and many other factors may affect your formulation choice or modifications you may make to it.

Before giving you some basic investment formulas to work with, it is best if you understand what the functions of the different formulation components are. Otherwise, if you develop problems, you will not have the basic knowledge to troubleshoot what's wrong and what you have to do to fix it. With this basic knowledge, when you get a formula from someone that works well for them but not for you, or you have a formula that works well with one kind of glass but not with another, you should be able to figure out how to modify it to suit your purpose. Although again you may decide to avoid this whole issue entirely and choose instead to work with a commercially formulated investment in this case we can recommend the products of Ransom and Randolf with which we have had good luck.

Even if you decide to purchase your investment, you should understand their composition. There are three basic components to an investment mold formulation: binders, high temperature refractories, and property modifiers. Each component performs a different function but which function an actual material is performing can sometimes be blurred in practice. To confound things further some of the materials that we will discuss may also be available in multiple forms.

Binders

Binders are those materials in an investment formulation that bind the other components of the formulation together. The most common ones used in kiln casting are gypsum plasters and cements. You can think of them as the mortar that holds all the individual bricks together to make a wall. In the simple investment formulation that we presented earlier, the binder was plaster. Each binder has its own operational temperature regime. As you exceed it, the binder loses strength. About half of a typical investment formulation consists of binder. As you decrease the binder fraction below this value the investment become weaker. A list of typical binders used in glass investment formulations and the temperatures regions in which they break down is given below.

Table 6. Breakdown temperature of common casting binders.

Binder	Breakdown Temp
Gypsum plaster	1300-1500°F
Hydrocal cement	1300-1500°F
Hydroperm cement	1400-1700°F
Portland cement	1600-1900°F
Colloidal silica	2300°F
Colloidal alumina	2300°F
Calcium alumina cement (fondu)	2800°F

Binders use three basic mechanisms to hold the other components in the investment mix together. The first and strongest is through chemical bonds that are formed between binder molecules and those of the other components in the investment formulation. The second and slightly weaker mechanism is by molecular attraction between the binder molecules and those of the other components. An example of such attractive forces are electro-static forces. The third and weakest mechanism is by physically trapping the other components within a matrix of binder molecules. Let's now look at some typical binders in detail.

Gypsum plasters and cements

Gypsum (calcium sulfate) plasters and cements are basically ground up gypsum stone (alabaster or selenite), which has been quarried, crushed, screened, pulverized and is then heated to around 350°F (calcined) to drive off both physically attached water, and chemically attached water molecules of crystallization. They differ somewhat in crystalline structure as a result of the different temperature and pressure conditions under which the calcining is done. After calcining, the gypsum is reduced to a soft material that is easily milled to produce a fine homogeneous product. The end product is thirsty and wants to return to its stone state. When mixed with water and allowed to recrystallize, gypsum plasters and cements will form a produce without grain, hardness variations, or lumps. They differ in the amount of water required to form a workable product. Plasters are combined with 65 to 160 pounds of water per 100 pounds of plaster to achieve a good pourable slurry while cements are mixed in the range of 22 to 45 pounds of water per 100 pounds of cement. They both are very hydroscopic, i.e. soak up water out of the air, off your hands or whatever. Any humidity contamination will not be immediately apparent in the powder but it will influence setting properties. Because of this you have to keep them in a warm dry place away from water sources like damp floors. The primary gypsum plaster and cement manufacturing company, US Gypsum (USG), recommends that plasters or cements should normally not be stored for longer than 90 days to retain their optimal properties, but if kept dry they can be stored for much longer periods.

We recommend that you keep your plasters and cements sealed in plastic bags closed with strong ties at the very least, or better still get some of those plastic buckets with tight fitting lids used to store flour which can often be found in the trash behind bakeries. You can also find them at some hardware stores. Transfer material from your larger strong container to smaller buckets for use in your mixing area. This is done in order to try to minimize air space over the stored plaster or cement. Doing this reduces the investments exposure to moisture from the surrounding air. Be careful not to get drops of water into your plaster or your mix may seem like it has pebbles in it. But if you do accidentally get water into your small plaster container while mixing up a batch of investment, you have not lost as much of it.

When mixed with water, gypsum plasters and cements slowly chemically change back into their original form, a rock. As they harden, they do not really dry, they set. Most of the water is still there but it is incorporated as part of long gypsum crystals. By changing the particle size and drying procedure, plasters and cements with different performances are produced. The different gypsum products that you will purchase may also have materials added to control setting expansion or time. For example materials such as alkali sulphates or chlorides are added to accelerate set while ones such as borax, gelatin or starch are added to retard it and the addition of either will usually reduce setting expansion. The different gypsum plasters and cements vary in strength, set time, expansion during set, shrinkage during firing, water requirements, and pour characteristics. They can generally be substituted for one another, but may require slightly different amounts of water be added to achieve the same degree of dry strength and can result in considerably different results. (This is not true of the gypsum cements as you will find out.) Some of the commonly available gypsum plasters and cements are listed in Table 7 with a few of their typical physical characteristics.

Table 7. Properties of typical gypsum plasters and cements.

Gypsum Product	water added (% of dry mix wt.)	Set time (min)	Dry density (lb/cu ft)	% Set Expand	Compressive strength (psi)
No. 1 pottery plaster	70	27-37	69.0	.210	1,800
No. 1 molding plaster	70	27-37	69.0	.200	2,000
Plaster of Paris	70	27-37	69.0	.200	
No. 1 Casting plaster	65	27-37	72.5	.220	2,400
Pottery plaster	74	27-37	66.0	.190	1,800
Hydrocal cement	45	25-35	90.0	.390	5,000
Hydroperm cement	100	12-19	<40	.140	-----
Hydro-Stone cement	32	17-20	119.4	.240	10,000
Ultracal cement (30)	38	25-35	99.0	.080	6,000

The strength of a plaster or cement is the result of the development during setting of a matrix of numerous needle-like crystals which become tightly interwoven. It is the density of this matrix that dictates its strength. Dilution of the mix with more than the desired amount of water results in a final matrix of crystals that are further apart from each other than desired and thereby weakening it. That is why the optimum amount of water to be added to the mix, usually referred to as the normal consistency (amount of water by weight to 100 parts of plaster to achieve a standard fluidity), is so important. As an example of this see the data in Table 8 which lists how setting time, compression strength and final dry density of a typical plaster varies with the plaster to water ratio. The amount of water a plaster is mixed with also affects other properties besides strength such as: chip resistance, durability, density and surface permeability.

If not stored properly, your plaster or formulated investment mix can rehydrate by pulling moisture out of its surroundings. If it has done so, it may not perform well anymore. This can cause it to take longer to set up because much of the recrystalization may have already occurred. This reduces the amount of interleaving of the needle-like crystals and thus the strength of the mold, resulting in increased mold cracking. Molds made from partially hydrated plaster many times will also be rougher to the touch because of clumping of the plaster. Two ways of determining if you have a problem come to mind. The most accurate is to compare weights of equal volumes of your suspect plaster and a known good plaster or "hot" mix. If its weight difference is more than 20% greater, get rid of that old stuff. Alternatively you can compare the setting time of the two. If the suspect material takes more than a couple extra minutes over the good stuff, it is most likely bad. Trying to save money by using bad plaster is just not worth it.

Table 8. Effect of plaster-water ratio on some properties.

Plaster-water ratio (by weight)	Setting time (min)	Compression strength (psi)	Dry Density (lb/cu ft)
100/30	1¾	11,500	112.7
100/40	3¼	6,750	96.6
100/50	5¼	4,500	84.4
100/60	7¼	3,250	75.3
100/70	8¾	2,500	67.6
100/80	10½	1,800	61.8
100/90	12	1,400	56.7
100/100	13¾	1,000	54.1

A description of some of the commonly available plasters and their properties follows:

USG #1 pottery plaster is a good general purpose plaster. Its strength and easy flow characteristics account for its popularity. It is generally recognized as the industry standard against which other gypsum plasters are judged. It is mixed with 70 parts of water per 100 parts of plaster. Pottery casting plaster has polymer and synthetic fibers additions that improve its performance in solid sculptural or slush casting applications. These increase the chip resistance and impact strength of the mold. It is mostly used by the ceramics industry for the construction of slip casting molds.

USG #1 moulding plaster, sometimes referred to as "soft plaster" or "Plaster of Paris" (so called because the raw material was once mined from the hill of Montmartre in Paris) is the softest and most porous of the different varieties. It contains no surface hardening agents and is thus the easiest to carve and use for making waste or throw away molds. Its nominal consistency is also 70 parts of water per 100 parts of plaster (any thing in the range 67-80 parts of water works well). It reproduces intricate detail well.

USG #1 casting plaster is another widely used utility plaster. It mixes easily and is slightly harder and denser than molding plaster as well as having better chip resistance. It contains small amounts of hardening agents to achieve harder surfaces and other additives to give it smooth working capabilities. This extra hardness results in decreased permeability, which is useful in normal model building because it reduces the amount of paint the plaster soaks up. For this reason it is also a good plaster for making wax master molds. It is mixed to a nominal consistency of 65 parts of water per 100 parts of plaster.

USG Hydrocal is a white gypsum cement. It has a much greater setting expansion (almost twice) that of the gypsum plasters which is also the greatest of all the gypsum cements. This expansion occurs uniformly in all directions and is controlled through the amount of water with which it is mixed. This greater expansion facilitates removal of models after complete set which is optimal anytime after about two to three hours from initial set. Hydrocal is fairly easily carved and will bond to additional pours after it is completely dry. It must be worked quickly because it has a fairly short period of plasticity and hardens rather rapidly. It is mixed with 45 parts of water to 100 parts of Hydrocal. There are actually a number of Hydrocal formulations available that differ mainly in strength and set expansion.

Hydroperm is another gypsum cement that is often used in the construction of molds for metal foundry casting. It is formulated with a foaming agent that causes it to produce a uniform matrix of bubbles throughout the mold forming a lighter, low-density mold. The size and distribution of these bubbles can be varied by changing mixing parameters. Once set up, the bubbles result in an interconnected cellular structure in the mold that makes it very permeable to gases. This is a desirable property for foundry applications since it prevents trapping of air in the mold as it fills and allows the molds to dry much faster. Its formulation also includes some refractory materials.

Hydrostone and Ultracal are two other gypsum plasters that we do not usually use because they set up too hard for mold making. You end up breaking the casting as you try to remove the mold. They can be put to good use though in making cradle molds to reinforce your casting molds or as a partial addition to strengthen molds if you are plagued with cracks.

Most glass artists will refer to any of the gypsum plasters or cements as plaster without recognizing that there is really any difference between them. Sometimes we are no different, although you would think that we would know better. As a general rule, we tend to use white Hydrocal cement for a binder in our investment formulations.

Cements

Portland cement is most commonly used in construction. In mold formulations, it is used with plasters to modify strength or set time. Unfortunately Portland cement becomes chemically activated during casting operations and would readily stick to the glass if it were used as the primary binding agent for high temperature (over 1200°F) applications. Portland cement can be used as a backup insulating refractory. It should not be exposed to direct contact with glass or flames.

Calcium alumina cement, commonly known as Fondu (a brand name), is a high temperature (up to 2500°F) binding agent commonly used in castable refractory formulations that need to withstand direct exposure to flames and furnace gases. Up to 15% by weight can be added to an investment mix to increase a mold's strength at high temperature. One down side to using it, is that its strength makes the mold harder to remove from the glass after firing. When added in amounts greater than 4%, small amounts of potassium sulfate are required to facilitate quicker setting of the investment. Calcium alumina cement is the binder used in the light-weight castable refractories manufactured by A. P. Green. It is also sometimes used by glass fusers in the construction of slumping molds.

Colloidal alumina is a liquid suspension of fine alumina particles. It is used as a binding agent for tightly packed olivine sand when doing sand casting. We glass fusers sometimes use it for rigidizing fiber paper and blanket in slumping mold manufacture. Although it can air set, colloidal alumina should really be fired to about 1100°F to reach its optimum strength. It does not become activated at high temperatures so it will not stick to the molten glass. This means that it can also be used as a good glass casting mold release. Its addition to an investment formulation will strengthen it and reduce glass sticking.

Colloidal silica has similar binding properties and uses as colloidal alumina. It is also used by many glass fusing artists to rigidized ceramic fiber molds. Unlike colloidal alumina, colloidal silica can become activated at high temperature causing it to interact with or stick to molten glass and therefore does not work as a mold release. It needs to be fired to realize its optimal strength but it only needs to be fired to about 800°F. If you use it as a binder you may find that a kiln wash mold release is required to prevent glass from sticking to the mold.

Refractories

The next major investment formulation component, refractories, are materials that are added to the formulations because of their high temperature stability. As materials go they tend to be stable both dimensionally and chemically at high temperature. It is for this reason that refractories also form a major portion of an investment formulation. Typical refractory materials added to investment mixes are: silica, diatomite, alumina hydrate, zirconia and olivine sand. These microscopic refractory particles influence the shrinkage of the binder matrix during firing. They do this by acting as a stable backbone to which the binder matrix can cling as it shrinks.

In adding refractories to a plaster-based mold formulation it is important to add a material or materials that provide a range of particle sizes. This allows you to more closely pack the refractory particles in the investment mix so that they form a stronger and denser matrix. Then when the plaster starts to shrink at about 1200°F, it can grab tightly onto this stable matrix resulting in increased mold strength and decreased shrinkage. This works well until about 1400-1550°F when the plaster starts to decompose and lose its strength.

Silica-based refractories

Silica may be added to an investment formulation as either a sand (120 mesh and coarser) or a flour (220 mesh and finer ground from flint). Particles larger than 80 mesh can be problematic because of their tendency to settle. This problem is worsened if vibration is used to try and release trapped air in the freshly poured investment. Silica can also cause problems in higher temperature molds for two reasons. First, because of its relatively low melting temperature, it can become activated and stick to the glass. Second, being a finely ground form of flint, it goes through a quartz inversion at approximately 1060°F. At this temperature, the crystals rearrange themselves with about a 2% volume change causing the silica to expand during heating and contract during crash cooling of your kiln. This can cause cracking of the mold if temperature is changed too quickly. Fine silica dust is a health hazard. It is much more damaging to the lungs to breath than plaster. Prolonged or acute exposures to free silica can result in a condition called silicosis, which is very similar to asbestosis. This can lead to reduced lung function (read as difficulty in breathing) and possibly cancer. So a respirator is definitely in order when handling it especially when it is in a finely ground form like silica flour. When using sand as a filler you may want to add a couple of size grades to get better packing. Its coarser texture will not necessarily lead to a coarser texture in the casting because the more liquid part of the mix will come to the surface to fill fine voids especially if used in combination with silica flour.

Another form of silica commonly used in investment formulations is crystobalite. It is a form of quartz with a very high melting temperature (3140°F) that has also been crushed and ground into a flour. Crystobalite differs from silica flour in that it has a higher degree of expansion. This material was discovered in the '20s and is thought to be the result in nature of lightening strikes. Now a days it is manufactured by high temperature processing of silica.

Diatomite, commonly known as diatomaceous earth, is the siliceous shell remains of microscopic single-celled algae. It is a porous crystalline material that is not as dense as silica and does not pack as tightly as silica flour. But like silica, it also becomes activated at higher temperatures and can stick to the glass. It is used in investment formulations instead of silica to form a lighter more porous mold that breaks apart easier.

Dry clay particles can also be used as a refractory filler. All clays, as described earlier, are mixtures of alumina and silica primarily differing from each other in the size and shape of their particle distributions as dictated by the processes of weathering, chemical interactions, and sedimentation that they have gone through. Some may still have unaltered fragments of feldspar or quartz. Particle size varies from 120-250 mesh for fire clays to 250-400 mesh for kaolin clays. Their addition to plaster-based investment mixes serves a refractory role by increasing high temperature strength and reducing shrinkage. Clays also act to help increase strength by providing a strong packing matrix of particles that form ceramic bonds to each other. Molds with clay additions to binder levels require firing to 1600°F or higher to completely develop this ceramic bond through vitrification which occurs as some of the clay components melt and bond together. This temperature is a function of the purity of the clay. High percentage clay molds may be too tough for casting and will not break away easily from the glass but could be useful for cradle molds.

Non-silica refractories

Alumina hydrate occurs naturally in a number of different crystalline forms that although they have the save chemical composition respond differently at high temperature. Dan uses it as a 50% additive to kaolin clay in making a kiln shelf separator or "wash" for his fusing work. In that application, a finely ground alumina hydrate (300 to 350 mesh) is used to give a smooth back surface to a fused piece. Coarser grinds are used for refractory additives to large open-face slumping molds that you have probably purchased. For kiln casting work, a 200-300 mesh grade is a good choice for use as a refractory filler. Alumina does not melt by itself until about 2040°F and thus does not become activated in the range of interest for glass casting.

Zirconia is an even higher temperature refractory material that is very stable over the entire temperature region of interest in kiln casting. It does not melt until about 3700°F and it will not react with the glass. It can be purchased in a wide variety of mesh sizes from 30 to fine flours. Take advantage of this availability and add a mixture of sizes to get a high density packing as was discussed earlier for silica.

Olivine foundry sand is made by grinding the mineral, chrysolite (magnesium iron silicate) to sand sized particles. In a fine mesh grind, it works as a good refractory additive to plaster-based investment formulations because of its low coefficient of thermal expansion. It is an expensive but extremely high melting temperature sand, 3470°F. Be aware that foundry sands, like olivine, are often characterized by an A.F.S. number that characterizes a specified mix of mesh sized particles rather than a single mesh size. As an example, olivine 120 is a mixture of 50 to 180 mesh particles. Unlike silica sand and clays, olivine sand does not suffer from the problem of expansion at high temperature from a quartz inversion.

Property Modifiers

Property modifiers are a collection of materials formulated as part of investment mixes to change any of a number of mold properties. Among these properties are included: increased wetting of models for more faithful reproduction, increased setting time, decreased drying time, increased porosity, decreased bubbling and internal compliance which allows absorption of the expansion or compliance of other components. Property modifiers are usually added in small proportions, not as major components, even if they are refractory in nature. They are often misused and little understood by most glass artists.

Grog is pre-fired clay that has been ground up. You will want a fine mesh grind, in the neighborhood of 120 to 200 mesh for investment formulation. It is used like a refractory to lower expansion and contraction rates of your investment mix. A similar material that is commercially available is Kitty litter. It is puffed clay and will work well for bas relief molds but is mostly put to use for making fusing slumping molds because its texture is too coarse for investment molds.

Ludo is the remains of previous investment molds that after firing and breaking them from the casting is crushed and screened. It is added to an investment mix just prior to pouring to prevent weakening the plaster matrix. Like grog it reduces mold shrinkage as well as accelerates setting time. It allows reuse of some of the more expensive refractories. You can also grind up "dead" or broken slumping molds for use as a filler. Hey no sense in wasting material.

Fiberglass fibers can be added to an investment formulation to increase its low temperature strength through cure and burnout. To use them for molding, it helps to first chop them in a blender with a little water, then rinse and drain. If used dry, add a little extra water to the investment mix. If used wet, do not add the extra water. Mix them up with the water just prior to adding the dry investment. Besides increasing tensile strength, the chopped fibers can be added to the formulation to enhance thermal shock resistance and mold porosity. They can generally be added in ratios of up to 1 cup of fiber to 10 cups of water without loosing too much detail. They will lose some of their strength near casting temperature (no surprise since they are glass after all) and become activated. But in small amounts they make an excellent modifier. Of course the fact that they are cheap and easy to come by helps some. Addition of any fiber material reduces the ability to do extra carving on molds prior to curing. We usually chop up fiberglass insulation for this purpose, but Anna Boothe says that she has a friend who chops up fiberglass mesh as used in boat building or car body work into one inch lengths for her which she then uses in her investment formulations.

Alumina-silicate fibers such as Fiberfrax® can be added to increase the mold's strength. They are light weight, have high temperature mechanical stability, low thermal conductivity, low heat storage and good corrosion resistance. They will not weaken at casting temperature but may become slightly activated. Use them as was described for fiberglass. They can even be used by themselves, bonded by colloidal alumina or colloidal silica, to make glass molds.

For a higher-temperature fiber that will not thermally activate, try bulk zirconia fibers from Zircar Products Inc. They have 3-6 micron diameter fibers about 2.5 mm long of 99% cubic zirconia and can be easily distinguished from diamonds. They have a melting point of 4700°F compared to the 3700°F for the alumina-silicate fibers. They show no shrinkage up to 2800°F compared to 2% shrinkage seen with the alumina-silicate fibers. Use them as described for the other fibers.

Stainless steel fibers are also available to be added as modifiers to increase the strength of your molds. RIBTEC has the capability to manufacture fibers in a range of sizes from .005" to .060" in diameter (.020" is their standard diameter) and from 3/16" to 3" in length (here the standard lengths are 3/4", 1" and 1 3/8".) These fibers provide the same kinds of benefits and problems as alumina-silicate fibers. You do not need to add extra water for these fibers and you will definitely not be able to carve investment molds with this modifier added.

Kaolin clay, or china clay, is as was discussed earlier, a high purity residual clay. It, like all clays, is a mix of alumina and silica. When added in large amounts, it may serve as a binder or refractory. Because of its low flux content, kaolin many times does not melt until around 3300°F. Thus when added in small amounts, on the order of 3-5%, it helps in separating the glass from the mold. Its tough, durable, and easy to use. Of the various types of kaolin clay, Edgar plastic kaolin works best for this purpose.

Safe handling of investment materials

Investment materials are very dusty and at the least may serve as an irritant to your lungs. Some of the materials, such as silica flour can, as has been mentioned, cause serious damage to your lungs. For this reason, you should always wear a respirator with a filter cartridge (purple) specifically rated for silica when mixing silica bearing investments. Details for using respirators and developing respirator plans are discussed in our chapter on safety. Mixing of investment materials should be restricted to a small designated area of your shop to avoid spreading the material all around. This area, as well as the rest of your studio, will need proper ventilation to remove any residual dust from the air. Ventilation along with other desirable hygiene practices are also discussed in greater detail in the chapter on safety.

Plaster-based investments can also be irritating to your skin. Besides for the fact that they suck the moisture out of your hands, they are mild alkalis and can produce burns similar to the lye in drain cleaners. You may find it necessary to use hand creams to replenish the moisture that is removed from your hands as you handle it. Some people seem to be more sensitive to this than others. If your skin burns, you may want to try neutralizing the alkali by washing your hands in vinegar and rinsing them well in water. Of course the better choice would be to avoid skin contact altogether by wearing gloves. It goes without saying that you also want to keep plaster dust out of your eyes.

Investment formulations

A number of investment formulations are presented in this section. These formulations have been obtained from various sources as well as our own personal experience and have been found to perform well in kiln casting of glass. They may be sufficient for most of your kiln casting needs. In fact you may find the first formulation is enough. Many glass artists do not go beyond it because of its good performance and its simplicity. With the basic knowledge that we have just presented on investment materials, you should be able to understand the purpose of the different components. Furthermore, if you are having difficulty with an investment mix, you should now have some ideas of how to modify it to make it work better for you. Remember less water generally produces a stronger mold. This is because plaster becomes a solid by the formation of tightly interlaced crystals of gypsum. As more water is added the crystals form farther away from each other and the structure is thus weakened. If your molds are fragile and crack, too much water could be the culprit. You can also try adding chopped fiber to a mix to strengthen it. When you add materials to modify a mix, you may or may not have to add extra water to the mix. The basic rule is that if the material absorbs water, add water; if not, then don't.

Almost all mold formulations are plaster-based mixtures with other materials added to increase strength and refractory (high-temperature) capability. As mentioned earlier, such plaster-based systems lose most of their strength in the range of 1350 to 1550°F. Mold formulations with greater than 50% plaster tend shrink unacceptably when fired over 1400°F. This causes them to crack and results in unwanted lines in the finished piece. Mixes for higher temperatures will replace some of or most of the plaster with cement and will add various refractories to reinforce the mold. Think about these things as you examine the following example investment mix formulations. To further illustrate this, we will examine the effect of changing an investment's formulation as we present our first investment mix by looking a the effect of varying its plaster/refractory ratio.

Before you start mixing any of these investment formulations, you might want to review the rules that we presented on mixing plaster-based investments in the chapter on the Basic Frit Casting Process.

Investment mix # 1:

1   part gypsum plaster or cement
1   part silica flour (200-300 mesh)

This is one of the easiest mold mixes to make and it is what Dan primarily teaches. Premix both dry ingredients. The dry mix is added 2 parts of mix to 1 part of water for optimum results. Good results from this mix are also obtained by measuring dry components by volume and adding the dry mix to water until islands form on top of the water as was explained in the basic process chapter. This mix works best at lower temperatures because of the high percentage of plaster and because the silica activates at higher temperatures. This mold achieves fine detail, can be carved prior to curing, and can also be successfully added to after set. It is a soft mix and larger molds may need reinforcement with chicken wire or chopped fiber especially after the mold exceeds about 7 to 10 lb. With your current understanding of the different investment components, you should be able to use this mix as a starting point and modify it at will to get the properties that you desire.

Frederic and Lilli Schuler did a study on the effect of varying the mix ratio of binder to silica flour for Hydrocal and Hydroperm cement on which they report in their book "Glassforming." They made a number of formulations of differing mix ratios and fired them to 1000°C. After firing the samples, they measured the percent shrinkage of each sample. Their results are shown plotted in Figure 47. In examining the data, you can see that Hydroperm is much more stable than Hydrocal as well as being much stronger. From the data, you would think that you

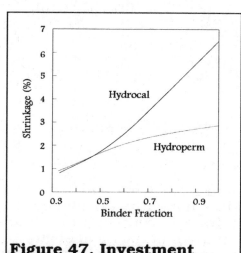

Figure 47. Investment shrinkage study.

would want to go to as low a binder content as possible. But obviously if you go too low, there is not enough plaster to hold things together. It also seems that for ratios of plaster to silica flour above 50/50, the Hydrocal samples always seemed to crack. Below that value, although the samples didn't crack, their strength was considerably reduced. The Schulers' recommended a 33/67 mix. Hydroperm mixtures. You can choose which to use yourself but Hydroperm mixes are sometimes difficult to demold. You may want to add a little to your Hydrocal-based mix to increase mold strength.

Some artists, such as Robin Grebe, prefer to use sand instead of silica flour because of the danger of developing silicosis. Silica flour is classified as a toxic dust by OSHA, so she prefers to keep its use to a minimum. She, like many of us kiln casting artists, lives in close proximity to her studio and thus has extra incentive to keep toxic materials out. Besides some artists claim sand performs superior to silica flour in preventing cracking of the mold at high temperature because of its gradation in particle size.

Investment mix # 2:

        28 parts gypsum plaster or cement
        12 parts calcined (pre-fired) kaolin clay
        13 parts sifted asbestos
        10 parts silica flour (200-300 mesh)
        37 parts silica sand (60-80 mesh)

This is a classical mold mix developed by Rousseau in the late 1800's for his Pâte de Verre work. Since asbestos is no longer in favor, people have modified this mix in a number of ways. Some replace the asbestos with some other chopped fiber. Others increase the calcined kaolin to about 22 parts and add a few parts of uncalcined kaolin clay. Without any chopped fiber, this mix makes a very soft mold, almost too soft for lost wax casting. The premixed dry mold materials are added slowly to water until build up appears just below the surface of the water. Then gently stir until you reach the consistency of cream and pour. (Always wear a respirator when handling dry ingredients because all can be irritating to the respiratory tract and some like silica can cause irreversible lung damage over time.) This mold can be used up to temperatures of about 1500°F.

Investment mix # 3:

        2 parts gypsum plaster or cement
        2 parts silica flour
        1 part zircon

Add 2 parts of premixed ingredients to 1 part of water. This mix does not shrink as much as the first mix because of its higher refractory content, but at the same time this reduces the overall strength of the mold slightly. The addition of the high temperature refractory, zircon, helps reduce the sticking of the glass to the mold at higher temperatures. This mix can be used for casting up to about 1600°F. It is also soft and easy to remove afterwards.

Investment mix # 4:

>   4   part gypsum plaster or cement
>   4   part silica flour
>   1   part kaolin clay
>   1-2%   chopped fiber

Add 4 parts of premixed powders to 3 parts of water. After slaking, stir one of the many types of chopped fibers, prewetted into the investment and then power mix. This mold mix also achieves fine detail and works well for lost wax casting. Molds should be cured to 1450°F to mature the kaolin clay binder and are good for casting up to temperatures of around 1600°F. The addition of the clay and the chopped fiber are attempts to make the mix stronger. Even so it is still a fairly soft mix and breaks away from the glass easily. Remember that the chopped fiber will severely restrict the carvability of the mold.

Investment mix # 5:

>   1   part gypsum plaster or cement
>   1   part diatomite
>   5% kaolin clay

Premix dry ingredients and add 5 parts of mix to 3 parts of water. Because of the porosity of diatomite, this mix air dries faster than the previous mixes especially as wall thickness increases. This faster drying is one of the primary reasons for adding diatomite rather than silica flour in an investment mix. The porosity of the diatomite also causes this to be a lighter mix and increases its carvability. The kaolin clay, which is used here as a property modifier, helps prevent the glass from sticking to the mold allowing use up to about 1550°F. If you don't have any kaolin clay available, you can add kiln wash instead.

Investment mix # 6:

>   4   parts Hydroperm cement
>   1   part diatomite

Combine 5 parts premixed dry ingredients quickly with 4 parts water. Let stand for about a half of a minute and hand mix to get all the lumps out. Then vigorously mix using a power mixer about 2 inches off the container bottom until you get the desired volume increase. As some large bubbles may also be generated during mixing, you should then slow down the mixer and coax large bubbles out by raising and lowering your mixer. As mentioned earlier, Hydroperm has a foaming agent incorporated in it and when correctly mixed will develop a homogeneous distribution of small air bubbles that are just barely visible — about .01" in diameter. This will cause the mix to increase in volume up to 3/4 of its initial volume, so plan ahead. If you vary the additives, be aware that the volume increase will vary also. Straight Hydroperm doubles in volume. This is a fast setting mix that can be deframed in about an hour and is ready for curing immediately. This mix has the capability to pick up fine detail and can be successfully fired up to 1600°F. One problem with Hydroperm molds is that they are fairly strong and may give you some problems in demolding your glass. So this type of mold would be used with models that have good draft and no undercuts. With careful demolding it may be reusable. Addition of about 5% kaolin clay in the dry mix will help prevent glass from sticking to the mold. Use of a separator compound is also suggested if this is used for the casting mold. We recommend a mix like this for use in construction of a cradle mold around your casting mold.

Investment mix # 7:

    1   parts gypsum plaster or cement
    1   parts Hydroperm cement
    1   part silica flour

Very similar to basic mix #1, but a little stronger and a little more prone to shrinkage. The foaming agent in Hydroperm helps to lighten the mold some allowing for faster drying and curing as in the last mix. Newy Fagan says that she uses this mix in some of her work.

Investment mix # 8:

    1   parts Hydrocal cement
    1   parts silica flour
    1   part Kast-o-Lite

Premix dry ingredients. Then add by feel to water and mix by hand. This makes a strong mold that is hard to break away but is good for bas relief and cradle mold purposes. The Kast-o-Lite refractory from A. P. Green will make the mold a little coarse.

Commercially available investments

If you do not want to deal with formulating your own mix, there are a number of commercial investments available that you might like to try. A number of kiln casting artists report that they have had very good success using the investments manufactured by Ransom and Randolf (R&R). They say that they very rarely get any mold cracking and can usually get by without even air drying their molds. The two formulations most commonly used for kiln casting are R&R 910 and R&R 965 investments. Both of these were formulated for casting aluminum and copper based alloys. They are both gypsum based but differ in their refractory and modifier components. R&R 910, the stronger, denser and least expansive of the two, is reported to be formulated using calcined silica, fiberglass and various specially graded refractories. Wetting and suspension agents are added to decrease chances of trapping bubbles on the surface of your wax replica. R&R 965 on the other hand uses cristobalite, crystalline silica and graded refractory additives. Both are recommended to be mixed to a consistency of 28 parts water to 100 parts of powder.

The instructions that I have been given by Donna Milliron of Arrow Springs on their use is as follows. To start out she estimates or measures the volume of her mold frame. This is made easier if you use things like tin cans for mold frames. She then measures out a volume of water equal to about two thirds that of the mold frame. Into this she sifts the investment until it peaks. To save money you can reuse up to one part of freshly ground investment from previous molds to 2 parts of fresh investment. Here you are using the recycled material as a refractory filler and the fresh investment mix as a binder. This recycle mix is slightly weaker than the original one, but retains finer detail than the original mix. The reused material has to be kept dry just as the fresh does to get optimum performance. It also has to well ground or it will form hard lumps. After peaking, allow about one minute for slaking and then mix. Continue mixing until the mixture will just coat your fingernail (about two minutes) and then pour your investment quickly because it will set up in a hurry. If you have problems finding this material, call Donna. She, as does Mark Abildgaard, uses it almost exclusively in her work and will usually have some around for sale.

Ullmann makes a Pâte de Verre investment that is available from Ed Hoy's in 50 pound lots for about $1.00 per pound plus shipping and handling. This mix only requires addition of water and is mixed like plaster. It survives to 1500°F with very little cracking and is easily removed from the finished work. It can also be reused by grinding up a used mold and mixing 3 parts of it to 1 part of fresh investment. It shrinks a fair amount when it sets though.

Satin-Cast is another prepared investment material that gives fine detail. It is most popular with jewelers, and since they work small and use materials in small quantities, it is likely to cost a bit more than some of the other commercial mixes.

Lab plaster (they choose a real exotic name for this product), manufactured by Columbus Dental, offers fine detail, thermal shock resistance and ease of break away. It might be a bit difficult to find but the effort is worth it.

Alumina hydrate and alumina silicate bonded with colloidal silica also makes a very strong mold material with low thermal expansion and excellent surface reproduction capability.

Remember there is a limit to the detail that can be captured in the glass. This limit is a result of its final strength for the detail to resist breakage during removal from the mold and during cleaning. There is also always a formulation tradeoff between ease of mold removal and durability at high temperatures. So you may need to experiment to find an investment formulation that works just right for you and your work.

Mold Construction and Processing

Now that we know more about investments let's elaborate on how they are used in making molds. Molds are the equivalent of a photographic negative only in the three dimensional sense. It contains a negative cavity in which the glass frit is consolidated to form our final positive product. As such, the mold represents an important intermediate step between our original model and the final pâte de verre or kiln cast piece. The complexity of its construction and the materials from which it is composed can vary widely depending upon your desires. For these reasons we believe it is important to present as thorough an examination of mold construction and processing as possible.

This is an important subject because your final product is an exact reproduction of your mold cavity and not your original model. Thus if you are not able to translate all that creativity that you put into making your model into a usable mold, you will not get it in your final piece. Sure you may be the recipient of a few happy accidents but the failure or success of your work depends upon being able to consistently produce a usable mold from your model.

Mixing large batches of investment

Earlier we discussed hand mixing small batches of investment. As your work gets larger, your batches will have to get larger and hand mixing may no longer be appropriate. With large batches of investment, you may want the assistance of power tools with mixing attachments like an egg beater, which by the way can be used for medium sized batches. Attachments designed for paint mixing are ideal for this purpose and can be purchased for use with a variable speed power drill to mix your investment. They come in many different sizes and configurations with most looking like two or three bladed airplane propellers. They may be mounted singly or multiply to a shaft. One of the best power attachments for mixing investment is illustrated in Figure 48. It is called a Jiffy mixer, and is available at your friendly neighborhood hardware or paint store in a variety of sizes. It is perfect for mixing investment.

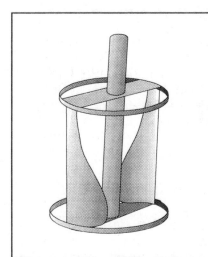

Figure 48. Jiffy mixer used for mixing large investment batches.

The two vertical blades help confine the main mixing action within the mixer while the horizontally opposed impellers force material from the lower and upper areas of the container into the mixer. The leading edge of the lower impeller can scrape the bottom of the container bringing all the heavy particles into the mix while the ring prevents puncturing the container walls. This design also helps minimize splashing and sucking of air into the investment mix as long as you keep the mixer head below the surface of the investment. They are available in a wide variety of sizes suitable for mixing investment batches anywhere from a pint to 100 gallons.

One thing to be aware of when choosing to power mix investment is the possibility of electric shock. Electricity and water don't mix too well. We know that you will try not to spill any water but sometimes in the heat of mixing investment we all get a little sloppy. Therefore to avoid getting shocked consider using doubly insulated drills with good ground wire connectors. The use of extension cords with Ground-Fault Interrupt (GFI) protection built in, as most new homes have in bathrooms, is also a good idea. This will cut off the power if you get a short and hopefully protect you from receiving too great a shock.

Deaerating investment

If you are lucky enough to have a vacuum pump, it helps at this point to pull a vacuum over the mix for about a minute to try and remove any gas bubbles. Otherwise they can end up becoming attached to your model and will show up as glass lumps on your final piece. A simple vacuum system can be realized using a rubber-gasketed lucite plate with a wet-dry shop vacuum hose connected to it that you push down on the top of your mixing bowl to pull the air out as shown in Figure 49. The sides of your bowl should be fairly high to prevent accidentally vacuuming up investment

Figure 49. A simple vacuum cleaner deaerating setup

mixture because some will boil up. This kind of accident can be hard on your vacuum. Another way to remove the bubbles that get into a mix is to vibrate it. The easiest way to this is just to bounce the mixing bowl on the table for a little bit. A more elaborate system that works a little better is to hold a vibrator against the side of the bowl. Later you can use it to work out all those aches and pains that you got from crushing your own frit or whatever else ails you. There are also small flat vibrators that jewelers use or if you are working really large scale a vibro-lap may do the job.

Alternate mold frame construction techniques

We have already discussed how to construct a relatively simple mold frame box from cardboard and hot glue. Another convenient material to have around from which you can rapidly construct round molds are strips of linoleum. Remnants can usually be obtained cheaply, if not for free, from a flooring contractor. Good sizes to prepare ahead of time are strips varying in width between 2 to 8 inches and ranging in length from 8 to 24 inches. You could also use heavy roofing paper if you have any of that lying around. When needed either of these strips can be coiled into a cylinder and held in place by duct tape or clothesline. With roofing paper, you will have to wrap it 3 or 4 times around to make a strong enough frame. The edges are then hot glued down to your pallet or clay dams can be built around them. A mold frame constructed in this way is commonly referred to as a coddle (good to know for those scrabble freaks out there). Early mold makers used leather strips for this purpose. These were tanned and waterproofed using soap. They would usually keep a number of widths available and would use one by wrapping it around a short round base. They would tie it in place with rope and would patch any cracks between the leather and the base with clay. Coddles are usually formed into cylinders because this is the shape into which the hydrostatic pressure of the fluid investment will try to force it. But since coddles are constructed from flexible materials, they can also be formed into other shapes such as ovals or rounded triangles. Unfortunately because of the flexible nature of these materials, non-cylindrical shaped coddles will require some reinforcement to hold their shape.

Figure 50. Mold coddle made from linoleum strip.

If you find yourself getting seriously into the production of kiln cast glass, you may want to make convenient, adjustable wood mold frames. Adjustable, wood mold frames can be made from closed grain hardwoods like maple, cherry or birch. These are usually preferred over softwoods like fir and pine because they absorb less water from the plaster and warp less. In addition, it helps to seal the wood with something like polyurethane. The adjustable frame illustrated in Figure 51 could be constructed from four 1" x 4" boards about a foot and a quarter long. Attached to the end of each board is a three inch right angle bracket that fits down over the next board. Since the brackets are only screwed into one of the boards, the boards can be slid relative to each other to quickly construct sturdy rectangular mold frames 4" high of up to about 1 foot on a side. To help seal the boards against each other, you can insert small wedges underneath the angle iron or add T-bolts to push them together as shown in the figure. If you need deeper frames, you can use 1" x 6" or 1" x 8" boards along with correspondingly larger angle brackets. If you need bigger mold frames, you can use longer boards. The only problem with these fixtures is that you are restricted to rectangular frames which may have excess mold material in the corners that is not needed. These areas can be blocked off with cardboard or clay as desired. The frames are held down on the glass pallet by weights placed atop of the wood frame or by clamping them to the table. If you encounter leaking problems, pack some clay around the base. Hot glue can also be used, but it may take a wood chisel and some time to remove the glue.

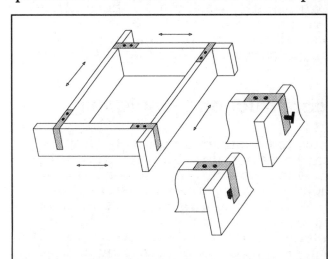

Figure 51. Adjustable reusable wood mold frames.

If you find your production work is consistently small and about the same size, you may want to consider using a jeweler's-like flask. This is useful for items like beads. To do this, find a regular metal can like those used to package vegetables and that is about an inch or two larger in diameter than the largest dimension of your model. The can should not be of aluminum or zinc. Aluminum will melt. Zinc is not compatible with glass and its fumes can have serious health effects. Cut off the bottom and top lids. If still too long, trim it such that it is about ½ to ¾ of an inch longer than the model mounted on its sprue and reservoir. Make a small base of clay around the reservoir and push your flask can into it. You are now ready to cast your mold into the flask. After the mold is setup, you really don't have to remove the flask if you don't want to. In fact you may find its strength helpful to alleviate problems associated with mold cracking. You can then proceed on as normal with drying, curing and casting. Just be sure to keep the flask away from the coils in the kiln and go a little bit slower in curing because water will not be able to get out the sides of the mold with the flask in place.

Reinforcing molds for frit casting.

A common problem with molds is cracking during curing or casting. This can be caused by a number of factors. The first, which has already been discussed, is that of plaster investment material that was not stored properly and was allowed to hydrate. The second is incomplete drying of the mold such that there was too much moisture left in the mold. The moisture breaks the mold apart as it turns into steam during the early portion of the cure cycle. This can be partially alleviated by going through this portion of the cure cycle slower, but this can be hard to control if you do not have a controller on your kiln. Another cause of cracking is improper screeding of the bottom of your mold such that it does not sit flat on the kiln shelf. This can be corrected by lightly sanding the bottom of the mold flat after it has set up and before it is cured. A "Sure Form" tool by Stanley also works well for this process, as shown in Figure 52, if used on the plaster before it is completely dry. We have also discussed how firing a mold causes the mold material to weaken and how large molds may crack from outward pressure of the molten glass.

Well what can we do to correct these problems? Some can be handled by better process control during screeding, curing and casting. Alternatively you can strengthen or reinforce your molds. We have already discussed how you can strengthen the mold by using stronger binders like cements or clays as well as strengthening modifiers like ceramic or metal fibers. Another internal strengthener you could use would be to embed a metal mesh like chicken wire into the outer surface of the mold. Cut up and fit your chicken wire so that it leaves a gap between it and the model to be filled with

Figure 52. Using a Sure-Form tool to trim a mold.

investment. If not it can end up discoloring your casting an ugly brown color. Unfortunately all these options make the mold harder to break apart after casting, possibly resulting in damage to the casting. For really large molds you can use a stronger wire mesh like that used for stucco or concrete. This is what Linda Ethier uses for some of her really large castings. She suggests that you wire the corners together for increased strength.

Another reinforcement option, that of providing external reinforcement for your mold, may be a better option. One way for this that we have already discussed is the use of a jeweler's-like flask with your mold. This provides great strength but ends up being size limiting and requires longer curing. Another simple technique that is often used is to wrap the mold with 18 to 20 gauge copper wire. This is applied in horizontal bands about the mold at about one inch spacing before or after curing. The wires are tightened by twisting it with a pliers. Dan usually applies them before curing when the mold is fairly strong. Jim applies them after curing and then, only to molds with cracks because the copper wire gets badly oxidized as well as softer at the high temperatures present in the kiln. If you decide to apply wire post cure, go slow with the pliers when twisting the ends of the wire because you can easily crack the mold which is actually quite fragile at this point. This would ruin your whole day. Hopefully the wire will hold the mold together so that those hairline cracks do not grow into gaping fissures.

Another way to provide external strength for your mold, we would suggest that you consider casting a cradle mold about your casting mold after it has set up and mold frame is removed. Add a second frame about the casting mold to allow for an additional ½ to 1 inch of thickness on the bottom and the sides of the casting mold. Then cast a cradle mold in the second frame about your casting mold using an investment mix such as #6 or a high temperature castable refractory as well as the adding hardware mesh. Cradle molds provide a strong mold around the casting mold while still allowing the mold directly around the casting to be broken away fairly easily. If you make the cradle mold without a bottom, it may be reusable and could be used as a mold frame in which to cast your next mold.

A cradle mold can also be approximated by stacking hard fire bricks or some other strong refractory material like slices of kiln shelves around your mold. Use your imagination to come up with other ideas.

Multi part molds

Most of the molds that you will make and we have described are single part throw-away or waste molds. We concentrate on these because usually molds are weakened so much by firing that they are not reusable and besides we are into making one-of-a-kind pieces of art. There are times though, when you may want to make a limited number of production objects from a low melting-temperature glass and would like to reuse the same mold. This might be possible with a one-part mold if your model has no undercuts and sufficient taper to it that the finished piece can be removed from the mold without destroying it. If not, you are forced to construct a mold with more than one part to achieve reusability. There are also situations where you want to intricately

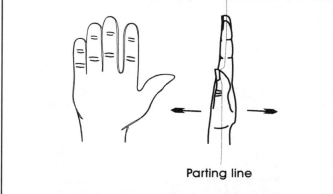

Figure 53. Choosing an orientation for making a two-part plaster mold.

want to intricately decorate a piece but it is impossible to reach into a single-part mold that will give the right shape. Or perhaps you want to work with materials that do not burn out well. In any of these situations, what you need is a multi-part mold. Such molds require more steps than a single-part mold but are not fundamentally any more difficult to make.

Two part molds

The simplest multi-part mold is a two-part mold. To make such a mold possible, the model must have a shape such that you can run a line around it, where to either side of that line the model has no undercuts and good draft. When you plan your two-part mold, look over your original model. Try to determine how you will have to construct the mold so that it allows disassembly. As an example let's look at making a model of an open hand. In this situation, the obvious way that the mold should disassembled from the model is in the direction away from the palm and the back of the hand and not in the direction of the fingers and the wrist as seen in Figure 53. If you look at your hand you can see how if you were to make

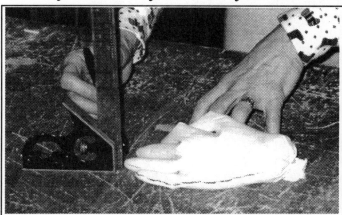

Figure 54. Determining the required mold parting lines.

a mold without undercuts that the mold will have to separate down the middle of you fingers. If your hand is flat then this will be pretty much a flat parting surface. If instead the hand is cupped slightly, the parting surface will no longer be a plane. We shall use such a cupped hand to explain how you can

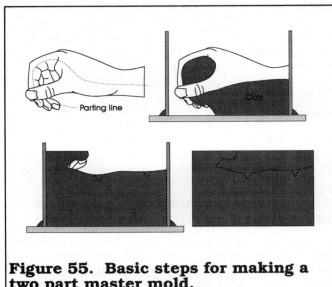

Figure 55. Basic steps for making a two part master mold.

go about constructing a two-part mold.

The first thing that you have to identify is the parting surface for the mold. Do this by taking the hand original and laying it down on your glass pallet. Position the model such that the nominal separation directions are up and down. You may have to prop the original up in one direction or another by using some clay shims. Next determine the parting line by rubbing pencil lead on a small carpenters square and then running the square around the object transferring lead to the high points of the object. If you have problems with this, just use a marking pen to mark the points the square touches as seen in Figure 54. This line should extend all the way around your object when you are finished and represents the line at which the mold should separate.

Once you have determined the parting line, block off the lower half of the hand on your glass pallet using clay as shown in Figure 55. The clay should come all the way up to your parting line. Construct your mold frame around the hand. Extend the clay bed out to the mold frame to fill its lower half. Smooth the clay out to make a uniform parting surface. Add a half of a sprue to the model for filling during casting. Spray on a parting agent of your choice. Then invest the upper half of your mold with plaster-based investment using the standard mixing procedures and allow it to set up.

Remove the mold frame and clean out the clay from the bottom of your original. Since it only takes about an hour for plaster to set, the clay should still be moist enough to be reusable. Carve some natches, V- shaped alignment features, into the parting surface of your mold so that

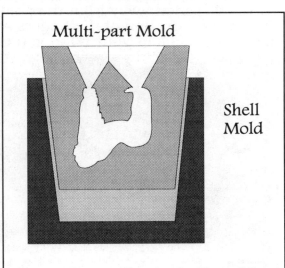

Multi-part Mold

Shell Mold

Figure 56. Using a shell mold to capture a multi-part mold.

the two mold parts will register. Invert the mold with parting surface up as in Figure 55. Add the other half of the clay sprue. Construct a new mold frame about the bottom half of the plaster mold. Spray the rest of the hand and the plaster with your parting agent. Then invest the upper half of your mold using standard practices. Once set up, your mold should now be complete. You should be able to open it up and remove the hand and the sprue. This mold is now ready for detailed filling. After the outer layers are decorated with a layer of glass paste, the two halves are put back together and secured.

Securing mold parts together

One thing that has to be considered when constructing multi-part casting molds is developing a way to hold the parts together during the casting process. Some artists put flanges on the parts that they can clamp together using a piece of metal that is bent in the shape of a U and acts like a paper clip holding the parts together. You can also use steel hose clamps to hold them together. Others use the technique shown here of casting a shell mold around the multi-part mold for the final casting step or you can make it so that the multi-part mold slides out of the shell mold. To do this you would cast your mold parts so that the assembled inner mold before casting the shell or cradle mold has a cross section of a trapezoid with the large base being the reservoir opening. This arrangement as shown in Figure 56. You can see how the shape of the multi-part mold allows slipping it out of the shell mold.

Multi-part molds

Now we are going to get a little more complicated. If your hand had been flexed differently, it might not be possible to construct a two-part mold that could be removed from the hand. You might need a three or four-part mold. In that situation you would start almost identically as with a two part mold. The difficult part is trying to determine where the parting lines should be. This means that you have to take some time studying the original model. Think about which surfaces have the proper requirements to serve as a mold section—no undercuts and good draft. Then go and mark your parting line on the model.

Make a bed of clay on some cardboard as before. Choose which section of the model you want to cast first. Block the model in with your clay such that only that section of the model is exposed. Build up the mold frame, apply mold release to the clay and the model, then cast the first portion of your multi-part mold and cut keys as before. Repeat procedure for the adjoining mold segments until all sections of the mold have been cast. The more parts that your mold has the more likely they are to leak. For more information on making multi-part molds see either *Plaster Mold*

and Model Making by
Chaney and Skee, *The*
Complete Book of Pottery
Making by Kenny or *Mold*
Making for Ceramics by
Frith.

Hollow vessel molds

One example of the use of
multi part molds is for
making hollow vessels.
Another is statuary pieces.
Both of these applications
require controlling access
to the surface of the piece
to get the final shape, thus
inhibiting the ability of
being able to decorate the
surface of the object.
Hollow vessels require at
least a two part mold
configuration because you
need a plug to form the hollow.

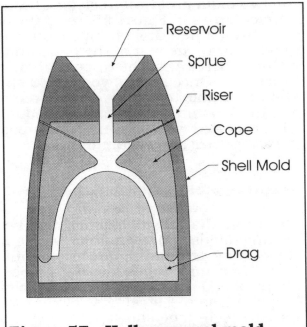

**Figure 57. Hollow vessel mold
similar to those for metal casting.**

Figure 57 illustrates the components of a hollow vessel mold used
for single color or poured layers of color. The terminology is the
same as that used in foundry work. The portion that shapes the
inside of the vessel is called the drag perhaps because you have to
drag it out afterwards. The part that forms the outside is called
the cope. Both of these pieces can be captured in a shell mold.
The shell mold may or may not allow disassembly of the cope and
the drag.

Such a hollow vessel mold is cast in a couple of steps. Figure 58
illustrates the basic steps for making a single-pour hollow vessel
mold. The way that we go about this is to first establish the
general shape of the
vessel by having an
insert of the general
size and shape that
we want for the
inner surface of the
vessel. A lot of time
this will consist of a
bowl, vase or
drinking glass. We
coat this core shape
with a release agent
like an oil or soap
and build up our
vessel model around

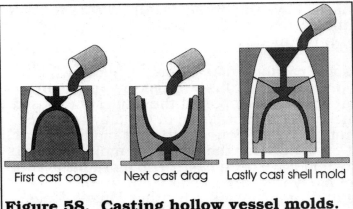

Figure 58. Casting hollow vessel molds.

it. (Nothing says that this could not be out of investment and thus be our drag.) We then develop the basic thickness of the vessel using our modeling media of choice—wax or clay. Upon completion of this, we build up any external surface decoration and add a base, a sprue and any other gating that may be required. The mold frame is then built up around the piece and the cope is cast.

Next we invert the mold, remove both the bottom of the mold frame and the central core former in order to set up for pouring of the drag. Here is where you find out if you applied enough release agent. If you want, you can also decorate the inner surface of the vessel at this point by adding material to or removing it from the inside. It is probably also apparent that it would be nice to use the same mold frame (except for the bottom which you had to remove) for this investment pour also. This will not be possible if you made your mold frame from cardboard which looses its strength after it gets wet. Coddles made from linoleum work just fine for this. If you use the same mold frame you can probably get away without putting a bottom underneath it, but we do not suggest it because the new investment will loose moisture too quickly through it.

Remember to carve some natches into the exposed surface of the cope so that it will be easy to align the cope and the drag later. Before casting the drag rewet the exposed surface of the cope and apply a parting agent to it. Here a slightly more viscous agent like Vaseline is preferred because it will help minimize water loss to the cope or interpenetration of the investment.

Figure 59. Mold for casting hollow vessels.

For extra strength you might want to cast a shell mold around both the cope and the drag. If you do, you will need to build up another mold frame. Smooth out the surface of the cope and drag as well as ensure that they have sufficient draft to be removable from the shell mold. Add any required extensions to the gating system and of course some more of the viscous parting agent before putting it in place in the mold frame. You may want to add some internal reinforcement to the shell mold by placing it inside the mold frame at this point. Now mix up a strong investment formulation and pour the shell.

Another way to make multi-part molds for hollow vessels was passed on to us by Anna Boothe who learned the technique from Karla Trinkley. In this technique, she uses a multi-part ring or step mold to build up a vessel with lots of detail. As an example, the mold for her "Neo-flower" bowl is shown in Figure 59. Here she has a solid core drag and a multi-part cope. To hold them in register she carves sharp natches into them as she casts each successive layer. The layers are constructed so that the bottom of the bowel remains exposed. Casting in this orientation allows the walls to fill better and makes them less likely to crumble or slump during the casting process. By casting the mold in steps, she can build up the frit in shorter sections which she can easily reach into to decorate and then adding each successive layer after the previous one gets filled. This kind of mold is still cast very similarly to the process that was illustrated in Figure 58 except that the cope is cast in multiple pieces and she did not make a shell mold. Then to hold the whole thing together, she forms a cradle mold by wrapping the exterior with wire mesh and lathering investment over it.

Figure 60. Mold set up in the kiln for wax melt out.

For hollow vessels, instead of building multi-part molds, the inside of the vessel can be packed with pre-fired mold material and chopped fiber paper instead to take place of the drag as will be seen in the next chapter. This mixture is pressed gently but firmly against the inside of the cavity to hold the glass frit into place during the final firing. If done properly this technique can prevent sliding of the glass in the vessel walls during the final firing. A solid cylindrical drag could be run down the center of the fiber paper if desired.

Wax melt out

For the many artists that use wax as their main modeling material the next step is to melt or steam the wax out of the mold. (The artists that use clay will dig it out and rinse the mold clean.) Which method you use depends upon what equipment you have available and how much of it you do. Steaming seems to do a better job than just melting wax out but we all have the basic equipment required to melt out wax—a kiln.   Ancillary melt out equipment to go with your kiln is cheap and simple. Use a cheap metal baking pan about three inches deep. Square or rectangular shaped ones are best since most of the molds end up being shaped this way also. This pan should be dedicated for this purpose and never used for cooking again since the wax is hard to clean out and not necessarily good to eat. You will also need a rack to hold the mold over the water. Quarter-inch mesh hardware cloth works well. For best support cut it about 2 inches longer and wider than the top of the pan. Then cut one inch squares out of the corners and bend over the flaps to strengthen the edges of the mesh.

To set up for melt out, place the pan in the kiln and put the grill in place. Pour about a half inch of water into the pan. Then place the mold, sprue cup end of the mold down, on the grill so that the wax will drain into the water as shown in Figure 60. You should have removed any clay from the mold ahead of time because it won't melt and will block the wax. Make sure that the water is not touching the bottom of the mold as this can also impede wax flow as wax floats on water but do not let the mold get too far from the boiling water or you may not get the mold hot enough. It also works better if the mold is wet because that will help prevent the wax from wicking into the mold.

Now you are ready to cook. Melting the wax out of a mold does not necessarily have to be done in your kiln but this is usually the most convenient heat source available in the studio. We recommend not doing it in your oven. Turn on the kiln and set it to soak at about 400 to 500°F. The trick here is in making sure that you don't run out of water. The water, besides for providing some steam to help melt out the wax, also prevents the melted wax's temperature from getting any higher than the boiling point of water. Otherwise the wax can burn and possibly start a fire. (Although I have been told by Mary Francis Wawrytko and others that they just catch the wax in a pan and never bother with the water without any problems. Although if you do this it is recommended that you keep the kiln temperature fairly low on the order of 225°F.) If you run out of water in the pan, make sure that the kiln is turned off and cooled back down below the boiling point of water before adding more. We know that it sounds a bit bizarre to pour water into a hot kiln but its really a lot safer than pulling the pans filled with molten wax out of the kiln and refilling them outside the kiln. Spilling hot wax on yourself is not exactly what the doctor ordered. Keep an eye on the kiln to make sure that it doesn't climb over 450°F. If you have a controller, this is not a problem. Also make sure to vent the top of the kiln with a small bone. When the surface of the water gets covered with wax, go into the kiln and examine some of the molds. Use a good set of gloves and remember to turn the kiln off first.

Make sure that you melt as much of the wax as possible out of your mold or you will have that much more smoky material coming out of the mold later during the burnout and heat curing phase. If you can get most of the wax out, you may be able to forgo a separate curing and burnout run. Once you decide that melt-out is complete, remove the mold from the kiln. Be sure to also remove the grill off the pan since it is more difficult to remove once the wax hardens. If using a kiln, its a safe idea to let the wax cool in place for about a half hour before trying to remove it. The wax will cool faster if the pan is on kiln furniture. Once the wax hardens, you will have some sheet wax which you can use in making your next model if you decide to reuse wax. If done right your molds will come out of the kiln clean and free of wax residue.

As we stated earlier, steaming wax out of a mold seems to work much better than melting it out and gets the molds a lot cleaner. You also do not load up the bricks in your kiln with moisture, which is not necessarily good for them. It also seems to be much faster. An ideal piece of equipment for steaming wax out of open faced mold is a canning steamer heated on a hot plate. It

Figure 61. Canning steamer set up to dewax molds.

has a nice heavy rack to hold the molds over the lower pan filled with water and a high top to put over the molds. Figure 61 shows a run set up in the bottom half of a canning steamer by Donna Milliron. If you don't have a canning steamer you can easily make a simple substitute by using heavy wire mesh to construct a rack that you stick into a large pot with a lid. Then you just add your mold and a little water and soon you will have a nice pot of wax soup. Sounds delicious doesn't it. The trick here, just as in melting wax out in a kiln, is to keep the pot filled with a little water or you might end up with blackened casting molds and a visit from the fire department. Steaming wax out this way from an open faced mold will usually get it clean enough that you will not have to go through a burnout phase later. If you cannot afford a canning steamer, you can do as some artists we have heard of and construct a large steamer by cutting old 55 gallon drums up into sections.

For large molds other than open face molds, steam injection seems to work better then steaming. Steam injection, if done right, can also get your mold clean enough that you will not have to go

Figure 62. Using a steam injection to remove wax from a mold.

through burnout. To be able to steam injection clean your molds you need a system to generate steam and channel it into your mold. For this you need an industrial steam pot to first generate the steam to which you attach some heavy black rubber tubing with a nozzle on the end which can be constructed out of copper tubing. Figure 62 shows Anna Boothe's setup in her studio. She sets the molds up on an old bed frame with the mold openings down and injects the steam from underneath. She runs her steam system at about 15 psi. The trick is to feed the steam through the nozzle into the mold opening and ensure that you melt all the wax out. Be sure to wear heavy gloves and splash goggles when you do this for protection from the steam and the dripping hot wax.

A poor man's steaming system can be constructed from a pressure cooker. The ideal thing is to remove the fitting from the top and attach a tee into it so that the base of the tee points to the side and the top goes up and down. The original fitting is then attached to the top section of the tee pointing up and the hose is attached to the base pointing to the side. You might be wondering why we just didn't attach the hose to the top fitting and use it like that. Well if the end of the hose got plugged by sticking it into wax or investment, the pressure cooker could build up too much pressure and blow its lid. Believe us, you don't want that to happen. Although we have heard of people doing exactly this and getting away with it. Some people will try anything.

We have also heard of people using wallpaper steamers and even vaporizers to steam wax out of molds. Look around, you may figure out a new way.

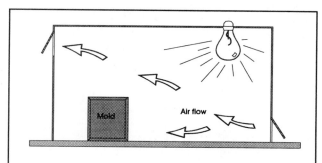

Figure 63. Air drying chamber for molds.

Drying molds

As described earlier, there are three stages to curing plaster-based investment molds. The first, which will is discussed in detail here, is air curing or drying. The other two stages, low-heat curing and mid-heat curing to remove physically bound and chemically bound water, will be detailed in our discussions of kiln procedures. Only molds that will eventually be used to cast glass need to be heat cured. Plaster master molds, which don't go into the kiln and are only used for making wax duplicates, only need air drying.

Air drying allows the plaster in investment to thoroughly set. This will take anywhere from several hours to several days depending upon the drying conditions and the mass of the mold. Conditions which enhance drying are low humidity, increased air flow and higher ambient temperature. A chamber to enhance drying can be constructed as shown in Figure 41 using a cardboard box and a portable drop light. Cut a small 1" x 4" vent in the top of one side of the box and a similar one in the bottom of the opposite side of the box. Put the mold under the vent in the top of the one side and the drop light near the vent in the other side. This will make the inside of the box warmer and will set up an air circulation pattern from the bottom vent to the top vent to help remove any moisture released by the mold. An alternate heating method would be to forget the light and the lower vent and instead poke a hole through that side for a cheap hair drier. Push the hair drier into the hole and turn it on low so that it will not burn itself out.

The larger the mold, the longer it will take to dry. This is because water vapor has to work its way through the torturous path between the plaster crystals to the surface of the mold. Drying time ends up being an exponential function of the thickness or size of the mold, such that doubling the size of the mold may increase drying time by much more than a factor of two. Incomplete drying of a mold can cause it to blow apart during heat curing or casting. So take that extra time to air dry the mold, it is well worth it.

Artists trying to achieve precise placement of color through the use of pastes will want to apply the pastes to a damp mold to prevent the paste from drying too fast. Any air drying is then done after application of the paste is complete.

Advanced Casting Techniques

In this chapter we discuss a few advanced kiln casting topics. The first topic is how to achieve variations in translucency, color and texture. Adding mastery of these techniques can add real pizzazz to your work. To that end, we will discuss the making of glass pastes and their controlled placement in a mold. Lastly we will discuss cleaning and polishing your casting. Each of these techniques add to the salability and uniqueness of your work. So their mastery is important.

Controlling the look of your work

Different effects can be achieved by varying how you mix and fill your molds with glass frit. These techniques vary from being very simple to being very detailed. The simplest glass placement technique is to fill your mold with a homogeneous load of frit. Here addition of the "frit de jour" will result in full density, single colored pieces. Although these pieces can be reinvested and cast in conjunction with single colored pieces of other colors to create a larger multicolored piece. This process is useful when you are trying to make multicolored pieces where you want to minimize any blending of colors as the frit slumps during melt and fill of the mold.

Even with one homogenous frit a number of different effects are achievable. The first of these has to do with the size of the frit. As mentioned many times previously, opacity varies with the mesh size of the frit used. Traditional pâte de verre pieces have a rather cloudy appearance. This is

Figure 64. Effect of using different sized frits.

the result of having been made from very fine frit (>100 mesh) which traps a multitude of small air bubbles. The temperatures used in kiln casting are not high enough to allow these bubbles to escape. Now-a-days it seems that most artists are striving for that dime store transparency that comes from using a slightly larger frit size range. Using 10 to 14 mesh frit will give this translucent look, while pieces made with larger chunks, "chunk de verre", or big pieces, "sheet de verre", will result in nearly clear castings. A second possible effect is achievable using a single multicolored mix of frit. Here different colors of frit are dry blended using a wooden dowel to give a spotted effect. You could probably refer to this process as "spotted dowel de verre" which is currently a rare and endangered art process. Use of mixes like this result in a finished casting with a look similar to marble.

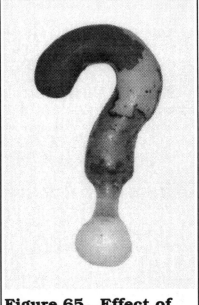

Figure 65. Effect of layering colored frits.

If you are going to fill your mold with a single color frit. There is an easy way to estimate how much frit will be needed to completely fill the mold. This tip was provided by a friend of Dan's, Scott Ingram. You take a jar of water and mark the water level. Then you quickly pour out enough water into the mold until it is filled to the desired casting level. You will have to fill quickly otherwise the water wicking away into the mold will cause you to overestimate the water needed to fill. (Obviously this is done before you dry out the mold.) The amount of water measures the volume of the mold cavity. Now by adding frit to the jar until the level comes back up to the original mark, you can measure an equivalent volume of frit. Then just dry out both the frit and the mold and you are ready to cook.

If you want to make a very fine-detailed, clear kiln casting, you can try suspending a crucible with a hole in it above your mold. This can be done by setting it on some soft fire brick or on a kiln shelf with a hole in it. Fill the crucible with relatively large chunks of glass to minimize air bubbles in the melt. Then as the glass heats up and melts, it will flow down through the hole in the crucible into the mold waiting below. Since the mold is also at the same temperature or slightly below that of the glass, the glass will more completely fill the mold and there will be no chill marks in the glass as seen in a typical casting process where the glass is rapidly chilled as it hits the mold. This will allow achieving clear castings with greater detail than typically attained by kiln casting. You usually have to put more glass in the crucible then is required to fill the mold because some will coat the crucible walls and not flow out. For this reason you will also often have overflow of the glass with this technique. This can lead to a problem with cracking of the casting as the over flow clings to the mold, fire brick, etc. To alleviate this concern, it is suggested that you kiln wash the top of the mold and any materials such as fire brick that might be present. Kathleen Stevens uses this technique in producing her trees. Instead of using a crucible though, she uses flower pots to melt her lead crystal in. With care to prevent thermal shock of the flower pots she can get four to five firings from one.

With some molds, especially bas relief, it may be possible to easily fill different sections of the mold with different forms of loose frit. They may be of different mesh sizes to achieve opacity variations, or of different colors to add depth. Figure 64 shows how different mesh sizes of window glass frit was used to accent features on a zany cat head piece. For different colors you could fill simply by pouring one color after another into the mold and get a Neapolitan ice cream effect as in Figure 65 (You are never quite sure what you will get in such a work.) or more precisely place it as is done in sand

Figure 66. Fine detail with precise placement.

painting. The Indian totem pole casting shown in Figure 66 was done this way. In such cases, when you cast a complete piece from different frit sizes or colors in a single firing, you will always get some blending of the glass as the frit shrinks in volume and moves about as it consolidates as well as colorant interactions. Depending on how much mixing you are willing to accept, you might trade off mixing against how fully dense you want the final casting. In other words, you might try fusing at a slightly lower temperature to allow the grains to tack fuse together without fully consolidating. Here the final piece will end up with a texture like sugar or if the particles are large enough you may get "pate de sushi." This is like the work of Karla Trinkley and Diana Hobson.

Techniques for fritting glass

We have already mentioned one way of making frit in the chapter on the basic kiln casting process, the newspaper and hammer method. There are many other methods that are more productive than this. A good way to produce a roundish frit of fairly uniform size distribution is to melt some glass in a clay crucible and then slowly pour it into a large container of water as Dan is doing in

Figure 67. The crucible that he is holding is a standard sized one available from most glass suppliers who sell fusing supplies. It is just the right size for this process. As the glass hits the water, it cools so rapidly that it can not contain all the stress within it and bursts apart into a fairly fine frit, on the order of 20 to 40 mesh.

This method is also what you use when you are coloring glass. Here since we are trying to make a bunch of frit at one time, we usually preheat the crucible in the kiln. Then when everything is hot, we add the dry mixed frit and colorants. This hot loading method seems to allow faster chemical burn off if it is going to occur. Since you will be melting, pouring and recharging the crucibles a number of times in a fritting session, some glass will inevitable run down the outside of the crucible. Some hot glass may also be spilled from the crucible inside or outside of

Figure 67. Pouring a crucible of hot glass.

the kiln if not handled carefully. Because hot glass is very corrosive, it can eat into kiln shelves, even when kiln washed, and will drill holes into soft brick or fiber blanket. For this reason, we like to lay a ¾ inch layer of silica sand directly on the bottom of the kiln as shown in Figure 68 and fire the kiln without a shelf so that the crucibles stand directly on the kiln floor. This may sound appalling to some kiln owners, but it is a whole lot easier cleaning some fused sand out of the kiln than replacing kiln bricking, especially if it is cemented in place—as most are these days. The sand will not melt since, as we discussed earlier, no glass kiln on the market gets hot enough to melt fused silica unless the sand is

Figure 68. Hot crucibles set up in a kiln.

highly fluxed. Thus if a spill happens, the sand will diffuse it and prevent the molten glass from reaching the brick kiln floor. It also adds some stability in standing the crucibles up, since they are slightly conical in shape with fairly small bottoms. When pouring crucibles from a kiln, a front loading kiln is the preferred configuration over a top loading one because it allows easier gripping of the crucible. So for someone who is going to do a lot of crucible work, such a kiln might make a desirable addition to your studio.

All activity, except heating of the glass takes place outside of the kiln. The crucible is best handled with some scissors-type, fireplace log tongs when pulling it out of the kiln, pouring it or for refilling it with a new colored frit mix. Using the log tongs may take a little practice but it is not difficult. If you have any doubts, try a couple of practice runs with a cold kiln. For better control, you may want to consider wearing only one of the soon to be suggested gloves. Being right handed, we find that using a gloved left hand and an ungloved right one works best for us as shown back in Figure 67. Then by approaching the kiln from the left side, the gloved hand can help protect the bare one. The left hand acts mainly as a fulcrum point, a weight support and a point to add a little extra squeeze on the tongs. It is the right hand which really controls the squeeze on the crucible though. Because the crucibles are slightly conical, it is best to approach them from the bottom with the jaws of the tongs open as you try to grab them. Then slide the tongs slightly upward and grab at about the middle of the crucible. The intense heat coming out of the open kiln may be a new experience for you and it can cause some people who aren't used to it to speed up their actions. Try not to let this happen as it can lead to a serious accident. Take your time, breathe

Figure 69. Aluminized coat for those really hot kilns.

through your nose and be sure to keep a commanding grip on the crucible. Use your body and gloved left hand to shield your right hand form the heat of the kiln.

Now since melting and handling crucibles requires the highest temperature exposures you are likely to receive during casting, we would like to suggest some basic safety practices to be followed. First and foremost, anytime that you go into an electric kiln, other than to just see the show, turn off the kiln. The heating elements are hot in two ways: thermally and electrically. If you should accidentally contact an electrical element with a metal tool, you can get welded to the concrete and support a hairstyle by General Electric—assuming that you live through it. We don't understand why every kiln manufacturer does not have a deadman's switch on the door that turns off the power whenever the kiln lid or door is opened or enclose their elements in quartz tubing. When doing crucible work, practice the buddy system. You will need that person to turn off the power and to open the kiln. Never wear polyester clothing or you may find yourself getting shrink-wrapped. Cotton works much better. Since you are getting radiantly heated when going in to pick up the crucible, it is best to wear long-sleeved clothes. A good denim jacket is best, south of an aluminized fireman's coat like Dan is wearing in Figure 69. When you go into the kiln you are exposing yourself to intense UV and IR radiation that can severely damage your eyes with repeated exposure. You need to wear some sort of protective glasses. We will talk more about this later in our safety chapter but suggest that a welder's green of at least a #3 shade is appropriate. A #4 shade would be better but you don't want them so dark that you cannot see what you are doing once out of the kiln.

High temperature gloves are a must. To many people, asbestos immediately comes to mind in one way or another. Asbestos is fibrous form of magnesium silicate. It is not toxic but the short fiber form, can be inhaled and lodge in the lungs. There it can act as an irritant—not a poison but a carcinogen. Asbestos gloves offer great protection from heat but the long fiber can break down with repeated heat exposure to form the bad short fibers. For this reason, it is best to avoid asbestos gloves, even if you can find them. There are other heat resisting gloves on the market based on Kevlar. Kevlar is basically a low expansion version of fiberglass that can withstand high heat, about 1000°F, for short periods of time. These gloves can be found at ceramics and welding suppliers under the name of Kevlar but for some reason are found at fusing suppliers under the name of "Zetex." What's in a name anyway. The important thing is that they should be double lined. A wool inner lining is the best. For better durability and higher heat resistance, PBI/Kevlar gloves are best, although of course they are more expensive. Pure PBI (polybenzimidazole) gloves are available but their price is out of sight and you don't really need something so high-tech anyway. Terry cloth gloves are all right for low temperatures (under 500°F) but they will flash at the temperatures that we are talking about here for crucible handling. Also avoid leather gloves, because once they get hot, they stay hot, and that can be rather unpleasant.

Now that you're all dressed up and have had a couple of practice runs, you're ready for the big event. Use two five-gallon buckets with one filled about ¾ of the way with water. Plastic buckets are okay for us but some people have had problems with them melting or scarring and for that reason have switched to large stainless steel mixing bowls in which to frit their glass. These will not melt nor will they allow the glass to get embedded in the bottom. So pick up the molten glass filled crucible out of the kiln with the tongs (don't forget to turn off the power first) and empty the crucible into the water. Go slowly at first because glass is viscous and tends to want to spill out as a big lump. A big lump could burn a hole in the bucket which can then flood the studio floor (not a good thing when working with electrical kilns) besides ruining a good bucket. After you are done pouring, fill the crucible with the next batch of glass and get it back into the kiln. If that was your

only or last batch, still put the crucible back into the kiln and let it
cool gradually or it may thermal shock
and crack on you. After the
completing the pour and replacing the
crucible into the kiln, you can pour off
the water from the one bucket into the
other bucket and dump the frit at the
bottom onto some newspaper to dry.
Repeat the process after each pour to
avoid mixing colors, wiping out any
fine frit residue with a paper towel. If
you don't like the colors that you are
getting at least you will have a couple
of gallons of warm water.

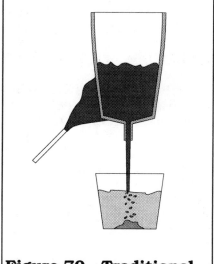

**Figure 70. Traditional
setup for fritting glazes.**

You can also melt your glass and frit it
as the old studio potters' used to make
their fritted glazes. Here you mix up
your raw materials (glass cullet and
colorants) in a funnel shaped crucible
with a small hole at the bottom. The
crucible is suspended over a bucket of
water. A flame directed on the outside of the crucible as illustrated
in Figure 70 heats up the mix to melt. Once molten, the mix flows
down through the hole in the bottom of the crucible and drips into
the bucket of water. The sudden change in temperature instantly
freezes the drops of glass and shatters them into a fine frit. Be
sure to provide plenty of ventilation if you try this because of the
high toxicity of many colorants.

An alternate method for producing frit from sheet glass is to pile
some compatible glass scrap on a kiln shelf, heat it to about
1450°F and allow it to tack fuse. Then after donning the
previously discussed attire and being sure to turn off your kiln (the
better to avoid any shocking experiences), reach into it with some
long hot dog tongs, pull the fused pile out of the kiln and dunk it
into a large container of water. If the container is plastic, hold the
glass off the bottom or it may melt through the bottom. The glass
will immediately start breaking apart into frit. This fritting method
also works well, but produces a frit with wider size and shape
distributions most of which is larger, in the 5 to 20 mesh range,
than that produced from the crucible method. The frit size
increases with the thickness of the glass pile you start with
because the glass does not chill as fast as with a thinner stack. If
you want bigger chunks still, allow the hot or molten glass to air
cool or thermal shock on a kiln shelf washed with separator.

Frit produced by any of these thermal methods can be broken
down finer by using mechanical methods because it will have
many more fractures that have not completely propagated. You
can wrap the glass in something like newspaper or canvas and
beat on it with a hammer as we talked about earlier. Wrapping it
helps prevent producing many flying shards. You should wear
safety goggles that completely shield the eyes just in case. Each

artist seems to have his or her favorite mechanical crushing method from industrial hammer mills down to a ball peen hammer in a coffee can. Dan likes one pound can of Folger's to 8 ounces of hammer. He can brew the coffee in the morning to wake up the red-eyed students and pound the can late at night to compete with the neighbor's rock and roll music.

Finer frit can be made from thermally preconditioned glass by working it in a porcelain mortar and pestle although because of the tempering effect it may be easier to further grind mechanically manufactured frit. To do this, you fill your mortar about 1/3 to 1/2 full with glass frit. Then pressing down hard, rock the pestle from side to side about a half dozen times, stir and repeat. This tends to be a laborious process and hard on your hands. So you may want to wear some light work gloves to prevent getting blisters. With perseverance you can produce a couple pounds of fine, 100 mesh or better, frit in an hour.

Steinert manufactures a large stainless steel glass crusher which is advertised as a heavy duty mortar and pestle for crushing glass. It is all stainless steel and has a pestle bowl 3-1/2" deep and 2-3/4" diameter in which you put the glass that you want to frit. The mortar tightly fits the bowl and has a 7" handle that you jam down onto the glass. It looks like a piston and a cylinder and sells for just under $100. We have found it hard to get a good punch on the glass because the fit between the pestle and the bowl is so tight that the air trying to escape as you push down slows the pestle. One possible way to fix the problem is to drill a couple of small vent holes near the lower edge of the cylinder to allow the air to escape. You can make your own version of one of these mashers by using pipe fittings that you can get from the hardware store. Frit made by mashing with iron implements will have a wide range of sizes and will also have metal impurities that need removal by using a magnet.

If you're a garage-sale-diva or a flea-market-master, you can also pick up used food blenders and garbage disposals for fritting glass. Boyce Lundstrum recommends using a ½ horsepower hammer mill garbage disposal mounted in the lid of a 30-gallon metal drum. If you choose this route, you should definitely wear safety glasses, gloves and a respirator. He connects a ½ horsepower shop vacuum to a hole in the side of the drum to pull dust out during operation. This should probably be a HEPA vacuum to prevent contaminating your breathing airspace with fine glass dust. He starts the vacuum and the disposal before dropping in small pieces of glass. Make sure that power is locked off before you stick your hand in it. (We pull the plug.) About a half minute after he turns off the disposal, he removes the vacuum from the side of the drum and uses it to clean out rounded glass chunks that will no longer grind from the inside of the disposal. He finds that he has to stop every 10 to 15 minutes to prevent overheating the disposal. If you fail to do this, you may have to occasionally unjam the disposal (done by inserting a long flat head screw driver into exit port and pushing against the underside of the hammer plate). This mechanical crushing method produces a frit 60% of which is finer than 17 mesh. For a real fine frit, use old blenders. Do not use these blenders for food anymore unless you want to grind down your teeth. They also make really gritty margaritas.

Commercial Glass Frits

Frit is available commercially from a number of sources. By far, the soda-lime glass frit used most often by studio glass artists with America is that from Bullseye Glass Company. It is available in the wide color palette and compatibility quality control for which Bullseye's fusing product line is known. It is comes packaged in either 1½ ounce tubes or five pound jars. The 5 lb. jars were seen pictured back in Figure 19. The available frit sizes they carry are listed in Table 9. They also have a clear non-lead crystal with negligible iron content which is available in either billet or chunk form.

Table 9. Frit sizes available from Bullseye.

Frit Designator	Size Description	Mesh Size	Particle Size	
			(in)	(mm)
01	Fine	14-70	0.008-0.047	0.2-1.2
02	Medium	10-14	0.047-0.106	1.2-2.7
03	Coarse	5-10	0.106-0.205	2.7-5.2
08	Powder	> 70	< 0.008	<0.2

The lead glass frits are mainly available from ceramic supply houses. For a possible supplier, you could try Standard Ceramic Supply. They still carried them when we started writing this book They are getting harder and harder to find though.

Traditional glass pastes

In molds with a lot of slope, loose frit will not work because it just slides down the side of the mold. In this situation, you can make use of the full potential of the pâte de verre process, i.e. make a paste of your glass. Here one uses the technique as it was developed and used by the French masters. It is also possible to achieve subtle shading of colors with this technique. To be able to apply your glass paste with control, you need a mold with large enough openings to allow complete access to all surfaces.

Making glass pastes

You make a glass paste by mixing your frit with water or water-based binding agents like those used in glass painting, pottery glazes or enameling. It can then be brushed or packed it into place. Water alone can be used to bind the paste and burns out clear (at least in most cities) but lacks the pastiness necessary to hold the glass frit in place on near-vertical surfaces. Oils as binders are not generally recommended because they can carbonize and there is usually no place for the carbon to escape as the oil burns. Of course there are exceptions to every rule. Donna Milliron has told us that she has had good success using squeegee oil which hardens almost like a glue and has not had any problems with either carburizing or color reduction. If you are going to use oil-based binders it is advisable to use them sparingly, to add a soak at 1000°F to burn them out during the firing and to have a fairly permeable or porous mold to prevent trapping organic vapors.

Traditionally one part of gum arabic (from the acacia tree) dissolved in one part of alcohol and then mixed with twelve to twenty parts of warm water was used to make the paste. Be careful with this though because it can carbonize and "fry," that is cause bubbling or crackling in the glass, if the solution is mixed too strong. It's a pretty strong binder. Other traditional gum binders include: gum tragacanth, dextrine, vee gum and CMC (sodium carboxymethyl-cellulose). They are all mixed similarly to gum arabic and can be found at many ceramics supply stores. A good binder found around most households is a diluted

Figure 71. Glass paste can be placed with palette knife.

solution of Knox gelatin. It doesn't take much gelatin to get the glass to stick and you can even drink the leftovers to get those chrome-molly fingernails we talked about earlier. Another simple water-based binding agent is sodium silicate dissolved in water. Any of these mixtures will harden when air dried so you should only mix as much as you need.

Thompson Enamels makes a good binding agent called Klyr-Fire. This is a methyl-ethyl-cellulose based binder that has given us good results. It burns out clean, is cheap and you don't need a letter from the governor to buy it directly from the manufacturer or its distributors. No mixing is required and it can be used straight from the bottle. Brushes used with it can be cleaned with water afterwards. The paste does not harden as much as some of the other mixes though and may move around some on you.

Glass pastes painted into your mold can achieve very subtle shadings of color through the use of a palette of colored frit or incorporation of metal oxides or enamels. The addition of 10 to 20% by volume of 80 to 120 mesh enamels is sufficient to create sufficient color density when used with a clear frit. Enamels work best with the low-temperature, high-lead (20 to 25%) glasses because their flex points are similar. Otherwise you may have to adjust the coefficient of thermal expansion of the enamel to fit the base glass frit that you are using. This can be done by mixing it with the desired base glass, melting the mixture in a crucible and refritting it by pouring the melt into water. Make sure that you allow the melt to sit at high temperature for a little while to allow good mixing of the components.

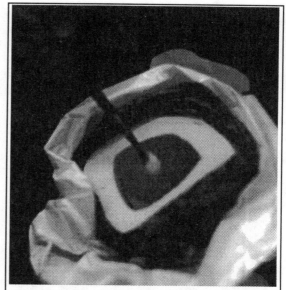

Figure 72. Keeping mold damp while applying a glass paste.

Using glass pastes

Once mixed, the glass paste is applied with the brush in thin layers to the low relief areas of the mold. A small flexible palette knife also makes a good tool for paste application. Remember that because the mold is a three dimensional negative of the finished work, these low relief areas will end up being raised areas in the final piece. First, fill in carved out or detail areas with color as your design dictates. Then continue applying paste until you have the entire surface of the inside of your mold covered to at least 1/16 of an inch thick. Sometimes it's a little tricky to get the paste into the neither regions of a mold and it may require considerable dexterity. A mini-mag flashlight can be helpful in exploring those really deep molds. It also helps to keep the mold wet by wrapping it with a damp towel as shown in Figure 72 while applying your glass paste. This prevents the water-based binder from drying too quickly. This technique will increase the working pot life of your applied paste, give it more strength and decrease your chances of forming air bubbles.

After application of the first layer, let the layer dry some to avoid disturbing it as you build up the thickness of the rest of the piece. You can let it air dry naturally or use a hairdryer if you are in a hurry. Then build up the thickness another 1/16th of an inch to about an 1/8th of an inch by applying color as desired to build color density. Many times the second layer of paste is used to form a lighter background or semi-transparent color to prevent the piece from becoming too dark or opaque. Try to gently pack the paste down to decrease movement during the fusing process. To help minimize color motion and mixing, it is recommended that these two layers be fired to consolidation or light tack fuse process temperature for three to four hours depending on the thickness of the mold. By then the glass will have shrunk to about 70% of its original volume. This is easily done if the mold does not have too vertical of sides.

Figure 73. Hollow vessel mold packed and ready in the kiln.

For highly sloping objects or hollow vessels, you will need to pack the inner surface with ceramic filter paper backed with ludo as shown in Figure 73 or insert an inner mold piece for a two part mold. This will minimize sliding of the paste in the mold as it consolidates. In the past, artists such as G. Argy-Rousseau, would pack the center of the vessel with asbestos fiber. That technique is not practiced now-a-days for obvious reasons. (For similar reasons many people are also becoming concerned about the health risks of using ceramic fiber paper.) It works best if hollow or lightly sloping modeled molds are fired opening down as this prevents the edges from collapsing or crumbling. Additional layers are then added and fired until you get the final thickness in which you are interested. In the last firing, you can continue up to full fuse temperature to get a full density casting.

Again there are really no hard and fast rules in kiln casting. By careful color placement and buildup, many glass artists are pleased with the results that they achieve from a single firing. To avoid problems of color movement, they will construct molds without steep sides or work mainly with homogeneous frits. In choosing the placement of your colors, it is often advisable to use your darkest and richest, or most opaque colors for the relief details sections as they will show up the best. Be careful in their application, because in thicker layers the light can be obscured to such an extent that the piece can end up looking like one big completely opaque dark mess. The glass core of your casting will usually look better if made of lighter tints of colors since the mass of the glass will intensify the effect. Don't be afraid to use those wimpy colors for the core since too strong a color will render the whole piece opaque, unless of course that is the effect that you are trying to achieve. One exception with using mainly more transparent glasses is when you are casting a hollow vessel like a cup, bowl or vase. Here the thin walls and the light entering through the center of the vessel allow use of richer colors..

Some artists find that they need to dilute their commercial transparent colors to get the color saturation that they want in their work. Most do this by melting some of the transparent glass in a crucible to which clear glass has been added and the refrit the melt. Jim has found that mixing a small amount of a transparent Bullseye powder with some medium ground clear frit and a little Klyr-Fire binder works as a fast and easy alternative to this. Add just enough Klyr-Fire to allow the powder to evenly coat the clean frit and it will achieve a good uniform color when fired. You have to be sure to mix it well to prevent color variations.

Inclusions

As previously discussed you can combine homogeneous frit cast pieces together by reinvesting them in a mold, adding filler frit and recasting the piece to join the components into multicolored pieces. Of course you are not limited to single color components with this technique. You are also not limited to just joining them. Why not use one as an inclusion inside of a larger work? You could make fish swimming in a fish bowl. When you use this technique you want to be sure that your outer glass is translucent enough to be able to see the included object in the casting. For this you want the outer frit to be a very transparent color and a larger mesh size.

You can also incorporate fused elements or trailings poured from crucibles. David Ruth likes to use a number of glass elements like this in his large sculptural pieces. He feels that they give his work more depth. They act as a focal point to draw the viewer into the piece. You do not need to restrict yourself to cast or fused glass inclusions. Many of you may have some skill with lampworking. Why not use that skill to make lampworked objects to use as inclusions. This concept can lead to many interesting casting possibilities. What about making lampworked insects that you then cast as inclusions in an amber colored glass. If you want to be more playful you could make small encased dinosaurs and sell them as dinosaur theme park starter kits.

You also do not need to limit yourself to glass inclusions. Thin metal foils, leaf and screens will also work well. Try to make sure that they are completely encased and keep them small if you want to avoid cracking.

Cleaning a casting

The final step in any kiln casting project is cleaning up your glass casting. How much cleaning you have to do may vary a lot. It is a function of what type of glass you used, how activated your mold formulation becomes at the process temperature and how hot you actually went in the firing. Generally speaking, the higher temperature you go to in a casting firing the more likely you are to get investment sticking to your casting. Let's look at the range of results that can be expected.

The easiest situation is where you have had virtually no mold-glass interaction and all you have to do is clean the dust from the mold off of the casting. For this situation, all that you need after breaking away the mold and picking off the small pieces with dental picks, is a little Bon Ami and an old tooth brush. Bon Ami is a low-caustic, mildly abrasive scouring powder available in most grocery stores. You just get the casting wet, sprinkle on a little Bon Ami and apply a little elbow grease with an old tooth brush. (Please don't ask where to get elbow grease.) After a good scrubbing, the casting should be clean with minimal dulling of the surface.

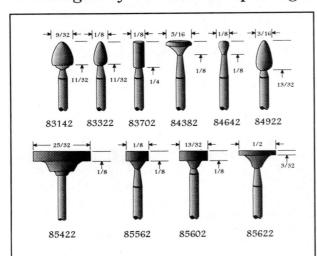

Figure 74. Available silicon grinding bits from Dremel.

Okay, let's suppose that everything did not go perfect and you have a fair amount of mold material that interacted with your glass casting. The easiest way to try and remove it, although not always the most successful and definitely not the least hazardous, is to try a little better living through chemistry. Many of the famous artists of old would use hydrofluoric acid to clean up their castings but we tend to avoid that stuff like the plague because of the great danger it presents if not handled carefully enough. Lime-Away will work to some degree to remove investment. It won't bring the casting up to a full shine but it may help remove some of the mold material. Muriatic acid can also be used for this task with soda-lime glasses but should be avoided like the plague with lead glasses, where it will dissolve the lead out of the glass leaving a soft porous casting that falls apart. (This also points out why lead glasses should not be used for food bearing surfaces, especially acidic ones.) Muriatic acid is a diluted form of hydrochloric acid and will dissolve or corrode metal, so store it in plastic or glass containers. It is a strong acid and should be treated with respect. See some of the precautions listed in the back of this book for dealing with acids and read the instructions on the bottle. Use it to try and dissolve some of the investment off the surface by dipping the casting into the acid for a few minutes and then rinsing the acid off.

If you still have a lot of investment tenaciously hanging onto the surface of your casting, then it is time for more drastic measures. If the surfaces of the casting are relatively flat, then you can attack the investment with wet and dry sandpaper. You can also use diamond embedded pads on the casting. Either should be used wet both to keep the dust down as well as to lubricate the pads. Pads and sandpaper come in a number of grit sizes and are numbered by the size of the grit similarly to mesh sizes. You usually start out with a coarse grit like 80 and work your way up to a grit like 800. Along the way you may make stops at sizes like 120 and 240. How fine you go to depends upon the final finish that you are trying to achieve. Since most pâte de verre has a matte or semi-matte finish, most artists do not go much past about 240.

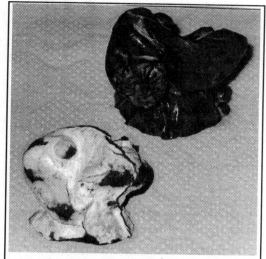

Figure 75. Pepper crevices were too small for grinding.

For surfaces that are not quite so flat, you are better off using a variable speed moto-tool like a Dremel ®. When using these it helps to have a flex-shaft attachment and a variable speed control—a foot pedal type is the most convenient to use. For bits you can use the gray-green silicon grinding bits made by Dremel ®. They come in a number of different sizes as illustrated in Figure 74. You can also purchase diamond coated bits from sources such as Lapcraft Co., Crystalite Corporation or Truebite. Either of these kinds of bits will have to be used wet and since a lot of silica loaded mist will be generated, we recommend that you wear a respirator with a combination mist/dust filter.

Because of the finite size of the heads on the bits, you may find that there may be small crevices in a casting that you will not be able to get the grinding bits down into. Figure 75 shows before and after shots of such a piece in the form of a curly pepper found in Jim's garden. Although much improved after grinding, it still has material down in the crevices too small to reach with the bits he had available. In a case like this, you may want to resort to sandblasting the last of the investment off to the casting. Although if you have a sandblaster, it is probably easier to start with it in the first place. Blast lightly so that you do not carve into the piece, unless of course that is what you are trying to do.

Shining up the cast surface

If you don't like the matte appearance you have on a raw or abrasively cleaned casting, you can make your piece appear more shiny and translucent by oiling or waxing it. This also eliminates accumulation of fingerprints later on. Oils will permanently change the surface of the glass making it look wet or damp. We have used a number of different oils for this purpose including salad oils. One spray oil that has been found to perform well for this purpose is Varathane Natural Oil Finish #66 Clear. It is a clear oil that does not yellow after drying. To apply the oil make sure that the casting is as clean as you want it — clean from fingerprints, etc. Spray a good coat over the entire surface being sure to get any deep crevices. Make sure that the entire surface is covered. Blot up any excess oil until the entire surface has a matte surface finish. If you see puddles in deep areas use the edge of a paper towel to blot them. If you get any dust on the surface wait until the oil is dry before trying to remove it. It will dry in about a half a day.

An alternative way to shine the surface of a kiln cast piece is to seal its surface with a clear acrylic or enamel. This will give the glass surface a wet look that is permanent. Like oils, the most convenient way to apply them is in a spray form. You might want to test these materials first on a piece of clear glass because some have a yellow tint to them. Make sure that the surface is clean and free of oils before starting. Apply the

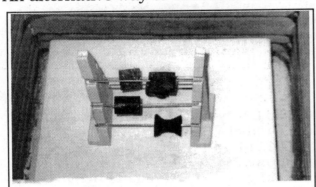

Figure 76. Kiln cast beads being fluxed on a bead stand.

spray with thin even clean strokes; starting each stroke off the piece and finishing it again off the piece. Allow each coat to dry before applying the next until you are satisfied with its appearance. Do not allow it to puddle in any of the crevices.

For soda-lime glass pieces, there is another alternative available to give your casting a permanent shiny surface. You can try using a low firing-temperature clear glass enamel, often referred to as a glass flux, to shine up the surface. For this we recommend Flux 92 by Standard Ceramics Supply, Inc. or Back Magic from Fusion Headquarters. (So named because it is used to make the backs of fused projects smooth and shiny.) Either will mature with a 15 to 30 minute soak at 1100°F. This technique will not work for lead glasses because the casting will slump at these temperatures. Be sure to ramp the kiln temperature up and down very slowly if you have much variation at all in thickness of your piece so that you do not thermal shock it. Jim has had this problem on more than one occasion and nothing is more frustrating than cracking a piece in the final step. Since these low firing-temperature fluxes are high in lead content you will not be able to use them on anything that might be used as a food bearing surface and there are no comparable non-lead bearing products.

Some artists don't like to use flux on their work because they say that these low melting temperature fluxes leave a hazy finish on their work. Instead they may "fire" polish their work. To do this they heat up the work in a kiln just to the point where the surface of the glass starts to get soft and smoothes out. This can be a real tricky process though because you get really close to the slumping temperature of the glass. If you are going to try this technique, you will need a very accurate and responsive kiln controller to avoid slumping problems. We have been advised that this can be achieved with Bullseye glass cast pieces by heating it into the range of 1275 to 1285°F for about one half hour. We suggest careful calibration of your controller to assure the proper temperature control prior to trying this.

Be aware that you will not be able to flux or fire polish all the surfaces of your casting because at least one surface has to be on the kiln shelf. That is of course unless you are making small items like beads which can be hung on a ceramics bead stand as shown in Figure 76. If you think about it, you probably also realize that you could decorate your work with low firing-temperature enamels which would allow you to add decorations to the exterior of your piece instead of fluxes. This idea may shock many pâte de verre purists but what the heck. You are the artist—you decide.

Kiln Procedures

The topic of this chapter is kiln operations. The two main kiln operations used in kiln casting are burning out molds and firing castings. Either of these operations can be broken down into three phases (heating, process and cooling) which we will focus on in great detail. We will also provide you some general rules of thumb for determining the parameters to use in each phase. After that we will finish the chapter with a discussion of different pieces of equipment for measuring the temperature of and for controlling your kiln.

Kiln operations

If you have been a fuser, one of the things that you will find interesting in our discussion of kiln operations is how in fusing and slumping we go to great lengths worrying about thermal shocking the glass and don't worry about the molds. Here in kiln casting it is exactly the opposite of this case. The molds are the vulnerable components and not the glass. In fact the molds help insulate the glass and protect it during cooling. Gypsum-based investments weaken considerably as they are taken to high temperatures and may crack if abused. That's why we went to the trouble to include refractory materials and property modifiers in the investment formulations listed previously.

As stated, there are two main kiln operations performed in kiln casting glass: burning out molds and firing castings. The first, burnout is done to remove any organic remains from your model left in the mold be it wax, wood, plastic or some other material. The other, firing your casting, transforms the frit encased in the investment mold into the final piece of kiln cast art. Let's briefly discuss each of these operations.

Curing and burning out of molds

After melting or steaming out any wax, air drying and reinforcing the mold, the next step in the kiln casting process is often to heat cure it or burn it out. (If you have been successful in completely removing all modeling material manually or by steaming it out as in case of wax, then these important steps can be included as part of firing the casting.) What we are concerned with in curing a mold is removing all the water and organic materials without cracking it. As explained earlier, any water remaining in your mold may be transformed into steam by the heat of the kiln. This phase transformation involves a tremendous change in volume that has to be resisted by the strength of the investment material. If not done carefully this can result in cracking of the mold in a similar manner to how volume expanding epoxies are used to break up granite boulders as an alternative to dynamite when building roads in the mountains. So to prevent cracking the mold, we want to remove this water slowly.

Water exists in the mold in two forms: physically adsorbed water and chemically bound water. Physically adsorbed water is that water which remains on the surface of the investment crystals after the casting process or has been attracted from the air. This water is loosely attached and can be removed slowly by air drying or more quickly by heating the mold to around to around the boiling point of water. At this temperature this loosely bound water is rapidly transformed to vapor. If you have thoroughly air dried your mold, you may have already accomplished this task and this portion of the cure cycle can be minimized. Chemically bound water, on the other hand, is that water which actually becomes part of the chemical makeup of the material. As in the manufacture of gypsum plasters and cements, the investment mold has to be heated up to at least 350°F to drive this water off. Therefore when curing a mold, dwells at both 225°F and 350°F are included during the heating phase to carefully remove both of these forms of water.

The other part of this operational discussion, burning out all organics in the mold, is done so that they do not coat the glass that you are casting with carbon. To completely decompose most organic materials, you have to heat them to temperatures of about 1000°F and sometimes as high as 1200°F. Make sure that the studio and kiln are well vented when doing this because there could be some smoke. If you were real diligent about steaming out your wax and don't have cavities to trap wax, then you probably will not have enough in the matrix of the mold to worry about carbonizing. But to minimize any chance of problems, you may want to include a dwell at a temperature between 1000 and 1200°F to burn off all carbon before proceeding on to casting temperatures. This will work well with wax but may not be sufficient to handle dense organic substances like woods or vegetables which often leave ash behind after burnout. Any such ash will have to be cleaned out of the investment mold before filling it with glass frit.

Firing a casting

When you have a clean mold and have filled it as desired with glass frit, you are ready to fire it to consolidate your glass. Figure 77 shows a kiln setup with molds ready to be fired. In this operation, if you have not previously heat cured or burnt out your mold, you will have to be concerned about any moisture present in the investment as was discussed above. In addition, you will have to be concerned about exposing the glass to the proper time-temperature conditions to achieve the final desired product. As any good glass fuser knows, your final project is a function of both the exposure temperature as well as the length of time you spend there. One can be balanced off for the other. Here the

Figure 77. Kiln full of filled molds ready for firing.

relationship will be a little different than what you may be used to for fusing because of the insulating nature of the investment mold and the greater amount of flow that is necessary. Time has to be allowed for the glass to change temperature after a change in kiln temperature.

The process temperature that you should use for kiln casting is a function both of the type of glass that you are using and the degree of fusion desired. Higher temperatures are required for harder glasses and greater density of casting. Remember also that darker colored glass will absorb heat better and appear softer.

Three phases of any kiln operation

Any kiln operation is basically divided into three phases: heating, process and cooling. This is seen in the typical pâte de verre firing schedule illustrated in Figure 78 that we repeat here from our introductory chapter. The heating phase for the most part is pretty self explanatory and our biggest concern in that phase is preventing thermal shock of the mold. The process phase is that portion of the firing at which the process, in this case kiln casting, is accomplished. Here the concern is getting the proper heat work into the glass to fully form and fuse the casting. Lastly is the cooling phase considered by many kiln casting artists to be the most critical phase because it is here where the glass must be carefully returned to room temperature in a minimum stressed condition to avoid possible cracking of the final work. This seems to be one of the least understood and easiest things to mess up. Let's look at each of these phases in greater detail.

Heating phase

In the heating phase of a kiln firing, you are concerned about not heating your piece so fast that you could thermal shock the glass in your project. Thermal shock is the result of stress building up from variations in temperature throughout the piece of glass and the corresponding relative expansion it undergoes. Here expansion of the hotter edges of the glass can pull at the cooler inner section such that you literally pull the glass apart. This is not usually a concern with kiln casting because the glass is usually already in the form of frit rather than large pieces. In addition, the thermal insulation of the mold slows the rate of temperature rise of the glass and smoothes out any gradients. Here the only time that this tends to be a problem is in refiring of a large bas relief casting still in the mold in an attempt to fill it up some more or when you are fire polishing a casting. In either case the thinner areas of the glass can heat up sufficiently faster than the thicker area or the areas buried deeper in the mold to cause them to crack. But if still in the mold, you are just heating it up to fusing again anyway, so it may not matter.

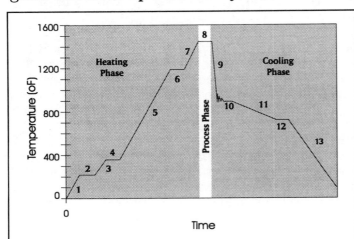

Figure 78. Three phases of a kiln operation.

Instead we need to be concerned about the mold. We want to avoid abusing it. So for that reason we will assume that it still has considerable moisture and maybe some organic materials in it. (This discussion can also be applied to a filled mold that did not require a separate burnout cycle.) With this in mind, let's discuss how you go about heating these puppies up to cure and burn them out. Start by putting them into the kiln with the reservoir opening up. Leave at least an inch between molds to allow good air circulation between them. Then close the kiln but leave the top propped open about an inch with a piece of kiln furniture. As in segment 1 of the kiln operation illustrated in Figure 78, we want to heat the kiln slowly to about 225°F. Now comes that age old question; how slow is slowly? This depends upon a lot of things. First, how wet is your mold? Did you do a good job air drying it? Second, how big is it? Are you modeling a small bug or King Kong? Third, how much time have you already invested in it and are you willing to risk having to start over? Fourth how strong is it? Did you use a reinforced investment? Lastly, are you a gambler or are you afraid to even test your luck at the lottery? If you answer all these questions and mail them in on a post card, we'll be glad to

misinform you. Slowly is something that you will have to decide.
We would suggest that you keep your heating rate in the
neighborhood of 50 to 300°F per hour per inch thickness of the
mold. Most of the molds that we construct are only about an inch
thick at the thickest point so we set the controller reach 225°F
somewhere between 30 minutes and three hours. Mold thermal
shock, although not likely at this point, is possible so don't push
the pedal to the metal too hard.

Once you reach 225°F, you will have to dwell (segment 2) at this
temperature long enough to allow the whole mold to come to
temperature, all the water to evaporate and be transported out
through the porous structure of the outer surface of the mold.
You're not going to ask how long is long enough are you? Go back
and look at your answers to those previous questions. The same
factors apply with the addition of how porous your mold is. We
suggest that long enough will usually lie within 1 to 2 hours per
inch thickness of mold. Again if you have thoroughly air dried
your mold, this portion of the cure cycle can be shortened.

Now that you have removed all the physically attached water, your
mold is through the most likely cracking region. But we suggest
that you continue heating slowly in segment 3, to 350°F where we
stop to remove the chemically attached water. Let's keep the same
definition of slowly, so it will take about the same amount of time
to reach this temperature as it did to reach 225°F in the first
heating ramp. Dwell at the 350°F temperature in segment 4 for a
little shorter amount of time than that of segment 2, say on the
order of ½ to 1½ hours per inch thickness of the mold. After this
dwell, you should have removed all the chemically bound water
and you can speed up in the next heating ramps as you go up in
temperature to burn out organic materials in segment 5. Doubling
the rate to about 100 to 600°F per hour range per inch of mold
thickness should work okay.

Any organic materials will start to burn at about 500°F and
produce smoke. This means that it is time for everyone to go to
lunch. At one workshop Dan gave, the kiln was in the employee
lunchroom. His class went out for lunch, but the employees ate in.
As you can guess, he was not the most popular out-of-town expert
that day. Obviously this should not be a common problem
because we are sure that most of you follow good work practices
and do not eat, drink or smoke in your studio anymore often than
you burn out wax in the employee lunch room.

Once the kiln gets to about 1000°F, most of the smoke will be gone
but burn out may not be quite complete. If you open the kiln for a
peek, the molds may "candle" or burn with a small flame. This
means that there is still some wax in there. You may also notice
that the mold has a black or gray carbon build up especially
around the reservoir opening. This carbon is what remains from
any organic materials that were in the mold and have to be cooked
until they completely disappear leaving a totally white mold.
Otherwise any residual carbon can fuse onto the surface of your

glass and will be very hard to remove. You can soak at this temperature or proceed on up to about 1200°F. Sometimes the soak at the top of this firing can last as long as several hours before you burn out all the carbon because the wax may have wicked into the mold especially if it were melted out rather than steamed out.

If the mold was empty when you started, you have a choice to make once burn out of the mold is complete. (Assuming of course that there is no ash that needs to be cleaned out.) You can fill the mold with frit or whatever size of glass pieces you prefer on the spot and turn this into a casting firing or you can cool the mold back down and fill it at your leisure. The first choice would save having to do another firing, but in return you forfeit the chance for any color placement. To fill the mold when hot, something like a lead ladle wired to a length of half-inch re-bar for stained glass is suggested. Most of you may have some old re-bar laying around since you were probably into stained glass at one time. Lead ladles may be a little harder to find since they are being unofficially considered as undesirable lead abuse paraphernalia. Try a plumbing supply shop or hardware store. Otherwise consider using a large serving spoon or non-aluminum metal scoop from the kitchen. You will need these rigs later anyway for topping off the glass in your reservoir at the top end of the casting firing. Try to get in and out of the kiln fairly quickly or you will risk thermal shocking the mold. It is relatively weak at this point and a cold blast of air is the last thing that it needs.

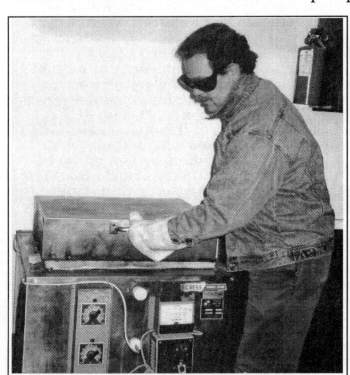

Figure 79. Proper protective clothing for kiln entry.

When opening the kiln at these temperatures, you have to be careful because of the extreme heat and all the electromagnetic radiation coming out of it. Besides making sure that the power to the kiln is turned off, make sure that you are not wearing any polyester clothing. If it gets too hot, this material melts and can do a shrink-wrap routine on you which we guarantee will not be pleasant. It does not cool off very fast afterwards either and will continue to burn you. Wear cotton clothing instead because it will start smoking long enough before anything worse happens that even we can tell that we have been "too long at the fair." Your protective clothing should be long sleeved of course. An old blue jeans jacket is ideal. Also use high temperature gloves that are from the Kevlar family. Avoid asbestos. Figure 79 shows Jim dressed out during kiln entry.

Instead of filling the mold at this point, most artists prefer to cool them back to room temperature so that they can clean out any ash and carefully compose the color placement of their glass powders, frit or chunks into the mold. This is where a lot of the real art in pâte de verre takes place. Cooling the mold should also be done with some care, because the chemically attached water has been driven off, the mold will now be rather fragile and must be treated with respect. It is vulnerable to thermal shock and will have to be cooled slowly. Oh! Oh! There's that ambiguous word again. Cooling in the range of 100 to 600°F per hour per inch of mold thickness should be okay. You can go on the fast end with small molds but take your time for those big boys. If you hear any pinging sounds while peeking at the molds in the vented kiln on the way down, this is probably indicative of micro thermal shocks that may lead to hairline fractures. These can further develop into cracks that may leave noticeable lines in your finished work.

All this was fine for a wet mold, but what about a reinforced one that has already had a heat cure cycle or was well dried. If your mold has sat around for a long time since heat cure, you might want to consider that it may have picked up physical water and give it a similar heating cycle to that for a wet mold. If not, you can do away with all this and heat right up to the process temperature without any stops along the way. This rate should be in the range of 100 to 600°F/hour/inch of investment thickness.

Also if you were able to steam out most of the wax, you may want to make only one operation and combine burnout and firing. Here you could heat the wet mold in the normal way to a burnout hold (segment 6) and spend an hour or so before going on to heating in segment 7 to the ultimate process hold (segment 8).

Process phase

In the process phase, we're still worried about the health and well being of the mold since you still can't do much to harm the glass. The mold is getting weaker and weaker the higher we take it in temperature. For this reason, pâte de verre has been traditionally done with highly fluxed lead-based glasses which don't require as high of process temperatures. Otherwise we would be completely happy using a soda-lime glass like Bullseye which has a complete line of colors available. This is all part of the trade off on which types of glass you want to use.

The pâte de verre process hold temperature is a function of the type of glass you are using and whether you are going for a full fuse or are just consolidating the frit before adding more. Keep in mind that what we are actually doing here is fusing, but now in three dimensions. The full fuse temperature is the same as that you would use in ordinary flat fusing, it's just that the process times are longer. Also if you are trying to minimize any air in your work, you may want to go slightly hotter than the full fusing temperature. Donna Milliron tells us that she routinely takes her castings to 100°F over full fuse to get complete consolidation of her work. Other artists, such as Mary Francis Wawrytko, prefer to hold the casting at lower temperatures, she goes to around 1400°F, for much longer periods of time. She does this because the mold remains stronger at this temperature and is less likely to crack on her. She relies on the longer time, sometimes up to a day to allow proper glass flow to fill her mold. You will have to play with this tradeoff to see what works best for you. We tend to use higher temperatures because we are impatient. Table 10 suggests processing temperatures for some of the glasses that you might use in kiln casting. In normal flat fusing, you only require about a 15 minute soak at temperature; kiln casting in a mold, on the other hand, requires soak times on the order of a few hours. Longer if you are trading off temperature for time.

Table 10. Kiln casting process temperatures for various glasses.

Glass type	Fusing Point (°F)	Tack Fusing Point (°F)	Softening Point (°F)	Annealing Point (°F)	Strain Point (°F)
Bullseye					
Transparents	1530	1430	1250	990	920
Opals	1550	1450	1270	935	865
Gold-pink	1450	1350	1180	882	820
Desag GNA	1575	1475	1325	960	800
Wasser	1500	1400	1250	950	650
Uroboros	1450	1350	1225	1000	800
Spectrum	1425	1325	1250	950	700
Plate glass	1450	1350	1275	1150	850
Pemco PB 83	1175	1050	950	775	650
Lenox crystal	1350	1300	1200	826	750
Kugler				875	750

The kiln casting process temperature that you choose also depends upon what you are trying to do at the moment. If you are trying to get a full density casting in a fully contained mold, you would process in the range of the full fusing point. If you are trying to get a near full density casting, while at the same time reducing frit movement, you might process at or just below the tack fusing point for your glass. If you are trying to consolidate your frit for subsequent addition of further layers with absolute minimal movement of the frit, you would process it at what we are calling the consolidation point. The lower the process temperature, the longer the process time will have to be to get flow. For gently sloping objects such as bowls, it helps to consolidate the frit first before proceeding on in temperature to generate a fully fused smooth shiny outer surface. For hollow objects do not go any higher than the consolidation point without packing the inside of your mold or you will get gross movement of the frit.

Those of you trying to get very clear castings by melting from a crucible into a mold may have to process at considerably higher temperatures than those stated in Table 10. As much as 300 to 400°F higher may be required to get the glass to the point where it will flow properly.

So here you are holding at the process temperature with great anticipation, waiting for the process to take place. This is only slightly more exciting than watching grass grow. How do you know when it is happening? You just open the door or lift the lid and take a peek. The sharp edges of the frit granules will start to round out and the whole thing will begin to look like orange sushi. Be sure to wear your protective glasses. Not so much because something will jump out of the kiln and bite or burn you, but because the glow from the kiln itself can be very damaging to those sensitive eyes. There is a lot of invisible infrared and ultraviolet radiation coming out of the kiln that will cook your eyeballs if you give it a chance. Imagine having to take glaucoma medicine for the rest of your life.

But you say that you are afraid to watch the show because your brand new kiln came with warning labels all over it saying "DON'T OPEN THIS KILN WHILE IN OPERATION!!" How else are you ever going to know what's going on inside that hot box? You almost have to visually monitor the big event because we're sure no one sold you a program. After all, kiln casting is a spectator sport for the tragically creative and sometimes even requires active participation of adding glass to ensure a proper outcome. But you can meet the main intent of those warnings even if you can't meet the letter of them—by turning off the kiln before you look or reach into it. This will help prevent you from electrocuting yourself. When you do so, you will also want to protect your hands, arms and body because they can be cooked also. Wear heavy cotton clothing, long-sleeve shirts and gloves. For a top loading kiln, it is suggested that you make a hook out of some re-bar to open the lid so as to not expose yourself to too much of the heat that will be rising out of the kiln while you hold the handle.

Anyway, let's get back to what's happening. In flat fusing, the glass only has to puddle out onto the kiln shelf once it gets soft. In kiln casting, the stuff has some traveling to do. It has to flow down into all the nooks and crannies inside the mold. Depending on the size of these passages and their depth, this journey may take anywhere from an hour to a full working day. So if you don't want to be chained to the stool in front of your kiln monitoring the infinite range switches, it is a good idea to consider getting a programmable electronic controller connected to a thermocouple as will be discussed later.

After you have practiced kiln casting for a while, you may find that a given size mold filled with a particular type glass will fuse to a full density casting at full fuse temperature over a set period of time. So you can just adjust your set point controller to that process temperature and come back to check on progress after that time. If it needs more time, then give it more until you have determined that the process is complete.

In most kiln casting firings, it is almost impossible to know ahead of time exactly how long the process phase will take unless you

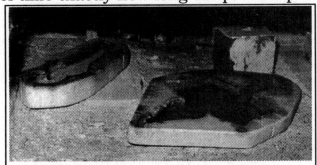

Figure 80. Hungry molds begging for more frit.

have done this same piece a number of times before. Usually you will have to visually assess the progress to be sure that it is done. A wind-up kitchen timer with an alarm to remind you to check the kiln is a good idea if you are as drifty or busy as we are. If you have a big studio or if you are hard-of-hearing, go to a photography store and purchase a GAR-LAB darkroom timer. The buzzer on that thing will wake the dead, much less the occasional sleeping glass artist. The noise is so disturbing that you may even develop a better biological sense of timing just to avoid hearing it. Either that or you may develop some other sort of Pavlovian response and start salivating or something.

Sometimes even though you have visually monitored the flow of the frit down into the mold you can not be sure that it has fully consolidated deep down inside there. If you cut the process time too short, you may notice a gradient in the degree of fusion in a piece. The section nearest the sprue will be more translucent and smoother while that deeper inside the mold will be more opalescent and rougher. So consider spending a little more time at process temperature on your next firing.

If you have a set point or programmable controller, you don't have to worry too much about having to get to the kiln right away to prevent over-cooking the glass. Although if your glass is susceptible to devitrification and some are much more susceptible than others, you don't want to spend much more time at temperature then you need to. Usually all that will happen if you stay longer at process temperature is that the mold will just fill a little better but devitrification can always creep up on you. If have to worry about anything, it's mostly about the mold strength. If it is going to fail at the process temperature it will usually happen in the first hour or so. Devitrification is the growth of an orderly crystalline structure that usually occurs at the surface of the glass and gives the glass a scummy look that obstructs the passage of light through it.

As you hang at process temperature, you should eventually notice that the glass frit is sinking down out of the reservoir and into the mold cavity. This will usually be apparent within an hour at process temperature. If that happens, what's a mother to do? You may have to refill the reservoir with more frit to insure that the cavity inside the mold completely fills. It helps to have marked your molds or to have made a map of mold locations in the kiln to know which mold gets refilled with which color frit. At temperature, they all look the same—like big glowing blocks. Topping off the mold may have to be done a number of times. Some of the more complex inner shapes

Figure 81. Refilling a mold during a firing.

may be like hungry dogs, eating everything you give them and more. Sometimes the frit will sink down at an almost alarming rate. Unless you see a big glowing mass of glass flowing from beneath the mold (in which case you have one sick puppy and don't need to feed it any more), you just keep feeding him. This is called "fill the mold again" and the procedure is the same as we explained earlier for a cured mold to which you were adding glass directly after curing by using some sort of scoop on the end of a long handle. Figure 81 shows a closeup of a mold being refilled with frit using a metal ladle that has been extended with stained glass rebar. It is fairly easily done if you can remember which color goes where. Otherwise read the map.

This is also the time to take the usual precaution of turning off the power before going into the kiln. We can not emphasize this point enough. **Always turn off the power before reaching into a kiln.** The kiln is thermally hot with no question but it is the electrically hot that can kill you. That is one mistake you will only make once. Also don't forget to turn the power back on again when you're done or the project will not get finished.

After you are finally satisfied that the mold is completely full and the glass is properly fused, wait and give it another hour or two just to be sure that it fills fully because the inside of the mold will be lagging behind in temperature from the outside. You can then declare the process phase officially over and proceed on to the next phase of the firing.

Cool down phase

The most important aspect of cooling is going slow through the non-brittle temperature regime also known as the annealing range. Annealing, as was discussed earlier, is the process of raising a material to a high temperature where the molecules become mobile enough to relieve internal stress and then slowly cooling the material to minimize any new stress build up. In this case we are already at the high process temperature, so all that we are really trying to do is minimize stress induced during cooling as we proceed through the annealing range.

The first step of the cooling phase, as it is in fusing, is to crash cool the kiln temperature as much as possible from the process temperature (which is in the lower end of the glass's fluid regime) down through the flexible range to the upper end of the non-brittle solid regime. You try to end up just above the annealing point. This crash (segment 9) is done to try and chill the amorphous glass liquid into a solid as quickly as possible. This minimizes the chances of developing devitrification and any time between end of process phase and the start of annealing is just wasted time. If you are operating your kiln with a programmable controller, you can probably get by without crashing, but as a general principle we recommend always crashing. Besides it makes great party chatter. "What did you do today? Oh, I crashed my kiln." We find that it usually takes between a half hour to an hour to crash a medium sized kiln.

We sometimes crash through the flexible regime by venting the kiln. You can do this by opening the kiln door fairly wide and closely watching the temperature drop on the pyrometer. As it comes down to the annealing point, we close the kiln and let the temperature within the kiln equilibrate. At this point some glass artists will repeat the crash process a couple of times until the kiln stabilizes about at the desired temperature. Others leave the kiln vented a few inches after the first crash cycle and allow it to crash the rest of the way more gradually. We have found through experience though that rapidly crashing the kiln in either of these ways can be hard on molds. You can hear them plink and chink as they crack before your eyes. Although this may not result in gross flaws, it will result in fine cracks in the mold that can mare your final casting. For this reason, many kiln casting artists just let the kiln crash as fast as it can under no power with the lid closed. This technique is much less likely to result in mold cracks.

In either case, we should realize that in kiln casting the actual temperature of the glass is probably lagging well behind that of the kiln air temperature because of the thermal inertial of the mold. For this reason, you will want to dwell for awhile at the crash temperature (segment 10) to allow the mold and glass to equilibrate. Remember it is the size of the thermal gradients during annealing that determine the amount of permanent residual stress in a piece. So you want to equilibrate the piece before proceeding on. The length of the dwell is determined by the mass of the glass and by the mass of the investment material (how well it insulates the glass) as well as to some extent by the composition of the glass.

The common fusing rule of thumb for soda-lime glasses is that 15 minutes of soak is required for every ¼" of glass thickness if cooled on all sides without any mold. Where the glass is cooled on a mullite clay kiln shelf, which is highly refractory (holds heat and releases it slowly), the time at the annealing point should be about four times as long. This means that 1 hour of soak is required for every ¼" of thickness to account for the mass of the glass. We use this same rule of thumb in kiln casting to calculate the portion of the dwell required to equilibrate the glass. This may sound extreme, but keep in mind that the kiln shelf is cooling through the glass. For small pieces, the soak time can be less. We have found a half-hour per quarter-inch of fused thickness will work. In addition you have to account for the insulative effect of the mold. Plaster-based investment molds hold in heat, but not nearly as much as the dense mullite clay. You should allow 1 hour per ½ inch of mold thickness to account for the time required for heat to flow out of the mold. If you have crashed more gracefully with a closed kiln this additional time can be reduced by ½ to ¼ of this value depending upon how fast your kiln cools; ¼ for most firebrick insulated kilns and ½ for fiber insulated ones. These two components, time for glass and time for mold, are summed to determine a value for the total annealing dwell. If you have trouble with cracking of castings or for larger castings, increase the annealing time dwell. After the mold has equilibrated you may want to add some fiber paper over the top of open face molds to make heat transfer from the casting be more uniform during high temperature cooling. It will slow loss from the exposed surface and make it closer to that through the mold walls.

After soaking at the crash temperature for the appropriate amount of time, it is now time to slowly cool the glass through the annealing range. In cooling through the annealing range, we are concerned with controlled contraction of the glass. As the glass loses heat through its outer surface, those areas contract first. The relative contraction between the outer surface and the inner glass is directly proportional to their temperature differences or gradients. Therefore we are trying to minimize temperature differences. If the glass is cooled too quickly, the outer layer of glass will exert compressive stress on the still flexible glass beneath it. This glass then moves around to minimize the current stress. As the hot interior starts to cool off, it wants to shrink in a different manner but is held in place by the cooler glass shell around it. This causes permanent stress to be locked into the bulk glass. If the glass returns down to room temperature with a grumpy thermal memory, it is more likely to break from subsequent temperature changes caused by sunlight or hot water.

Thus it is controlled cooling through the annealing zone which is really critical to the ultimate longevity of our work—assuming of course that it makes it through your critical artistic review. This region of the firing is also sometimes referred to as the high temperature cooling zone. It is important that the temperature is reduced evenly through this zone, otherwise the work will not be completely annealed. This is where, in doing large works, that it really pays to have a programmable controller. If you are firing down manually, make sure that you do not fall out of the zone too quickly or you will have to reheat the piece back up to the annealing point and start over. There is no credit for partial time served.

Determining the annealing schedule for solid glass invested in a mold can be a bit tricky but anything that is not a mystery is really just guesswork. The thickness of the glass is the most important consideration, along with its mass. The larger the work, the longer the required annealing times. The refractory character of the investment material, as explained earlier, also influences this. The heat has to pass through the investment material to escape and this can make the effective annealing times as much as four or more times longer than if the glass were cooling directly from all of its surfaces. We usually account for this by longer dwells at both ends of the high temperature cooling stage.

If you happen to be lazy and haven't determined the exact thermal properties of your glass by doing a slump test, there is always the "best guess" method. This is where you cool slowly through the zone where the annealing range is expected. If you figure that the annealing point is at 950°F, then "crash soak" to at most 980°F. (We usually use 1000°F because it is easier to remember and calculate.) This soak at just above the estimated annealing point remember is only to minimize temperature gradients within the glass and the mold before continuing on. The high temperature cooling phase which follows is what determines any permanent residual stress. This consists of an approximate 150°F drop in temperature from the annealing point to the strain point for soda-lime glasses. To be sure we have completely annealed our work we usually go down in a slow controlled ramp to about 700°F. Once at the strain point, soak again (segment 12) to let the heat in the glass pass out through the mold. Here you should only have to soak for about ½ the crash soak time since the descent through the annealing zone was much slower.

Cooling rates, as was explained before, are controlled mainly by glass thickness. Refer back to Table 4 in the chapter on glass to determine an appropriate high temperature cooling rate for your firing. (You may also want to review the discussion there to refresh yourself on how those cooling rates were derived and how they may change some with different glasses.)

With small pieces, several cubic inches or less in size, the mold can serve as an advantage since it slows the heat loss down through the annealing range. In such cases you may even be able to turn off firebrick insulated kilns after the process phase and allow the piece to drift down naturally through the annealing range. As your work gets larger, controlled annealing time becomes a definite necessity. This is because as your should remember annealing times are calculated based on the thickest part of the glass to be safe. For really large work like that done by Linda Ethier or David Ruth, the annealing cycle can take as long as a month. Here besides size, the shape of the work is also a factor in how much annealing is required. A regular shape, like a square or a sphere, will require a much less annealing time than one with the same maximum thickness but having a lot of thickness variation. This type of work is more likely to develop large temperature variations and thus stress. Residual stress seems to concentrate at the thin points causing the piece to snap apart at this cross section.

Once safely below the strain point and out of the annealing range, we transition to the low temperature cooling portion of the firing. Here the cooling rate is not as critical as in the high temperature cooling range since all permanent stress is already frozen into the glass. There is no changing the glass's thermal memory in this zone, and all temporary strain caused by thermal gradients in this stage will dissipate as soon as the glass stabilizes back at room temperature. Of course if you go too fast, the temporary stress can still build up to high enough levels to crack or thermal shock your work. This is not as likely in kiln casting as with fusing though because the mold usually slows down heat loss enough; unless of course it's an open-face mold. So many times you can just turn the kiln off after the high temperature cooling phase and allow it to drift back down to room temperature on its own. To help make an open face mold cool more uniformly you again might want to lay some fiber blanket over the top of the mold. Our firebrick kilns will take about 8 hours to cool back to about 200°F from the strain point. It is usually only with larger works that you have to fire down through this phase since they are more susceptible to thermal shock.

After the kiln has cooled, allow some time to ensure that the mold and the glass have really returned to room temperature. Since the glass cools through the mold, it could still be warm inside. In other word, even though you can lift up the mold with your bare hands, the glass on the inside can be hot enough to burn your fingers. It is better to allow some extra time for the glass to cool than to chance having to go through all this a second time to make a new piece.

So how much time do all these steps add up to anyway. Table 11 lists all thirteen firing schedule steps that we have discussed in this chapter, gives some suggested ranges of both temperature change rates for the heating and cooling ramps as well as example dwell durations that might be spent in each phase for small projects on the order of an inch or so in thickness encased in an inch thick mold

Table 11. Summary of a typical firing schedule.

Segment	Description	Temp Change (°F)	Rate Range (°F/hr/in)	Fast Time (hr)	Slow Time (hr)
1	Low temperature heating ramp	RT-225	50-300	½	3
2	Physical water removal dwell	225		1	2
3	Low temperature heating ramp	225-350	50-300	½	2½
4	Chemical water removal dwell	350		½	1½
5	High temperature heating ramp	350-1200	100-600	1½	8½
6	Organic burnout dwell	1200		1	2
7	High temperature heating ramp	1200-1550	100-600	½	4
8	Process temperature dwell	1550		3	4
9	Kiln crash ramp	1550-1000		½	2
10	Crash equilibration dwell	1000		1½	4
11	"Annealing" cooling ramp	1000-700	25-150	2	12
12	Strain point dwell	700		¾	2
13	Low temperature cooling ramp	700-RT	75-300	4	8
Total				17¼	55½

RT is short for room temperature.

Kiln controllers

As you can see, the process of kiln casting of glass is rather lengthy. The total kiln time itself may vary between hours and days depending on the size and intricacy of your work. To achieve optimum results your kiln will need close control. So if you do not want to be a slave to your work, you will want to consider getting some sort of electronic controller for your kiln. We will finish out this chapter with a discussion of kiln temperature control and measurement.

The standard control mechanism on most kilns are infinite range switches. They are the dials that have low, high and a bunch of other settings in between on them. They are seen on the left of the kiln in Figure 82. They control the amount of time that electricity is flowing through the wires of your kiln elements. They work in a similar manner to the thermostat for your house. Inside they have a bimetallic strip (two metal strips welded together) that bends as it heats up from the current flowing through it. So current will flow through it for a while until the strip heats up

Figure 82. Kiln with various control devices installed.

enough to bend and break electrical contact. Then as the strip cools, it straightens out enough to again make contact. By rotating the dial on the switch, you control how far the strip has to bend before it breaks contact and thus the fraction of time that the kiln is on.

You might think that this would be a good way to control the temperature of your kiln. Unfortunately it isn't. It does not read what is happening in the kiln and must be manually adjusted. You have to work a lot with your kiln to get a feel for how the different infinity switch settings control its rate of temperature rise. Figure 83 illustrates the rate of temperature rise for different infinite range control switch settings on one

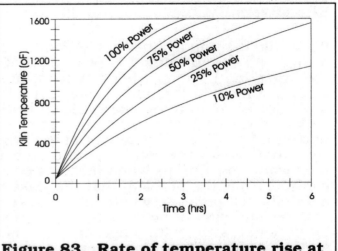

Figure 83. Rate of temperature rise at different infinity switch positions.

of our kilns. From this figure, you would think it possible to choose a setting that plateaus out at the temperature that you want. There are two problems with this approach. First, the rates and final plateau temperature vary some with the mass of the material in the kiln. Second, you usually want to get done as fast as possible because kiln time consumes electricity which isn't free. This means you want to raise temperature as quickly as possible regardless of final plateau temperature. For that reason, you may want to consider some sort of electronic controller.

Set point controllers

The simplest form of intelligent controller is a set point controller. It holds a kiln at a given temperature indefinitely. It will keep your kiln within a few degrees of your set temperature by turning the power off when it is too high and turning it back on when the temperature drops too low. The controller will not regulate rates of temperature rise or fall. You have to do that by adjusting the infinite range control switches. They act as a governor for your kiln, setting the maximum operating power fraction to help keep the kiln from getting out of control. In this way, they can be used to act as a manual override over any electronic controller. So with a set point controller, you can set your infinite range control switches for the approximate rate of temperature rise that you want and the set point controller for the final temperature. Then when the kiln reaches the set temperature, it will hold at that temperature. If already at that temperature, it will stay there by allowing the elements to come on and off as necessary to remain there. Set point controllers are not nearly as expensive as they used to be and many kiln manufacturers now include them as a standard option on new kilns.

Kiln sitters

We would caution against using "kiln sitters" to control glass firings unless you think it is possible that you might forget about the firing and have no other way to automatically turn it off. A kiln sitter is a more or less idiot-proof device that shuts off the kiln after a given amount of heat work. It works by having a small weight in the form of a lever arm resting on a cone placed in a horizontal position. The weight of the arm exerts a force on the cone that causes the cone to slump over time. The cone measures heat work and slumps when that has been achieved. This type of controller has the problem that the glass may need its heat work at a specific temperature where its viscosity is lower while the cone may register what it believes is the approximate heat work at a lower temperature with longer time. This type of control is also not appropriate for a situation where we want to go to peak temperature for a while and then ramp back down in a controlled manner since the kiln sitter will turn the kiln off. As you can see in the lower right side of Figure 82, Jim has on still installed on his work horse kiln. Here he uses it mainly as a backup timer for ending a kiln run in case his computer based controller develops bugs. (Actually the kiln came that way and he was really just too lazy to remove it.)

Programmable controllers

Programmable controllers can control just about every aspect of your firing — ramps, dwells, etc. They vary in how much power they are rated for, the number of program segments a firing program can have, how many programs they can store, how many kilns they can control and how they control ramp segments. Let's discuss each of these points in greater detail.

Most kilns will run either on normal household power of 110 volts or on larger appliance power of 220 volts. They can not be switched from one to the other. At the very least, the power relay of the controller, the device that turns on and off the power to the kiln at the command of the controller, will have to be changed to a new one of the proper voltage and power rating to match the kiln. By power, we mean that besides voltage, the relay will also have to be rated to carry the current required by the kiln to heat the elements. The product of current (amps) and voltage is power and is measured in watts. So when you go looking for a kiln controller be sure that it is rated for the current and voltage required for your kiln.

The next features under consideration have to do with how versatile you will find your controller. The first of these, the number of segments allowed in a program, is the number of ramps and dwells that you will be able to have in a firing. As we saw in this chapter, a typical Pâte de Verre firing may have as many as thirteen segments or more. Some controllers only offer a limited number of control segments and therefore are not quite as useful.

If you do more than one kind of firing with your kiln, it would be nice not to have to completely reprogram the controller every time you want to do a different operation. This is where the feature of being able to store more than one program in the controller comes in handy. You could have programs already entered for a number of different operations (wax melt out, mold burn out, initial consolidation, final casting, fusing, slumping, etc.) and just punch a button for whichever one you wanted at the time.

As your studio grows, the number of kilns that you have may also grow. You might start doing techniques that require more that one kiln to be operating at a time—like pouring molten glass from a crucible heated in one kiln into a preheated mold in another kiln. Alternatively just the long firing times of large pâte de verre pieces may convince you that you need more than one kiln.

Lastly let's discuss the two different methods that manufacturers have implemented for ramp segment control. They are end point and rate control. In end point control, you program the time and temperature for each change in your program. Thus for a simple program where you go from room temperature to 1000°F at 200°F/hr, hold for an hour and cool at 200°F/hr back to room temperature; you would have to program four points. First you program the starting point as 0 time 0°F (easy math temperature or very cold room). Next you program the end point of the first ramp of 5 hours (1000°F/200°F/hr = 5 hr) or 300 minutes and end point temperature of 1000°F, the controller will recalculate the rate and control appropriately. The third point will be 6 hours (5+1) or 360 minutes and end point temperature of 1000°F. The last point will be 11 hours (5+1+5) or 660 minutes and an end point temperature of 0°F. In rate control, you program the temperature rate and the length of the segment. So for the same program you would program three segments. The first segment would be a rate of 200°F/hr for 5 hours or 300 minutes. The second segment would be 0°F/hr for 1 hour or 60 minutes. The last segment would be -200°F/hr for 5 hours. Either of these techniques works just fine. End point control is the most common type on the market. Dan has a Digital controller of this type. Some people prefer thinking in terms of allowable rates and for that reason prefer rate control.

Most of the controllers have a keypad and a small LED or liquid crystal numeric display where you step through each program, one segment at a time. Because of screen limitations, they may also require that you learn some sort of a simple program language to

communicate with the controller. There is also a PC run controller
— Kilntrol IV — that allows you to visually program your kiln with
a mouse on a computer screen. It displays where you are in the
program but this controller requires a 386 or newer PC. This is
the type that Jim uses and is the reason that he has the laptop
computer out in the left of Figure 82.

Whichever kiln controller you purchase, it won't be long before you
become proficient with it and wonder how you ever got along
without it. So why wait? Go get one.

Pyrometer calibration

To accurately control your kiln and determine glass properties, it is
required that you have a well calibrated temperature measurement
system as seen in the center of Figure 82. The preferred
temperature measurement system is a pyrometer. A pyrometer
(translates literally to mean fire meter) uses a thermocouple made
from wires of two dissimilar metals that is inserted into the kiln to
monitor its temperature. Heating the welded junction between the
two wires causes the metal in one of the wires to pull electrons
from the other wire. This physical effect, called the Seebeck effect,
causes electricity to flow around the electric circuit from the
thermocouple to the pyrometer. It is actually a quite common
effect between metals, but certain metals produce much higher
voltage potentials than others and are therefore used for this
purpose. Some specially developed alloys, like chromel, alumel
and constantin have been developed to enhance the Seebeck effect
and make thermocouples so sensitive that they can measure the
temperature increase from holding them in your hands. A
pyrometer actually measures the amount of current that is flowing
through it, but since the current is directly proportional to the
temperature of the thermocouple, the readout is calibrated in units
of temperature. The markings on the meter are equally spaced but
this is really only an approximation. The Seebeck effect is really
non-linear so the readout is only accurate over a narrow
temperature range.

Another thing that you should be aware of is that not all
thermocouples are created equal. They vary in materials used,
wire diameter and sheathing technique. Table 12 lists some
thermocouple types, the metals from which they are made and
their applicable temperature range. They each provide different
electromotive force potentials for a given temperature and thus
shifting from one to another would require recalibrating your
pyrometer. Wire diameter and sheathing technique both affect the
responsiveness of your thermocouple. The thicker the wire or the
more sheathing insulating the welded junction, the slower its
response will be to temperature changes. But at the same time,
the thinner the wire and sheathing, the sooner the thermocouple
will burn out. The function of the sheathing is to protect the
thermocouple from attack by the kiln's atmosphere especially a
reducing one which can eat away at the metal. Stainless steel

sheaths are usually used but we have also seen good quality thermocouples where fast response is desired use quartz as sheathing.

Table 12. Some common thermocouple types.

Thermocouple Type	Metal pair	Electromotive force (mV/°C)	Temperature range (°C)
T	Copper Constantan	0.0509	-200 to 300
J	Iron Constantan	0.0529	-200 to 1100
K	Chromel Constantan	0.0720	0 to 1100
E	Chromel Alumel	0.0407	-200 to 1200
S	Platinum Platinum-Rhodium 10	0.0105	0 to 1450
R	Platinum Platinum-Rhodium 13	0.0117	0 to 1450

Since the most critical temperature region for kiln casting is in the annealing range around 1000°F, we usually calibrate our pyrometer for this region. To do this, we place a large # 022 cone in a wire stand near the thermocouple junction. This cone will indicate a temperature of 1090°F. As you may know, cones actually indicate heat work, the integrated time/temperature history of your firing, and not the exact temperature of the cone. But by controlling the temperature rise rate of your kiln to one of approximately 270°F/hr as used in calibration of the cone material, it will give a fairly accurate indication of 1090°F.

The cone is set in the stand at an angle of eight degrees. When the cone slumps to "wicket," which is where the tip of the cone bends over and touches the deck, you have achieved the calibrated heat work. You might also want to place a # 021 cone in there with it in case there is an over firing. This cone will indicate a temperature of 1130°F. Ceramic artists will usually use three cones when doing a firing. One rated for just over the firing temperature and one rated for just under it. The third is for the desired heat work. The problem here is that a # 022 cone is the lowest temperature cone currently available and is closest to the temperature range in which we are interested.

Other more accurate tools that can be used in calibrating your pyrometer are chemical temperature indicators marketed by Omega Engineering, Inc. They have tablets, labels and lacquers that change color or melt at different temperatures, many of which are lower than a # 022 cone. There are indicators for over 100 different temperatures ranging from 100°F to 2500°F some of which may be more appropriate for calibration in the annealing range. We use a 950°F lacquer that works well. In fact it works almost too well because if you aren't watching closely it will be there one minute and gone the next. One call to Omega's economically correct phone number will get you 25 pounds of free catalogs without the hassle of a resale number or the governor's signature.

Once you have determined your pyrometer reading at a precise test temperature using cones or some other means, you can adjust the pyrometer or controller readings, if necessary, to indicate the correct temperature reading. On the common needle-type pyrometers, there is a set screw on the front of the meter to adjust the reading. Turning the screw gives you access to about 50°F of adjustment one way or the other. You will find though that adjusting it in one range will not assure a correct temperature reading in another range. When calibrated to 950°F, it may be as much as 50°F off at 1550°F. This is because, as was mentioned, the temperature induced voltage of the thermocouple is not necessarily linear as interpolated by the meter. This problem in not the case with a digital electronic readout pyrometer which is a good thing since it is much more difficult to determine which series of screws to turn. Of course reading the directions might help but that takes the fun out of it. All those adjustments compensate for the non-linearity of the thermocouple response and once calibrated a digital pyrometer will indicate temperature accurately over the complete range of interest.

Safety

Safety should always be your number one priority during kiln casting even above producing a quality product. The best way to stay out of trouble is to understand your materials and equipment. This understanding will allow you to realize where the potential dangers lie in your work and how to minimize them. In this chapter we will remind you of many of the hazards we have touched upon previously and provide you with some general safe operating rules.

Fires

In working with your kiln or hot plate, a number of general rules should be followed to avoid starting fires. First is the proper maintenance and location of your equipment. So check it out occasionally to see that everything is working correctly. Let's now reexamine some of the general safety rules for setting up your kilns.

Positioning your equipment to avoid fires

1) Mount a kiln on a stand to allow air circulation around it. Have a non-flammable floor surface underneath your kiln. Concrete is best, ceramic tile or brick is second best and some sort of non-asbestos fire-resistant board is the minimum requirement. Position your kiln at least 2 feet away from sheet rock walls and 3 feet from exposed wood.

2) Make sure that no flammable liquids are stored near your kiln. If some are stored in the same room, provide sufficient ventilation to prevent build up of vapors and store them in a flammable liquids' storage cabinet. It helps to have floor vents to carry away the heavy vapors from such materials.

3) Check all natural gas sources in the area, if any, to make sure that you have no leaks. Do this by painting all the joints with a soapy water solution and looking for bubbles.

4) If you work in your garage, back your car out before you start working so that there are no gasoline fumes around.

5) Try not to leave your kiln unattended. If you must leave your kiln, try to pop in and out to check on it. If you are the forgetful type, we suggest using an interval timer to remind you to check up on it. Even with kilns on a controller, problems have been known to happen. Dan had his controller go crazy one night, possibly because of a power surge and returned to find the kiln glowing bright.

6) Know where to go and how to remotely cut off the power to your kiln. This will most likely be at your fuse or breaker box.

7) Always keep at least one ABC rated fire extinguisher nearby. Position it so you will not have to reach over a fire to get to it, preferably near an exit, and know how to use it.

8) Keep a clear exit from your work space at all times through which to escape in case of a fire.

9) Have your kiln properly set up and fused or breakered by a qualified electrician. It is best to have a separate dedicated circuit for each unit. If you have more than one kiln on the same circuit, only run one at a time.

Proper operation of your equipment to avoid fires

1) Never allow children to play around your equipment.

2) Do not allow combustibles to build up in your work area.

3) Read and follow the manufacturer instructions for your equipment. Never lay anything on a kiln that you would not be afraid to stick into a kiln. The "cold" face of a kiln can get hot enough to ignite paper (451°F) and other materials.

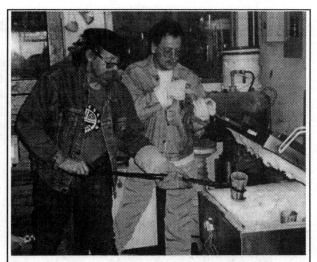

4) When working with crucibles, never work alone. If nothing else, your assistant can act as door jockey as Jim is doing for Dan in Figure 84, and let's

Figure 84. Have a door jockey when doing crucible work.

hope that's all. Then if anything does go wrong, there will be someone there to assist.

5) Be careful in heating wax not to get it so hot that it can flash into flame. A double boiler arrangement is the preferred heating configuration. Remember not to let the water boil out. Do not use open flame burners for heating wax.

6) Never put a 30-amp fuse into a 20-amp receptacle or you're just asking for trouble. Also if you're not getting enough juice out of your kiln, do not switch your breaker for a higher service one. These are intended to be the weakest part of the circuit and have been sized so that the house wiring does not burn or catch fire.

What to do in case of a fire

Besides taking the safety precautions listed above you need to understand how to extinguish a small fire so that it does not get a chance to grow. To do this you must, as was mentioned, have a good fire extinguisher. The right kind of extinguisher for our work is an ABC dry chemical extinguisher often referred to as a tri-class dry chemical fire extinguisher. This type of extinguisher uses nonconducting chemicals (good for use around kilns) that effectively suppress the three main types of fires. As you may know, these are: (A) fires involving combustible materials like paper, wood, cardboard, cloth or other similar materials; (B) fires involving oils, paints, gasoline, chemicals or other flammable liquids; and (C) fires involving live electrical equipment, such as kilns, crock pots, etc. ABC fire extinguishers are available in easy-to-store wall mounted units weighing between 2 ½ to 30 pounds.

You should read over the instructions that come with your fire extinguisher and ensure that you understand how to use it. General rules for operation and use of a typical ABC dry chemical fire extinguisher are as follows:

1) Most extinguishers have a safety pin that you have to remove first to be able to pull the trigger and start dry chemical flow.

2) Don't get too close to the fire. Stand about 8 feet away. Hold the extinguisher upright during use so that the dry chemicals feed properly.

3) Aim the extinguisher at the base of the fire. Squeeze the handle to start flow of the dry chemical and sweep the chemical spray from side to side to completely cover the fire.

4) In order to ensure the proper functionality of your extinguisher when you need it, you should inspect it periodically, monthly or more often. They will usually have a pressure gauge which should read in the proper range.

5)   If you ever use your extinguisher for any reason, have it recharged and checked out by an authorized distributor since they are more prone to leakage after once being used.

6)   After use, clean off all surfaces coated with the dry chemical because it is fairly corrosive.

If your fire gets too big, evacuate the building and the nearby area. Notify the fire department.

Burns

Burns can be caused by exposure to caustic chemicals, electricity, radiation or heat. In kiln casting of glass your main concern will be hot equipment and wax, although we may occasionally use chemicals or can be exposed to electricity. Burns as you may know are classified by their severity as first, second or third degree burns. First degree burns are usually characterized by reddening of the skin and pain. This type of burn, although painful, will heal fairly quickly. Second degree burns are characterized by the development of blisters and swelling. They heal a little slower but are usually not serious enough to require medical attention. Third degree burns involve damage to deeper skin layers and may have a charred appearance. They are often not very painful because the nerve endings in the skin may have been damaged. Third degree burns need medical attention because of the damage that has been done to the body's protective layer to infection.

What to do to avoid getting burns

In kiln casting, burns are usually a result of inappropriate attire or not paying proper attention to what you are doing. Here are some general purpose rules to help avoid situations that can result in burns.

1)   When working around hot kilns protect your body parts from the heat by using gloves, long sleeve shirts, light jackets, long pants and closed shoes. These clothes should be natural fibers like cotton or wool, not synthetic ones like nylon or rayon. Synthetics will melt and shrink when exposed to heat earning them the pet name of "shrink wrap."

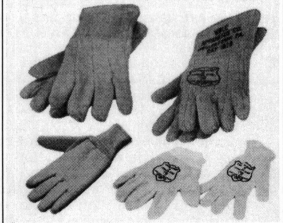

Figure 85. Temperature protective gloves for kiln work.

2) For high temperature work use Kevlar or Kevlar PBI gloves. The "Zetex" gloves are a type of Kevlar. Stay away from asbestos at all costs. Some examples of the kinds of high temperature resistant glove that you shoul use are shown in Figure 85.

3) Always turn off a kiln before you reach into it. We seriously suggest the installation of a dead man's switch on the top of the kiln that automatically turns it off for you whenever you lift the lid.

4) Be aware of which objects are hot and where you may have set them down so that you will not touch these areas until they have cooled. Even the outsides of gloves can become hot enough to burn you after reaching into a kiln.

5) Be careful when heating wax. Be sure that it is dry when adding it to the wax pot. Water sinks to the bottom of the pot and will flash boil causing wax to erupt from the pot. Put a cover on that pot.

6) Don't splash wax around. Better yet don't even carry it around when liquid, except in your injector. Be careful when injecting wax that it does not squirt out in unintended directions.

Whenever you are handling acids like muriatic acid or hydrofluoric acid to clean your casting, you need to wear special equipment to prevent receiving chemical burns. The following list of protective gear is suggested if you decide to use acids. Of course how much of this you wear depends on how much acid you are handling. We suggest considering goggles, gloves and a rubber apron as the minimal protection necessary.

1) Splash goggles that seal to your face to protect your eyes with a face shield over the goggles to protect the rest of your face.

2) Rubberized clothing which may include: laboratory apron, shirt, hat, boots and full length rubber overalls that fit down over your boots.

3) Gloves appropriate for the material being used. Natural rubber is good for dilute acids, alkalis and alcohols. Neoprene rubber is good for dilute acids, alkalis, alcohols and ketones. Butyl rubber is good for acids, alkalis, alcohols, ketones, esters and many other solvents. Nitrile are good for dilute acids, alkalis, petroleum solvents, oils, grease and amino acids. You may also want the gloves long enough to roll the top down to make a cuff to prevent solvents from running down your arm if you are not wearing anything else rubberized under the gloves (such as a shirt.)

4) Of course, a respirator with appropriate mist and acid cartridges.

What to do if you get a burn

Treatment for a burn depends on the type and severity of the burn. Very severe burns may also involve shock. This is a protective mechanism of the body to reduce the demands it places on its component systems. Factors that may contribute significantly in inducing shock include: loss of blood or chemical balance, extreme pain or traumatic experiences. A person in shock may look pale, feel clammy and be nauseous, dizzy, disorientated or headachy. In the event of shock, you should lie the victim down to allow better blood circulation, cover them to preserve body heat, and administer fluids if requested in the form of sips of water or water mixed with baking soda to the ratio of 1/2 teaspoon to a quart of water. Always seek medical attention immediately if shock is suspected.

Let's now look at what you can do in the way of administering first aid treatment for the different types of burns.

Thermal burns

First-degree burns are treated by cooling off the affected area by running cold water over it. Then if necessary apply a dry compress to protect the area.

Second-degree burns can also be treated immersing them under water for up to a couple hours. Then, if desired, use cold compresses to cover a second degree burn. After you are done cooling them, blot them dry and cover them with a sterile compress. Do not apply antiseptic preparations, ointments or sprays if the burn is severe. Also never pop blisters or intentionally remove skin from a burned area because this opens you up to infection. For large burns you may also want to elevate the affected limb to prevent swelling.

Third-degree burns are usually just stabilized and then medical attention is sought. Do not clean the burn nor try to remove attached clothing. Cover the burned area with a clean compress of freshly laundered material and then possibly cover this with a clean plastic bag to keep out germs. Elevate the affected limb. Have the person sit down and not walk if possible. Be wary of the possibility of shock. Seek immediate medical attention.

Chemical burns

If the chemical burn is to the skin, quickly rinse away as much as possible of the chemical with large amounts of water using a shower or hose for at least 5 minutes. Remove any articles of clothing from the affected area. Do not scrub the area. If any directions for treatment of burns are present on the chemical container, follow them. Apply a bandage and get medical attention. Notify medical personnel what material you were working with or better yet bring the can or label off it with you.

If chemicals get in your eyes, rinse them with large volumes of water as quickly as possible for at least 5 minutes for acid burns and 15 minutes for alkali burns. (Alkali burns are more tricky because the eye might appear at first to be only slightly injured but this can progress to develop deep inflammation and tissue damage.) While washing out the eye, ensure that the face and eyelids also get washed since they probably have been affected. If only one eye is affected position that eye down and rinse from the nose outward so that you are not transferring material into the other eye. For acid burns, if a weak solution of 1 teaspoon of baking soda in 1 quart of water can be made in a timely manner, rinse with this solution after the water rinse. For alkali burns, check the eye for any loose particles of dry chemical and remove them with a sterile gauze or a clean handkerchief. Rinse some more and then cover the eye with a dry pad or protective dressing. Try not to have the victim rub their eyes and seek immediate medical attention.

Electrical burns

Electrical burns are treated like thermal burns. With the exception that shock and CPR treatment may be necessary. You should consider getting CPR training from the Red Cross for just such an occasion. Be sure to turn off any live electrical equipment before touching a victim if he or she is still in contact with it. Otherwise you may become a second victim.

Toxic materials

The first step in evaluating what type of material toxicity plan you need for your studio is to examine which materials you are or will be using in your work. What are they? What is in them? Are they hazardous? How hazardous? What form do they take? How might they enter my body? The more informed you are about these materials the better you will be able to evaluate what you need to do to protect yourself, your employees and your family.

As an example, investment materials tend to be respiratory irritants at the very least. Free silica exposure (silica, as you may remember, is used as a refractory additive in many investment formulations) if inhaled can lead to a disease of a progressive nature called silicosis after heavy exposures of only a few months duration. Of course we are talking of heavy industrial exposures here, but the same thing can happen from low level exposures, it just takes more of them over a longer period of time. Thus, it is important that you observe good hygiene practices whenever working with molds and investment materials. If you mix any of your own colored glass, be aware that many of the colorants are toxic materials. They are usually heavy metals, like lead, that are poisonous and not easily eliminated by the body. Operations like scrapping kiln shelves or grinding glass creates dust containing silica. Other bad actors include: fiber paper that has been fired to high temperatures, overglazes since they are frequently high lead glasses, enamels and paints since they contain lead and other heavy metals, very fine frits, plaster, cements, etc. Even things that seem as innocuous as vermiculite can pose a health hazard. Its chronic inhalation can cause asbestosis-like reactions or cancer and ingestion can also cause cancer.

The degree of toxicity of a material describes its capability to hurt you. Highly toxic materials may only need a little bit to cause problems. So you can not always judge danger by how much material you are using. You also have to consider how often you use the material. Long-term usage of less toxic materials might also lead to health consequences. As an example, cancer is now suspected to be a result of chronic exposures to low levels of many chemicals called carcinogens. In fact it is not understood if there are any completely safe exposure limits to carcinogens. So the best practice is to minimize possible exposures to all toxic materials. To accomplish this, you have to understand how toxic materials can get into your body. There are three main routes of entry into the body: skin contact, ingestion and inhalation. We have already discussed how to avoid skin contact with toxic materials when we discussed what to wear to avoid chemical burns — gloves, glasses, etc. Ingestion can be avoided by restricting eating, drinking, chewing gum and smoking from the work place. Inhalation is harder to control because we can not restrict breathing. Let us look at what you can do to avoid problems with toxic materials in your work.

Good work practices to avoid toxicity problems

One of the best ways to avoid problems with material toxicity is to develop good work practices that incorporate a high degree of cleanliness. Examples of good work practices when dealing with powdered toxic materials like those present in investment mixes are as follows:

1) Isolate a work area for mixing these materials so the chemical powders do not get spread all around your studio. (If you do not have the space to dedicate to the mixing process, create one temporarily when mixing the materials and then clean it up right after you are done working with them.) This does not in any way mean that you should not keep an isolated work area clean. This work area should also have adequate ventilation to help remove airborne dust without at the same time tending to create it.

2) Consider using even more restricted volumes for the handling of your more toxic materials to help contain them. You could mix colorant powders in a small home-made glovebox, as illustrated in Figure 86, or confine all spray painting to a paint hood to help minimize your exposure to them.

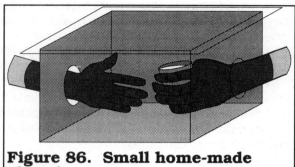

Figure 86. Small home-made glove box

3) If you have two processes using the same toxic material, try to collocate them so the materials do not get spread all around the work place.

4) Clean your work place regularly by either wet mopping or using a HEPA vacuum cleaner. Other methods such as sweeping or using an ordinary shop vacuum will just spread the dust around into your breathing air and contaminate your whole work space.

5) Store all materials in covered containers like those seen in Figure 87 to prevent them from being spread around. This also helps in preventing some of these materials, like plasters, from absorbing water from the environment.

6) Make sure that all the materials are properly labeled as to what they are and what hazards they present. Obtain and keep on file Material Safety Data Sheets (MSDSs) for all toxic materials that you use in your work. Understand how to read them and what they mean.

Figure 87. Wear a respirator when mixing investment.

7) Whenever you have the choice between using either of two materials, use the least toxic one. Such as using non-asbestos rather than asbestos gloves in kiln work.

8) Have a training program for both you and your employees so that you are sure they understand the hazards of the materials that they are working with

and proper work practices for their use. Besides protecting them, this will also help protect you from them.

9) When mixing investment materials, lead based glasses or colorants you should wear a respirator as Jim is doing in Figure 87 rated for the type of material and process you are engaged in. Make sure that your respirator fits and that you are wearing it properly. Respirators are not 100% effective and should not be substituted for proper ventilation.

10) Acquire and have on hand at all times, the proper safety clothing and equipment for handling the corrosive materials that we have talked about previously if you choose to use them. These may include the following: face shield, goggles, gloves aprons, safety shoes, etc.

11) Do not eat, drink, chew gum or smoke in your studio. You shouldn't smoke anyway, but don't compound the problem by having that habit result in ingesting other unintended materials at the same time.

12) Don't take toxic materials home with you: leave them in your studio. Wash your hands as you leave the shop or as you arrive home. (Please, not in the kitchen sink.) Change your clothes before leaving the shop, or at the very least, wear a long shop coat over your normal clothes which you leave in the shop. Wash and dry work clothes separately from family clothes.

13) Dispose of all chemicals properly to avoid exposing your friends and neighbors.

14) If you have a cat, keep the critter away from the work area when dusty or toxic powders are being used. Cats lick themselves clean and will ingest all of the nasty stuff with which it comes into contact. Dan almost lost a cat this way from exposure to toxic colorants during one pâte de verre class. Don't worry as much about dogs because they only bite mail carriers and eat homework.

Ventilation

As we have discussed, the route of entry of toxic materials into the body that is probably hardest to guard against is inhalation. Whenever materials are heated to the melting point and above, mixtures of particulate matter and gases are released. Inhaling large amounts of metal fumes can cause both immediate and long term effects. Acute exposures can cause flu-like symptoms within about 6 hours that can last for up to 24 hours. Chronic low level exposures to toxic metals such as lead can cause permanent neurological damage and reduced brain function. Small amounts of lead fumes are released during high temperature processes such as when using low melting-temperature lead glasses and fluxes. Some of these fumes are heavier than air, so you should ventilate your workspace both high and low. You should consider direct ventilation of your kilns. Kiln ventilation systems that draw air out through a hole in the bottom of your kiln seem to be the most effective. Burning wax out of your molds releases toxic fumes such as acrolein and formaldehyde and it is better if they do not get out into your work space.

Before we discuss how to guard against inhalation problems, let's devote a little time to understand what we are guarding against. Inhalation hazards can come in a number of different forms: gases, vapors, fumes, mists and dusts. Gases are materials in the air that we breath that do not have a solid or liquid form at normal pressures and temperatures. Vapors are gaseous forms of solid or liquid substances such as steam that may or may not be the result of increased temperature. Fumes are extremely small solid particles created by heating metals to above their melting point or by chemical reactions. Mists are small droplets of liquid which are released into the air by mechanical actions such as spraying, splashing or bubbling. Dusts are solid particles of many sizes and shapes that are generated by mechanical actions such as grinding, crushing, sanding. The smaller or more gaseous the material, the easier it is for that material to penetrate deep into your lungs and be absorbed by your body.

Ventilation tries to solve the problems caused by these materials by either of two methods: diluting them or removing them. In dilution ventilation, the objective is to try and reduce the concentration of toxic materials in the air we breath by mixing it with large volumes of fresh air. This is accomplished by exhausting large volumes of air and replacing it with new air. This does not mean installing a room air conditioner in a shop window. They do not exchange anywhere near the amount of air that we are talking about. Local ventilation in most cases is a better solution. Here an attempt is made to remove the toxic materials from the workplace at their source by sucking them out at the point where they are generated such as in ventilating the kiln.

When considering ventilation plans, here are some general principles to consider:

1) Try to remove contaminated air at its source. Pull it away from you and your employees. It is easier to control contaminated air by pulling it out of your workspace rather than by trying to push it out.

2) Exhaust systems are more efficient if they minimize the distance they have to move the air. Have them exhaust the air outside of the shop as far from air intakes as possible and be sure to discharge your effluent air in a responsible manner. Do not pollute someone else's air.

3) Air flow is more controllable if you avoid unwanted cross drafts and add sufficient supply make-up air through a planned intake system.

4) Ventilation systems work best if they are under negative pressure. This is accomplished by positioning the fan at the exit of the system not the source.

If you are really interested in installing your own ventilation system, we suggest that you contact an industrial ventilation specialist or get the reference book by Clark, Cutter and McGrane on this subject listed in the reference section of this book.

Respirators

Sometimes when doing especially dirty operations or when doing temporary dirty operations in a general workspace, you may want more protection than is offered by your ventilation system. This is the time to use a respirator. It should be stressed that respirators are usually considered temporary measures and should be used as the primary protective device only when no other means is possible or the contaminant is so toxic that a single control measure is not felt safe enough. Your primary means of inhalation protection should always be your ventilation system.

If you are an employer and decide that your employees need to periodically use respirators, you should know that OSHA requires a written plan for their use. This plan is to acquaint your employees with respirator use and selection. It should include a medical screening to look for proper respiratory system function, a fit check of the respirator, training in their use as well as their limitations, and setting up procedures for their maintenance.

Choosing a respirator

In choosing a respirator, you need to first consider what form of airborne toxic material you are trying to protect yourself from. Does it contain dust, mists, fumes, vapors or gases? Next you should consider how long you may be working in that atmosphere. Longer times require larger respirator canisters. How toxic is the material? Lastly you need to look at how the respirator fits. They should be comfortable, leak proof, easy breathing, and non-interfering with vision. Some of these questions may be difficult for you to answer. If so, you should consult a reputable respirator consultant.

The type of respirator that most artists will use is a quarter mask respirator that covers only the mouth and nose as shown in Figure 88. The figure shows a front and inside view of a typical quarter mask respirator as well as a part break down of it. The individual components shown are:

A. Headband assembly
B. Face piece
C. Exhalation valve seat
D. Exhalation valve flap
E. Exhalation valve cover
F. Cartridge
G. Assembled cartridge adapter assembly
H. Gasket
I. Cartridge adapter
J. Inhalation valve flap

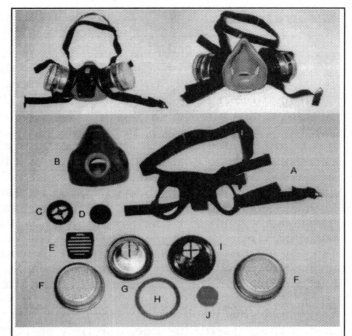

Figure 88. Different parts of a respirator.

To get proper protection from your respirator, it is essential that you have the proper fit. Otherwise instead of the inhaled air passing through the filter it will take a shortcut through a leak path. You check its fit by holding you hands over the ends of the filters and sucking in. You should feel the mask pull against your face. The longer the face piece remains pulled in the better the fit. It should remain for at least five to ten seconds. Next with some chemical filters in place, fan some strong smelling chemical vapors for which they are rated near your face and see if you can smell them. Be careful not to splash anything into your face. (You may want to wear some splash goggles when doing this to protect your eyes.) If both of those tests are successful, your respirator fits and you have a good seal. You guys with beards and/or long side burns should be aware that there is no way that you are going to get a good seal and that the respirator will not be completely effective for you. The fit of your respirator should be checked periodically to ensure that physical changes such as weight loss or gain have not altered it.

Once you have a good fitting respirator, you need to decide what type of filters that you need. As should be obvious, this is a function of the materials with which you are working. Dusts and fumes usually just require mechanical filtration of the air. This is provided by a filter made of folded felt or paper. Mists, vapors and gases will require cartridges incorporating chemicals that purify the air by trapping the materials. Some examples for which chemical cartridges are available include: acid gases, organic vapors, paints and ammonia.

Respirator care

Like any piece of safety equipment, respirators require periodic maintenance to ensure their proper operation when you need them. After each use, they should be cleaned and checked for worn or broken parts. Look for deteriorating plastic surfaces, rusting metal and cracked glass. If okay they should be stored in plastic bags. The plastic bags ensure that chemical absorbents are not being exposed to atmospheric vapors when not in use. This can greatly reduce the useful lifetime of a respirator cartridge because they become saturated with these vapors even from air exposure without use. For the same reason, careful records should be maintained of the amount of time that they have been used. They should be kept in a place that is out of the way but at the same time is easily accessible in the event of an emergency. This location should also protect them from sunlight and temperature extremes. You should always keep replacement cartridges and filters on hand and they should be stored similarly.

You can usually tell when filter cartridges are starting to reach the end of their useful life because they start to get harder to breath through as they get clogged up. Chemical filter life is not so easy to judge. They just stop absorbing the chemical agents without any warning. You might be able to test using less toxic aromatic chemical agents but sometimes not. For this reason, they are usually considered to be consumed after 8 hours of use or two weeks after being unpacked. Even if never removed from the package, some chemical cartridges may become ineffective over time. Such cartridges will usually come stamped with an expiration date. Also respirators are designed to be effective for what are considered normal exposures and will just not be effective against very high concentrations of contaminants. They will not be able to absorb all the material and will wear out quickly.

Optical considerations

In working with high temperature kilns, beside fumes and toxic gases you also have to worry about more esoteric things like exposure to non-ionizing electromagnetic spectrum. This is the portion of electromagnetic radiation with which we are most familiar. It is the result of electrons that have been thermally excited to higher energy states falling back down to lower energy states. Each transition from energy level to energy level results in the release of a photon with an energy equal to that of the difference between the two energy levels. This cycle is repeated as long as heat is applied to the glowing material. The entire conglomeration of photons taken together at on time form the electromagnetic spectrum. Lets examine this spectrum and then focus in on the part of it of concern here.

Electromagnetic spectrum

The electromagnetic spectrum is just what its name implies, a complete spectrum of radiation with wavelengths which, as illustrated in Figure 89, range from angstroms to meters. From examining the upper chart in the figure, you can probably guess that the shorter the wavelength the more damaging the radiation. The area of the electromagnetic spectrum of concern for us is that from 200 to about 2000 nanometers A nanometer, abbreviated as nm, is 1/1,000,000,000th of a meter (10^{-9}). The lower cutoff is 200 nm because radiation with wavelengths shorter than this are usually effectively absorbed by air.

The different portions of this spectrum have been labeled based on some combination of properties such as wavelength, common use or biological activity. Visible light is that portion of the spectrum that humans have evolved to use in sight. This familiar span ranges in wavelength from about 400 nm for violet to about 700 nm for red light. The exact range visible to each individual varies slightly. Radiation with wavelengths longer than visible light is referred to as infrared radiation (IR) and that with wavelengths shorter is referred to as ultraviolet radiation (UV). The ultraviolet region is usually further subdivided into smaller bands on the basis of phenomenological effects. Because these effects do not have sharp wavelength cutoffs, the effects may carry over somewhat between bands. The lowest band UV-C (200 to 290 nm) is not present in great quantity in nature because it is absorbed by earth's atmosphere. The band from 290 to 320 nm is called UV-B and is that band of radiation usually known for causing sunburns. Lastly the UV-A band from 320 to 400 nm is that spectral region that was used in the 60's to excite those fluorescent hippie posters.

Electromagnetic radiation damage mechanisms

When a light photon is absorbed by tissue, all of its energy is transferred to the absorbing atom or molecule. This energy puts the atom or molecule into an excited state — the mode of which depends upon the wavelength of the photon. The shorter the wavelength, or as you may remember the higher the energy of the photon, the more energetic the result. In increasing order of energetics the following may occur:

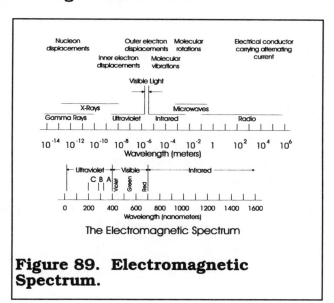

Figure 89. Electromagnetic Spectrum.

molecular rotations, atomic
vibrations in the molecule,
changes in electronic energy
state or expulsions of
electrons. This highest energy
result is known as ionization
and usually takes more energy
than is available from the
region of the spectrum with
which we are concerned. That
is why we originally said we
are dealing with non-ionizing
radiation.

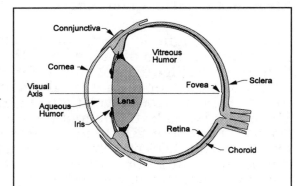

Figure 90. Cross section of the eye.

Infrared radiation may induce
rotational and vibrational states in a molecule. Visible and
ultraviolet radiation may induce higher vibrational states or
electronic excitations. Vision and photosynthesis are two
beneficial results of such interactions. Once the energy is
absorbed by molecules within a cell any of a number of results are
possible. The energy could be dissipated as heat. The molecule
may be structurally altered or even break apart. The molecule may
react with another molecule. The overall result to the cell from
these changes may vary from changes in cell function to death.
The question is what effect does this have on the eye.

The eye, as illustrated in Figure 90, is essentially a near-spherical
organ with a transparent window on the front called the cornea.
The cornea is part of the exterior sheath of the eye called the
sclera. The eye is sheltered from the outside by the brow and the
eyelids of which the conjunctiva is part. The iris divides the eye
into two chambers filled with clear fluids or humors. It also serves
to regulate how much light enters the eye. Rays of light enter the
eye and are focused first by the shape of the cornea and second by
that of the lens onto the retina. This is where the chemical
reactions that the brain interprets as sight occur. Electromagnetic
radiation of different wavelengths interact differently with the eye.
Let's examine how these different spectrum ranges can damage the
eye.

UV-C is essentially totally absorbed in the cornea. Its effects wear
off relatively quickly because of the fast growth rate of corneal
cells. Acute effects of its absorption by the cornea are essentially
pain and inflammation. It may feel as if sand is in your eyes.
These symptoms are usually felt sometime between 30 minutes to
24 hours after the exposure, depending on its severity. More
severe exposures are felt sooner. The worst of the symptoms are
usually over after about 6 to 24 hours and rarely last longer than
48 hours, again because of the rapid cell growth rate. Very rarely
does permanent damage result but also, unlike skin, the cornea
does not develop increased tolerance with repeated exposure. The
one type of permanent damage that can result to the cornea is

through the growth of a pterygium over the surface of the eye with its associated asphericity.

UV-B is partially absorbed by the cornea (about 40%) and partially by the aqueous humor (about 10%.) It has similar effects on the cornea as UV-C. The rest of the photons (about 50%) are absorbed by the lens. The primary effect of repeated exposures of the lens is decreased transmission or increased scattering of visible light. The basic mechanisms or fundamental changes that result in this phenomenon, called cataract formation, are poorly understood. They are thought to be due to changes in cell structure, fluid imbalances, mineral buildups or protein aggregation. The damage is cumulative and permanent. Lens replacement is required to restore unobscured vision.

UV-A has less and less absorption by the cornea and aqueous humor as the wavelength increases toward visible light. So more and more is absorbed by the lens until the lens too starts to become transparent as the wavelength approaches visible light. As this occurs, the UV-A is passed onto the retina. This exposure can lead to accelerated aging of the retina, but far and away the primary damage again done by UV-A occurs in the lens as with UV-B.

Visible light can also cause damage to the eye and this will primarily occur in the retina. Because of the eye's sensitivity to visible light, protective reactions such as iris constriction, squinting or closing of the eye will generally protect it. If you persist in viewing bright visible light, you may suffer photochemical retinal injuries that can reduce the eyes ability to detect light.

Near infrared radiation (700 to 1400 nm) is more dangerous than UV because a good portion of it penetrates through the various ocular media and is actually focused onto the retina. This results in heat buildup that can not be felt because there are no pain sensors there. The buildup of heat leads to denaturation of the biomolecules in the retina. In addition absorption by the other features such as the lens and the iris can also takes place. Here the lens is primarily damaged by tissue peeling off of the posterior surface of the lens. Damage to the iris is usually in the form of hemorrhages and inflammation.

Far infrared (1400 nm to 100 μm) is again primarily absorbed in the cornea. Delivered at low power it can again lead to itchy sore eyes. At moderate power, opacification caused by protein coagulation can result but pain felt on the skin usually causes you to close your eyes.

You have to understand that some eye damage is actually done by ambient levels of UV, visible and IR light all the time, but that this level is low enough that the natural on-going cellular renewal process is able to keep up with it. Something that upsets this balance, by decreasing the body's recuperative powers, can only make the situation worse. Chemicals or medicines that make the eye tissue more photosensitive can do this. Tetracyline, a common antibiotic is an example of a common drug that is a photosensitizer. You may also be interested to know though that individual or racial features do not seem to play as important role in eye sensitivity to light exposure as they do with the skin sensitivity. People with lens implants are also more sensitive to damage from light exposures.

There are a number of factors that dictate the severity of an optical exposure. They include: the temperature of the object, its size, distance from your eyes and the length of the exposure. The hotter an object is the more light that it emits and the wider the spectrum of the emitted radiation. Both of these are a result of the electrons getting raised to higher energy levels. This allows them to either have more small energy transitions as they fall to their ground state or have larger ones. More transitions mean more photons although of longer wavelength. Larger transitions means more dangerous light of shorter wavelength. The size of the hot object defines the amount of material that is heated to high temperature. This translates directly to more electrons getting excited and thus more photons released. The next factor that effects the exposure is the distance from it. The light from a kiln seems much brighter from 3 feet away than it does from across the room. This is because the density of photons decreases as you get further from the light source. Thus the farther away you are the fewer photons that hit your eye. The last factor, the length of exposure, can be minimized by keeping the amount of time in the kiln to a minimum.

Threshold limit value (TLV) standards have been set for UV, visible and IR light exposures by the American Conference of Governmental Industrial Hygienists (ACGIH). These standards are published as part of their annual booklet on TLV's for chemical materials in the workplace. These limits have been established to avoid injuries to the eye of the type listed above. To determine whether the exposure you receive as calculated from the factors described above is bad or not you have to first evaluate the frequency distribution of that exposure. The radiation exposure is then weighted by the eye's sensitivity to that region and these products are summed over the three regions — UV, visible and IR. The weighted UV exposure should be less than 10 mW/cm^2 for exposures less than 1000 seconds. The weighted visible light exposure should be below 100 kJ/m^{2}sr for exposure less than 10,000 seconds. Lastly, the time that the weighted IR exposure should be viewed is less than the square root of 10,000 divided by the product of the weighted exposure and the angle subtended on the eye. If these calculations are a little daunting don't feel alone. It took Jim a long time to work this out. Of course, if at all possible, you should always operate by the ALARA principle. Keep your exposures As Low As Reasonably Achievable.

Eye protection

The basic type of protection from electromagnetic radiation for use by you in kiln casting of glass is absorbing filter glasses. One type of absorbing filter that you may already be aware of are welding filters. They are characterized by shade numbers where the higher the shade number the darker they are. They have the problem of making it hard to distinguish colors when wearing them; everything looks green, but this is not really be a problem in kiln work because all you are doing is topping off the glass anyway and everything is so hot they all look the same color. Another type of protection used by some kilnworkers is didymium glasses like those used by flameworkers. These are not really protective enough for kiln work.

So to investigate the effect of kiln peeking exposures Jim constructed a spreadsheet to calculate them. It first estimates the radiation spectra of the light coming out of the kiln by modeling it as black body radiation. From information in the scientific literature, this is a

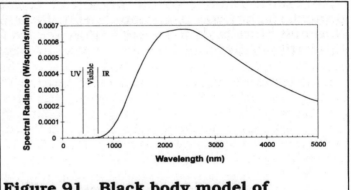

Figure 91. Black body model of radiation from a hot kiln.

pretty good model except for the characteristic sodium flare. This distribution is illustrated in Figure 91. The graph shows the black body spectral distribution predicted for a kiln at 1700°F. From this figure you can see that almost all of the radiation given off from the kiln is in the IR portion of the spectrum. Next this spectral distribution has to be weighted by the transmittance of whatever protective goggles are being used. The transmitted spectrum is then weighted by the eye sensitivity functions and compared to exposure standards.

For kiln work, we chose a test case of where a person is standing looking down into a partially open kiln at 1700°F. The kiln is 18 inches wide and open 10 inches high. The persons eyes are 30 inches from the open kiln. (Note that hotter kilns, larger openings or being closer to the eyes would all increase this exposure.) For this situation, an unprotected person would be receiving approximately a 315 mW/cm^2 exposure. This is more than 30 times the recommended exposure of 10 mW/cm^2. It could result in retina burns in as short an exposure as 24 seconds. Rose didymium glass would cut this exposure down to about 76 mW/cm^2 but this could still result in retinal damage in as short as 26 seconds. A #4 or #5 green didymium shade would reduce this exposure down to about 2 mW/cm^2 and would allow viewing times up to about 7 minutes without damage. These shades are so dark though, that you will not be able to see very well what you are doing outside of the kiln. Therefore we recommend wearing a #4 shade as you look down into the kiln.

Our recommendation is thus to wear glasses (not a face shield) that transmit only about 1% of the incident IR radiation. The advantage of this is that it allows your face to feel hot at about the same time as your eyes are starting to receive dangerous amounts of radiation. American Optical supplies goggles made with Calobar lens in three shades. Medium transmits 52% of the visible light and 9% of the IR. Dark transmits 33% of the visible light and 4.5% of the IR. Extra dark transmits 17% of the visible light and 1% of the IR. Extra dark provide the right amount of protection for looking into your kiln, use them if at all possible. Other manufacturers offer similar protection capability. Any face and eye protection that you use should meet the standards of the American National Standards Institute's "Practice for Occupational and Educational Eye and Face Protection" (ANSI Z87.1).

Glossary

Alginate	a gelatin molding material made from algae that is useful for making short-term master molds.
Annealing point	temperature at which stress in glass is relieved in a few minutes (viscosity of 10^{13} poise)
Bas relief	a simple form of three dimensional sculpture which is like a plaque
Burnout	heating a mold up in the kiln to burn out any organic material
Calcine	process of heating up a substance to drive off water. Gypsum is calcined to make plaster.
Cire perdue	French term for lost wax casting
Coddle	a cylindrical mold frame constructed by wrapping a strip of flexible material like linoleum up
COE	coefficient of expansion of a glass
Colorant	material added to color glass - usually a metal oxide
Compatibility	ability to use two glasses in a casting without problems cause by their having differing coefficients of expansion
Compression	stress state where the atoms are closer together than they want to be
Consistency	amount of water used in preparing plaster—usually expressed in parts of water per 100 parts of plaster.
Covalent bonds	highly directional bonds where electrons are shared between two atoms
Density	property which is defined as the weight of an object divided by its volume
Devitrification	loss of vitreous (unorganized) structure of a glass
Dwell	section of a firing where the kiln temperature remains constant
Fining	process of allowing bubbles to rise to the surface of batched glass
Fins	casting defects similar to flashing on injection molded plastic parts that occur when the mold cracks.
Firing	a run in the kiln to process temperature and back
Flask	cylindrical metal mold frame used by jewelers
Flux	low melting-temperature enamel
Frit	crushed granules of glass
Fused silica	glass composed only of silica (silicon dioxide)
Fusing	process of joining pieces of glass together by softening them in a kiln
Gypsum	material (alabaster) from which plaster is made—

	chemically it is calcium sulphate ($CaSO_4 \cdot 2H_2O$)
Hard glass	glass that softens at a higher temperature
HEPA filter	high efficiency particulate filter
Insulation	a material with poor heat conduction
Investment	mixture of materials from which refractory molds are cast
Ionic bonds	non-directional bonds consisting of one negatively charged and one positively charged ion held together by electrical forces
IR	light with wavelengths just longer than visible light
Jiffy mixer	bladed attachment used with a drill to power mix investment
Kevlar	low expansion form of fiberglass used to make heat resistant gloves
Kiln	heated chamber, usually electrically, use to cast glass
Lime	calcium carbonate (CaCO3) which decomposes to calcium oxide (CaO) by release of carbon dioxide during batching
Master mold	a mold used to cast multiple wax replicas of your model
Mesh size	measure of the size of particles based on the size of particles that pass through a wire mesh. Meshes are numbered by the number of openings per linear inch
Mold	a spatial negative of your model in which a casting is made
Mold frame	container in which the refractory mold is invested
Natch	a locking or keying feature added to allow easy registry of multi-part molds
Opacity	inability of a glass to pass an image through it
Pallet	base upon which model is constructed and mold frame is anchored to during investment
Pâte de Verre	literally translated from French as "paste of glass"
Plastecine	oil-based clay with properties almost like a wax. (Will not mix well with waxes.)
Poise	a measure of viscosity
Ramp	section of the firing where the kiln is changing temperature by either heating or cooling - usually at a constant temperature
Peaking	point in hand mixing of investment where little islands or peaks form above the water surface.
Refractory	a material resistant to high temperatures and attack by materials at high temperatures
Reservoir	cup-like addition to the top of a mold to hold extra glass needed to fill casting as glass frit consolidates
Screeding	scraping the top of an investment pour with a flat instrument to get a flat-bottomed mold
Separator	material used to coat a model or mold frame to make removal easier
Slaking	process of plaster combining physically with water. A few minute time period allowed after adding plaster to water but before mixing.

Soda	sodium carbonate (Na_2CO_3) which decomposes to sodium oxide (Na_2O) by release of carbon dioxide during batching
Soda-lime glass	glass whose composition is based on silica, soda and lime
Soft glass	glass that softens at a lower temperature
Softening point	temperature at which glass sags quickly under its own weight (viscosity of 4×10^7 poise)
Strain	differences in length between two marks caused by stress (expressed in micro inches/inch)
Strain point	temperature at which stress in glass is relieved in a few hours (viscosity of 3×10^{15} poise)
Stress	interior forces in the glass resulting from differences in strain or thermal gradients
Tap density	density achieved by gently tapping a container of frit on a table
Tension	stress state where the atoms are further apart than they want to be
Tetrahedron	four sided solid with triangular shaped sides
Thermal shock	fracture of the glass in a kiln by thermal gradient induced stresses
Translucency	measure of a the amount of light a casting transmits through it
UV	light with wavelengths just shorter than visible light
Viscosity	a material's resistance to flow
Working point	temperature at which glass can be manipulated and formed by hand (viscosity of 10^4 poise)

Suppliers and Manufacturer Sources

A. P. Green Refractories Co.
Manufacturer of a complete line of refractory products including firebrick, ceramic fibers, insulation and castable refractory mixes.

Arrow Springs
4570 Tennessee Drive
Shingle Springs, CA 95682
(916)677-9482
Distributor of Ransom and Randolph investments, wax working tools and Bullseye frit. Manufactures kiln and tools.

A.R.T.C.O.
348 N. 15th St.
San Jose, CA 95112
(408) 228-7929
Manufacturer of glassblowing supplies. Carry an assortment of high temperature gloves; Kevlar, Kevlar/PBI blend and pure PBI.

Carborandum
Fiberfrax Insulation
Standard Oil
Engineered Materials Co.
Fibers Division
P. O. Box 808
Niagara Falls, NY 14302
(716) 278-6221
Manufacturer of alumina-silicate based fibrous ceramic insulation materials such as bulk fiber, fiber blanket, papers, textiles, coatings and boards.

Bullseye Glass Co.
3722 SE 21st Ave
Portland, OR 97202
(503) 232-8887   Fax (503) 238-9963
Manufacturer of compatible colored sheet glass and frit (CTE 90) in opals, transparents and some dichroic. Will not sell direct, but they will advise you as to the best source of supply for your area. Publish a newsletter on their products and program.

BVC Inc
1425 Thistlewood Way
Carmicheal, CA 95608
(916) 482-6251
Manufacturer of set point and multi-ramp programmable controllers.
They have one system based on IBM compatible systems that allow
very easy input with visual feedback.

Ceramic Craft and Supply Co.
490 5th St.
San Francisco, CA 94103
(415) 982-9321
They had Pemco PB83 at the time of this writing.

Columbus Dental
1000 Chouteau Ave.
(P.O. Box 620)
St. Louis, MO 63188
(314) 241-2988
Distributor of dental investment plasters.

C & R Loo
1085 Essex
Richmond, CA 94804
(800) 227-1780   FAX (510) 232-7810
Distributor of colored frit from Germany. Also Bullseye frit and
Lenox crystal. Proof of being a wholesale business is required.

Crystalite Corporation
8400 Green Meadows Dr.
Westerville, OH 43081
(614)548-4855   (800)777-2894   FAX (614)548-5673
Manufacturer of diamond tooling for lapidary and glass market.
Large wheels to small bits.

Digitry Co. Inc.
108 High St.
Portland, ME 04102
(207) 774-0300   FAX (617)484-5220
Manufacturer of multi-ramp programmable controller for kilns.

Douglas and Sturgess
730 Bryant St.
San Francisco, CA 94107
(415)421-4450   FAX (415)896-6379
Distributor of a number model and mold making supplies such as
waxes, latex, plaster, moulage, etc..

Dremel
P. O. Box 1468 Dept 57
Racine, WI 53406-1268
Manufacturer of compact power tools used for grinding available at
most hardware and hobby stores.

Ed Hoy's
1620 Frontenac Rd.
Naperville, IL 60540-1762
(800) 323-5668
Distributor of complete hot and cold glassworking equipment and supplies. They have crucible, frits, glasses, investment mixes, Zetex gloves, etc. Strictly wholesale.

Edmund Scientific
101 E. Glouecester Pike
Barrington, NJ 08007
(607) 573-6250
Distributor of polarizing filters for testing compatibility as well as a multitude of scientific curiosities.

Fenton Glass Studio
4001 San Leandro St. #8
Oakland, CA 94601
(510)533-5515   Fax (510)533-9983
Classes in many glassworking topics which include: pâte de verre, fusing, enamels, sandblasting, stained glass, beadmaking, etc.

Frei & Borel
P. O. Box 796
Oakland, CA 94604
(415) 32-0355
Distributor of jewelry making supplies and equipment including waxes and wax working equipment

The Edward Orton Jr. Ceramics Foundation
6991 Old 3C Highway
Westerville, OH 43081
(800) 999-5442   FAX (614) 895-5610
Manufacturer of pyrometric cones, kilns and kiln venting systems.

Georgia Pacific
Gypsum Division
900 South West 5th Avenue
Portland, OR 97202
Manufacturer of many kinds of gypsum plasters and cements.

Glass Fusion Studio
1618 S. E. Ogden St
Portland, OR 97202
(503) 235-2284
Distributor of hot glassworking equipment and supplies.

His Glassworks Inc.
91 Webb Cove Rd.
Asheville, NC 28804
(800)91-GRIND   (704)254-2559
Distributor to glass artists of grinding equipment and Crystalite diamond tools.

Jiffy Mixer Co. Inc.
4120 Tigris Way
Riverside, CA 92503-4843
(800)5602903   (909)272-0838   FAX (800)666-4120
Manufacturer of efficient mixing heads that work well for power mixing of investment it minimizes splashing and air entrapment.

Lapcraft Company
195 West Olentangy St.
Powell, OH 43065
Manufacturer of diamond grinding bits available at many lapidary shops.

Lenox Crystal
Mt. Pleasant, PA 15666
(412)547-4541
Manufacturer of clear lead crystal cullet. Will deal direct.

OMEGA Engineering, Inc.
P.O. Box 2284
Stamford, CT 06907-0047
(800) 222 2665   Fax (800) 622-2378
Manufacturer of temperature measurement and control systems. Call number to order catalogs. Fax number for customer service.

Pacific Glass
125 W. 157th St.
Gardina, CA 90248
(800) 421-5170   FAX (310) 516-0335
California (800)354-5277
Distributor of Bullseye frit and fusing supplies including crucibles. Wholesale only so you need to qualify.

Polytek Development Corp.
P. O. Box 384
Lebanon, NJ 08833
(908) 534-5990
Manufacturer of all kinds of flexible molding materials including polyurethane, silicones, latex's, & alginates.

Premier Wax Co.
3325 Hidden Valley Dr.
Little Rock, AR 72212
(501) 225-2925
Manufacturer of a variety of different waxes

Ransom and Randolph Div.
120 W. Wayne St.
Maumee, OH 43537
(419) 893-9497   Fax (419) 893-4988
Manufacturer of a number of different castable refractory materials. Will sell direct and ship from nearest warehouse.

RIBTEC
Ribbon Technology Corporation
6270 Bowen Rd.
Canal Winchester, OH 43110
(800) 848-0477
Manufacturer of stainless steel fiber reinforcement.

Rio Grande Jewelry Supply
6901 Washington N.E.
Albuquerque, NM 87109
(800) 545-6566
Distributor of jewelry supplies including waxes and wax working equipment

Standard Ceramic Supply
P. O. Box 4435
Pittsburgh, PA 15205-0435
(412)276-6333
Distributor of ceramic supplies including lead based frits. We recommend # 28 which is 65% PbO, 1% Al_2O_3 and 34% SiO_2.

Sundance Art Glass Distributors
231-G. S. Whisman Road
Mountain View, CA 94041
(415)964-7248   (800)9HOTGLASS
Manufacturer of kilns.   Distributor of Bullseye frit, kiln controllers, fusing, beadmaking and stained glass supplies.

Thompson Enamels
P. O. Box 310
Newport, KY 41072
(606) 291-3800
Manufacturer of enamels and fine frits as well as Klyr-Fire binder. They will sell direct, although they may have distributors closer.

Trinity Ceramic Company
9016 Diplomacy Row
Dallas, TX 75247
(214) 631-0540
Distributor of ceramic supplies including Pemco PB 83.

United States Gypsum Company
Industrial Gypsum
125 South Franklin
Chicago, IL 60606-4678
(800)487-4431
Manufacturer of gypsum plasters and cements.

Uroboros Glass Studios
2139 N. Kerby
Portland, OR 97227
(503) 284-4900
Manufacturer of expansion 90 & 96 colored sheet glass mostly in dichroics. Will not sell direct but will advise. Publish a newsletter.

Wale Apparatus
400 Front St.
Hellertown, PA 18055
(215)838-7047   (800)444-WALE   FAX (215)838-7440
Protective gloves and glasses.

Wisconsin Aluminum Foundry Co. Inc.
South 18th and Franklin Str.
Manitowoc, WI 54220
Manufacturer of industrial steam systems as well as heavy cast aluminum pressure cookers/canners that can be modified for steam systems. The 21 ½ quart size is about $125 and the 15 ½ one is about $110.

Zircar Products Inc.
110 North Main St.
Florida, NY 10921
Manufacturer of fibrous ceramic insulation materials such as alumina-silicate and zirconia fibers.

References

Algeren, Ray. **Fusing with Spectrum Glass**, Spectrum Glass Company, 1986 *This short paper gives the only instruction on how to perform the bar test for compatibility. It is out of print, but if you call the company they might send you a Xerox.*

Ammen, C. W. **The Metalcaster's Bible**, Tab Books Inc., 1980. *A basic book on casting of metal. Discusses mold making, core molds and mold making tools. It also has an extensive dictionary of casting terminology.*

Bloch-Dermant, Janine. **G. Argy-Rousseau Glassware as Art**, Thames and Hudson, 1991. *A beautiful book with lots of delightful pictures of Pâte de Verre by G. Argy-Rousseau with some description of his techniques.*

Bovin, Murray. **Centrifugal or Lost Wax Casting Jewelry Casting for Schools Tradesmen Craftsmen**, Bovin Publishing, 1977. *Basic text on metal casting. Good set of conversion tables in the back of book.*

Chaney, Charles and Skee, Stanley. **Plaster Mold and Model Making**, Van Nostrand Reinhold Co., 1973. *This one is in print as a paperback and is available at most ceramic suppliers. The chapter on mixing plaster alone makes it worth it. It goes into two-part molds and then on to multi-part molds.*

Clark, Nancy; Cutter, Thomas and McGrane, Jean-Anne. **Ventilation: A Practical Guide for Artists, Craftspeople, and Others in the Arts**, Lyons & Burford, 1984. *Gives a good basic description of ventilation systems with examples. It also provides much of the information needed to size your own system.*

Cummings, K. **The Technique of Glass Forming**, B. T. Batsford (London), 1980. *Printed by the Anchor Press Ltd., 4 Fitzhardinge St, London, WIHOAH. Encouragement to experiment with kiln working. It was out of print almost before it was published. A must for the book collector but keep in mind that much of the material is theoretical.*

Denol, Edutions, **La Pâte De Verre**, 1984, ISBN: 2.207.1006.7. *You might have to go to France to get this one. It is written in French. Good photos of late 1890's European work. The best of pâte de verre, but we can't read it.*

Eliscu, Frank. **Sculpture Techniques in Clay, Wax and Slate**, Chilton Company, 1959. *Out of print. Gives some basic information on sculpting with these materials.*

Fielder, Larry. "Mold Casting of Glass" **Hot Glass Information Exchange 1979**, John Bingham ed., 1979. *This is an oldie and only 1,000 copies were printed. These are some of Larry Fielder's first writings on pâte de verre. Collectible if you're a glassomaniac.*

Fielder, Larry. "Pate de Verre, adapted from a Larry Fielder workshop." **Glass Art**, Vol. 6 No. 6 (Sept/Oct 1991). *These are some of Larry's later writings on the subject of pâte de verre. You should still be able to get copies of it.*

Frith, Donald E. **Mold Making for Ceramics**, Chilton Book Company, 1985. *A bit pricy but a good reference text on slip casting mold manufacture using plaster.*

Gardner, Paul V. **Frederick Carder: Portrait of a Glass maker**, The Corning Museum of Glass, 1985. *A good book showing a cross section of the life's work of Frederick Carder including some of his kiln cast work. Limited discussion of techniques.*

Halem, Henry. **Glass Notes — A Reference for the Glass Artist**, Second Edition 1994, Halem Studios, Inc., 429 Carthage Ave., Kent, OH 44240-2303 Tel (216) 673-8632, *Contains a wealth of information about glass, casting, equipment construction, etc.*

Hollister, Paul. "Pâte de Verre: The French Connection." **American Craft**, Vol. 48 No. 4 (Aug/Sept 1988). *A description of the rediscovery of Pâte de Verre and work of around the turn of the century.*

Kallenberg, Lawrence. **Modeling in Wax for Jewelry and Sculpture**, Chilton Book Co. 1981. *Excellent book on the modeling techniques used with wax by jewelers. Good discussions on the making of multiples using RTV.*

Kenny, John B. **The Complete Book of Pottery Making**, Chilton Book Company. First printing in 1949. *May or may not still be in print. A really good book on working with plaster and making molds of all configurations.*

Kervin, James E. **More Than You Ever Wanted To Know About Glass Beadmaking**, GlassWear Studios, 1994. *In print and available. Has a chapter on how the Pâte de Verre process can be used to make glass beads. It's chapter on fused glass beads is also applicable.*

Lillie, H. R., "Basic Principles of Glass Annealing" **The Glass Industry** Vol. 31 No.7 (July 1950) *Formed the basis for the classical understanding of glass annealing. Not for the weak of math.*

Lundstrom, Boyce and Schwoerer, D. **Glass Fusing - Book One**, Vitreous Publications, 1983. *It is still in print and is probably the best book available on basic fusing. An excellent chapter on testing for compatibility. Also a good basic overview of kiln firing procedures and glass annealing.*

Lundstrom, Boyce. **Advanced Glass Fusing - Book Two**, Vitreous Publications, 1989. *Still in print. Good chapter on bas relief glass casting.*

Lundstrum, Boyce. **Glass Casting and Moldmaking - Glass Fusing Book Three**, Vitreous Publications, 1989. *In print and available. It is worth it. Discussions on pâte de verre, frit casting and mold making.*

McCann, Michael. **Health Hazards Manual for Artists**, Nick Lyons Books, 1985. *Basic discussion of many of the hazards associated with different art forms and how these materials can affect your body.*

McCreight, Tim. **Practical Casting**, Brynmorgen Press, 1986. *Good practical book on metal casting. Jam packed with information on lost wax casting.*

McLellan, George W and Shand, E. B. **Glass Engineering Handbook**, McGraw-Hill Book Company, 1984. *Lots of technical information on glass properties and processes. In print. Not for math weenies or faint of chart.*

Midgley, Barry. **The Complete Guide to Sculpture, Modeling and Ceramics Techniques and Materials**, Chartwell Books, Inc., 1986. *Nice book on working with these materials. Lots of good pictures.*

Miller, Richard McDermott. **Figure Sculpture in Wax and Plaster**, Watson-Guptill Publications, 1971 *In print in a paperback edition by Dover last we looked. This is one of the better books on describing how to go about doing sculptural work with wax. It also discusses preparing for lost wax casting. Its description of plaster work also gives one a feeling for that material and how molds can be built up around large pieces.*

Morman, Shar. **Warm Glass**, CKE Publications, 1989. *In print and available. Very comprehensive in all aspects of kilnwork. She also addresses the mold and plug method of casting vessels. There were some technical glitches in the first edition so make sure that you get the addendum when you buy the book.*

Narayanaswamy, O. S. "Annealing of Glass" in **Glass Science and Technology** Edited by D. R. Uhlmann and N. J. Kreidl **Volume 3 Viscosity and Relaxation**, Academic Press, Inc. 1985. *A good summary of the modern theory of annealing. This book puts even Jim's grasp of mathematics and thermodynamics to the test. We suggest a Bachelor's in Engineering before you even attempt reading this one.*

Reynolds, Gil. **The Fused Glass Handbook**, Hidden Valley Books, 1987. *In print. Good introduction to testing for compatibility. He has written more detailed articles since the book.*

Rhodes, Daniel. **Clay and Glazes for the Potter**, Chilton Book Company, 1971 *The definitive work on clays and glazes. Good information on colors and composition of glazes which are really glasses.*

Rosenblatt, Sidney. "The 'Lost' Art of Pâte de Verre" **Hobbies**, Vol. 73, No. 8 (Oct 1968). *A short general introduction to the pâte de verre process.*

Rossol, Monona. **The Artist's Complete Health and Safety Guide**, Allworth Press, 1990. *Another basic discussion of many of the hazards with different art forms and how these materials can affect your body. A little information on the current practices and regulations.*

Scholes, Samuel R. **Modern Glass Practice**, c 1935 7th revised edition, CBI Publishing Company. *This is a highly technical engineering manual. Much of this book is difficult to understand. The first chapter will give you an understanding of glass as well as its material properties. There is also an excellent chapter on the classical theory of annealing.*

Schuler, Fredrick and Lilli, **Glassforming**, Chilton Book Company, 1970. *Out of print. Has an interesting chapter on annealing. It also has a small section on mold and plug casting for forming bowl-shaped vessels.*

Weinberg, Steven. "Glass Casting Techniques" **Hot Glass Information Exchange 1979**, John Bingham ed., 1979. *Out of print. Discussion of the basic casting process.*

Weyl, Woldemar A. **Coloured Glasses**, Society of Glass Technology, Sheffield, England 1951. *In its 5th printing, it is still one of best books around on the coloring of glass. It is fairly technical though.*

If you enjoyed this book, you may be interested in Jim Kervin's book on glass beadmaking!!!

More Than You Ever Wanted To Know About Glass Beadmaking

With that book, you can master the many different techniques of glass beadmaking

You will discover how easy it is to:

Wind beads — Using the techniques of lampworking, you will learn to melt glass in a torch flame and wind it around a mandrel to form beads. You will then embellish these beads with the many decorations that you will learn to make at the torch.

Blow beads — You will learn to blow tubing to form light-weight hollow beads that can be shaped and decorated. These beads can even be made to contain small objects.

Fuse beads — Using a kiln, you will fuse sheet glass together to form pendant and tubular beads. Fine granules of glass will be fused together in a mold to make Pâte de Verre beads.

Draw beads — Using the techniques of glass blowing, you will learn how you can blow bubbles and then stretch them out to make bead tube stock. Decorations can be added by adorning the bubbles.

Press beads — You will see how equipment can be made to squish molten glass into shaped beads. Removable jaws allow you to make different sized and shaped beads.

Decorate beads — You will learn many different bead decoration techniques including: frits, dots, trailing, distortion, canes, latticino, ribbons, murrine, and much much more. The book also has a whole chapter devoted to the technique of making mosaic canes.

> **This is the most complete manual on glass beadmaking available. It is a must for anyone seriously interested in making glass beads.**

Listen to what others have said about that book:

Glass Line — *"As far as the reviewer is concerned this is the best book on glass beadmaking yet published and he is half tempted to apply the adjective "encyclopedic" to it."..."If you have an old edition, you should get a copy of the new one and make a gift of the old one to a novice glass beadmaker."*

Stained Glass — *"... the book could be titled, All That You Should Know About Glass" ... "I had the feeling as I was reading the book that someone was standing over my shoulder guiding me - a real bonus for a beginner."*

Common Ground Glass — *"The book is more than a lighthearted romp through the world of glass beadmaking, and goes beyond the capabilities of any video. If you are serious about beadmaking, you will want to add this manual to your reference collection."*

Glass Patterns Quarterly — *"Do you have questions on beadmaking? I'm betting you will find the answer in ..."* (this book)

Lapidary Journal — *"We wanted to know! And you'll find out"*

Contemporary Lampworking — *"extensive text on making beads"*

The Glass Library — *"How did he do it? What a book!"*

Wale Apparatus Co., Inc. — *"This is a must"*

Frantz Bead Company — *"I highly recommend this book."*

At 254 pages, 113 figures and 22 tables, this is no picture book — it is all information. Whether you are a veteran glass beadmaker seeking specific information or a newcomer looking for the basics, this book answers all your questions. It also makes a wonderful instructional text for those of you teaching glass beadmaking. It is the only book that adequately covers beadmaking equipment and safety.

Order your copy of **More Than You Ever Wanted To Know About Glass Beadmaking** today. It is only $40 which includes shipping and handling. Send your check to:

GlassWear Studios
1197 Sherry Way
Livermore, CA 94550-5745
or call (510)-443-9139